GLORIA MONTERO

We Stood Together

First-hand Accounts of Dramatic Events in Canada's Labour Past

James Lorimer & Company, Publishers
Toronto 1979

ISBN 0-88862-268-6 cloth
ISBN 0-88862-269-4 paper

Design: Don Fernley

6 5 4 3 2 1   79 80 81 82 83 84 85

Canadian Cataloguing in Publication Data

Montero, Gloria, 1933-
We stood together

Bibliography: p. 260
ISBN 0-88862-268-6 bd.   ISBN 0-88862-269-4 pa.

1. Labour and labouring classes – Canada – History. 2. Trade-unions – Canada – History. 3. Strikes and lockouts – Canada – History. I. Title.

HD8104.M66   331′.0971   C79-094484-7

James Lorimer & Company, Publishers
Egerton Ryerson Memorial Building
35 Britain Street
Toronto M5A 1R7, Ontario

Printed and bound in Canada

CONTENTS

For David

FOREWORD

Canadian history is a passionate, turbulent affair. Unfortunately, most of our historians have recorded it largely through the exploits of the "national dreamers" – the men who forged Confederation, built the railways and set up huge industrial empires. But there is another side to the history of Canada – that made by the ordinary working people, the men and women who together with extraordinary courage fought battles that have had a profound effect on all our lives.

Where our "national dreamers" gambled with their fortunes our working-class heroes risked their livelihoods and sometimes even their lives as they organized into trade unions and worked toward their vision of a better life for themselves and their families.

Their struggles generated an excitement which we too readily forget forms part of our national temperament. Their victories laid the basis for the comfortable standard of living many of us enjoy today. Their stories are part of the history we too often have never been told.

In this book, I set out to explore a segment of this history through the personal stories of some of the men and women who made it. Against a vivid background of human detail they paint a vast panorama of twentieth-century Canada. We see the changing dynamics between government, labour and industry as the country lives through a period of phenomenal development, a devastating depression and two world wars. Each story traces a new aspect of trade unionism in Canada, adding in broad strokes the different elements that have played a role in building the Canadian labour movement.

We are hurtled through events from the early days of the Socialist

Party of Canada and the dream of the One Big Union to which all Canadian workers would belong, to the euphoric solidarity of the Winnipeg General Strike in 1919. As the Great Depression hits the land we are swept through the anguish of the one million Canadians who find themselves without work. The unemployed on relief form a union and trek east across the country to demand work and wages from an apathetic government.

From this period on, the labour movement gets new impetus from the communist-led Workers' Unity League. In a big drive all over the country industrial workers fight for union recognition. Cape Breton steelworkers and gold miners in northern Ontario are organized into the new Committee for Industrial Organization which is transforming the continent, challenging the conservative attitudes of the long-established craft unions in the American Federation of Labour. In Quebec, textile workers fight the big Anglo industrialists who dominate their industry, the oppressive Duplessis regime and the corrupt international executive of their own AF of L union.

Then in 1946, the Ford automobile workers in Windsor, Ontario, win a stunning victory with the famous Rand formula. Now, in principle, workers are promised union security with automatic checkoff of union dues.

All through this period, strong national unions are growing up challenging big business and raising questions about the autonomy of the Canadian labour movement and the power wielded by the U.S.-based international unions to which most organized Canadian workers belong. But militant unions that consistently question the status quo are vulnerable targets as the chilling winds of the Cold War reach northward into Canada. Then, union is set against union, workers against their brothers and sisters, creating fear and schisms that will take years to heal.

The Canadian Seamen's Union is brutally smashed and their jurisdiction handed to the Seamen's International Union. Fishermen manage to stay afloat but are forced to keep fighting the big monopolies as well as the Combines Branch of the Department of Justice.

By the 1960s the labour movement officially aligns itself with the New Democratic Party and a new force comes into play. "White-collar" workers begin to see themselves as trade unionists, too. Public employees join forces in a big, new national union bold enough to stand up to outdated government attitudes to labour relations.

In Quebec, public-sector workers go even further. They join ranks across union lines as the province's three big labour centrals take on a Quebec government, nervous and uncertain after the drama of October 1970.

As collective bargaining becomes an accepted principle, workers focus more attention on health and safety. The last story shows asbestos miners in Baie Verte, Newfoundland, confronting a powerful multinational corporation in a battle to protect their lives and the safety of their entire community.

A recurring theme throughout the stories is the relentless struggle of Canadian workers to assume control of their own affairs in building a truly autonomous Canadian labour movement. But more than anything else, perhaps, we are faced again and again with provocative questions about the role of government in labour disputes and the right of the state to intervene on the side of industry against workers.

There is no neat end to the labour struggle. The perspective has broadened but the protagonists and their interests remain exactly the same. Hundreds of thousands of Canadian workers remain unorganized. Immigrants, women, workers in small industries still face the exploitative tactics that create fear and make organizing a test of courage and endurance. In ways not too different from those told in some of these stories, men and women in workplaces in every Canadian province continue to be fired because they attempt to form a trade union. And this, despite the fact that we now have laws to protect them.

Even as I travelled across Canada gathering material for this book, Canadian businessmen in cities across the country were paying $500 to attend two-day seminars run by a New York firm of management consultants. Their object was to learn how to keep unions out of their operations.

When I began this book it was part of our working-class history I wanted to reclaim. I didn't set out looking for particular personalities but for the stories that might give us an understanding of the struggles

Canadian workers have waged in the past sixty years.

I ranged from one coast to the other, seeking out the people who might tell me about these struggles from a personal vantage point. I met them in their homes, on fishing boats, in mines and offices, over dinner and bottles of wine, through long evenings and breakfasts together, tracing the stories that are told here.

The storytellers vary widely in background, age and even in their political ideals. The one quality they all share is a conviction that only by working together for their common interests can men and women build a better future.

Some of the names are well known. A few still figure prominently in current Canadian affairs. Others have faded from the public eye, forgotten already by a nation that sets little store by its labour past. Without exception, they were cooperative and generous with their time and with their memories. I thank them all for the long hours they spent telling me their stories, patiently answering my questions and helping me unravel the facts and sort through the anecdotes.

For me, these firsthand accounts tell the story of twentieth-century Canada from the point of view of the ordinary man and woman who, thrown into extraordinary events, finds the solution that seems most valid at that particular time. The doubts that are sometimes expressed about decisions made, the satisfaction when they have been proved right, the anguish over old betrayals, the pride, the fear, the anger and the immense courage help us to understand what motivated these Canadians who battled against overwhelming odds for social and economic justice.

No one ever makes labour history alone. Without exception, the men and women represented here stressed the fact that theirs is only part of the story. Other workers involved in the same struggles may have perceived and experienced them in different ways. Where political differences are involved, these will inevitably colour individual points of view.

There will be readers who will argue with some of the rationalizations presented by the storytellers in the book. But I make no defence of oral history. Always subjective, sometimes biased, occasionally even imprecise as the years play tricks with memory – some might argue it is an imperfect tool for recording events. And yet oral history is one of the few techniques which allow us to become voyeurs of our own past. Sifting through the intrigue, the coercion and the back-room deals, we start to understand what decisions have been made about our lives and who has made those decisions. We even begin to see how our country has developed and where we might go from here. This, after all, is *our* story.

Many people helped me research this book. Others read parts of the manuscript. I want to thank them all. I am especially grateful to Phyllis Clarke, David Millar, Norman Penner, Margot Trevelyan, Bruce Magnusson, Isabel Murphy, Dan Daniels, Stan Wingfield, Winston Ruck, Margot Holmes and Otis Sawyer.

I must give very special thanks to Mark Czarnecki of James Lorimer & Company for his humour and flexibility when I most needed it.

G.M.

1

BILL PRITCHARD

Winnipeg 1919 and After

"I had never seen anything like Winnipeg in 1919. Despite the stories of blood running in the street, Winnipeg when I got there was the most peaceful city I had ever been in. And the most orderly. That's when I learned about the working class – when they have to they can meet a problem and deal with it."

As Bill Pritchard begins to talk to me I wonder at the irony that has brought me to Los Angeles to learn firsthand of a time in Canada when working-class consciousness was a force to be reckoned with. William A. Pritchard celebrated his ninetieth birthday in 1978. He still writes articles on socialist philosophy and current events and belongs to the American Society of Composers, Authors and Publishers (ASCAP). His hair is white and when he moves around his bones and muscles need a little more care than they once did. But all the stories I have heard about this man identify readily with the voice.

It is an orator's voice, strong and compelling, marked still with the Lancashire accent that places him as a son of Manchester, though I keep hearing traces of a Welsh lilt that must have been part of the heritage left him by his parents. It is easy to imagine this voice ringing with passionate emotion as Pritchard ended his two-day defence to a jury in Winnipeg sixty years ago with the prophecy: The union of the workers will be the peace of the world.

In a slightly darkened room with the California sun beating down mercilessly outside, this man who tells me he is "chock-full of anecdotes, haunted by reminiscences and sometimes filled with remorse" explains what brought the son of a Welsh miner to Winnipeg and the dock of one of the greatest state trials in Canadian history.

"My father was a miner but he also worked as an ironworker in steel construction. He helped to organize the steelworkers in Britain and he went down into Staffordshire to organize the women chain-makers of Cradling. Those women were stripped to the waist and were making chains. All of them burned ... and underpaid. Terrible.

"The part of Lancashire where we lived is either textiles or mines, but mother kept my brother and me out of the mines. I left school at thirteen and went to work in a construction company. My father was in Canada by then. He stayed here twelve years and became a socialist when he got to the coal-mining camps on Vancouver Island. Then he came back. And by this time, of course, I was an adult.

"I came to Vancouver with him in 1911 and for the first time in my life I went to work with a pick and shovel. I was twenty-three. I joined the Socialist Party of Canada and started to attend the classes the party held. We had a class on history. Not history as it comes from the ordinary school textbooks but history as it has to do with the movement of peoples. You might look at the pyramids and think of the glory of Tutankhamen. He had nothing to do with it but to go there and sleep. Who built the pyramids? Or, as one writer asked about the Great Wall of China – Where did the masons go for their coffee break? Dynasties didn't build these things. It was the people.

"Every Sunday night we had meetings in a theatre that would hold two thousand people. At one time, we had three theatres going in one night and the speakers went from one to the other. After some little trips on the soapbox outside, I got to where I used to speak too.

"I eventually got a job as accountant for a heating, plumbing and electrical firm. I stayed there until the 1913 depression came. Then I didn't know what to do. Everything went flat."

Still in his twenties, Bill Pritchard was becoming known as a speaker and party organizer. The Socialist local paid him a few dollars to take care of the party accounts then gave him an editorial job on the *Western Clarion*, the party paper. Requests started to come in for him to speak. He was away from home a great deal at this time, travelling and lecturing on political and labour issues. It meant leaving his wife and young babies but it gave Bill Pritchard a chance to see something of the country and learn firsthand what it meant to be a Canadian worker.

"I had my first view of a logging camp, several miles from Enderby. It was winter and plenty of snow around. I addressed the boys in the bunkhouse, shrouded in steaming fog produced from the wet clothing of the loggers hanging from a line which ran the length of the place. Shortly after, the Cumberland local asked that I be sent there for a series of lectures. The island coal companies were on strike.

"Then in 1915 a request came from Alberta that I be sent on a three-month propaganda tour. I went first to Calgary and then to Hannah on the newly opened CNR line. The train had just been made up and no heat had been generated. For miles I sat there, huddled up on the seat cold and shivering. During the whole of that three-month trip the temperature never went above forty below."

The tour wound up with meetings in the Crowsnest mining towns of Fernie and Rossland just over the B.C. border and Pritchard arrived back in Vancouver early in April 1916. It was a homecoming he has never forgotten.

"I lived in a little apartment on Alberta Street. To get there I had to take the Fairview beltline car. I dozed off during the ride and found that I had overrun my street and was downtown again. So I had to make a second trip. I arrived at the apartment house and wearily climbed the stairs to the second floor and opened the unlocked door. No one was there but the little fellow I had left three months before. Then I heard voices and footsteps. It was the wife and my elder son, two years old. They'd been to the doctor who had been attending the baby for what was diagnosed as a cold. The wife had become anxious but told me that the doctor said there was no cause for alarm. We retired early that evening. Around two in the morning my wife woke me up tugging at my arm. 'Will, Will,' she cried, 'look at my baby.' I jumped out of bed and went to the crib. The little fellow had passed away."

This was only one of a series of tragedies Bill Pritchard's family was to sustain over the years. But world events made no allowances for personal anguish.

The First World War dragged on in Europe and Canadian workers were up in arms about conscription. The country was rocked by labour disputes and strikes. Then came word that labour organizer Albert "Ginger" Goodwin had been shot. At a specially called meeting of the Vancouver Trades and Labour Council angry delegates passed a resolution that a call go out to all affiliated bodies for a twenty-four-hour strike the following day.

"Goodwin had organized the miners of the hard-rock camps around Trail and earned the enmity of the Consolidated Mining Company. That was his particular and personal crime. He was afflicted with respiratory complaints and ulcers and when he reported to the draft board was naturally pronounced 4F and dismissed. This, however, didn't sit well with the Consolidated corporation – Cominco – the world's biggest smelter. The management contacted the draft board and had Goodwin called back for a further examination where he was classed as A.

"Realizing what had been cooked up for him, Ginger hurried back to Cumberland and went out into the almost impenetrable woods high up in the mountains back of Comox Lake. He was there for quite some time. But one day he went out with a .22 rifle to seek some bird or a deer for the camp's larder and was walking down an almost invisible trail when he was shot by a Dominion policeman.

"I viewed the corpse in the funeral parlour. On one side of the neck just below the ear were powder marks surrounding a clean bullet hole. On the other side, a big wide horrible wound. From the position of these wounds the Cumberland police chief concluded Goodwin must have been shot from an elevated position, that he must have been walking down the trail unaware of what lay in store, and that whoever shot him must have been concealed in the bush at the side of the trail. The clean hole with the powder marks clearly visible meant that a soft-nosed bullet was used. The evidence was quite plain. Goodwin had been taken unaware by a minion of the government at close range.

"On the afternoon of the following day was the funeral procession – a mile long – organized by the police chief who marched at its head. I paid the final tribute. From the cemetary we returned to Cumberland.

Here was an expression of grief and rage. Some of the workers were inclined to all sorts of wayward acts. I understood their frustration, anger and grief but we had to face reality. Ginger was gone – nothing could change that. To engage in unlawful acts would play into the hands of the authorities. I urged them to leave it in the hands of the Cumberland chief of police, a returned soldier on the side of the workers.

"Meantime, back in Vancouver, chaos reigned. Many returned soldiers, some from their beds in Shaugnessy Hospital, were given shots of booze and coached by overzealous ladies of the 'better' class into trying to run the streetcars, etc. Others were influenced by certain business people and made violent attacks on labour officials and on the Labour Temple."

Pritchard was met at the Vancouver CPR dock by his father who told him that Mayor Gale had produced a list of names of seven labour men who had to be out of the city with their families within the week. Bill Pritchard's name headed the list. A tough, determined committee of union men demanded an audience with the mayor. They informed him that another list of seven names had been prepared and paired with the seven listed union men. Anything that happened to any one of the union men would bring down the same fate on the man whose name stood opposite his. These names were to be kept secret but for the top name on the list – that of the mayor himself. A wary truce was declared.

"The First World War ended November 11, 1918. The war to end all wars and make the world safe for democracy. But the Treaty of Versailles ripped all the pretensions and hypocrisies to shreds. The war was now seen for what it was – a clash between rival economic groups.

"Labour was particularly restive. Returned soldiers developed a more realistic view of the situation. Their wives, for the greater period of the war, had been held to the same meagre allowance that had first been established despite the rapid rise in prices. Children were kept from school for lack of proper footwear. I was a member of a delegation sent by the Trades and Labour Council which joined returned soldiers and their wives in a visit to City Hall to inform the mayor of the wretched conditions now facing these men to whom the promise was given: Nothing is too good for men who have done what you have done.

"In those early days of 1919, there was a spirit of rebellion against the government in the ranks of western Canada's trade unionists. It was reinforced with opposition to the reactionary policies of the union bureaucracy of eastern Canada. Resolutions from unions throughout the West poured out in volumes against continued censorship of books, restrictions on right of assembly, free speech and so on. Many called for secession from the Labour Congress. Finally, a convention of all affiliated bodies of unionists from the West Coast to the head of the Great Lakes was called in Calgary.

"Delegates at this convention carried resolutions for secession from the American Federation of Labour, the international unions whose headquarters were in the United States. They asked that a group be appointed to devise ways and means of bringing into being a new organization free of bureaucracy – democratic, based on industrial lines as opposed to craft, with officers who were to receive approximately the average wage of the workers they represented. All of this and much more.

"The United Mine Workers were already organized on an industrial basis. And in British Columbia five thousand loggers had been organized too. These couldn't have been organized on any other basis. And in any case, no effort had ever been made by the American Federation of Labour to even approach the question.

"The first vote taken of the membership showed overwhelming support for the proposed new organization, named the One Big Union. But while plans for the OBU were still in the infant stage, the General Strike in Winnipeg hit the country like a bolt from the blue."

Some 35,000 workers went out on strike in solidarity with Winnipeg's building and metal trade unions as they struggled to win collective bargaining rights. Almost every family in the city was affected. The rest were easily persuaded that this was a monstrous plot to take control and set up a workers' soviet. After all, not even two years had passed since the Russian workers had overthrown the might of the Czar.

Winnipeg's business and financial interests worked quickly to organize the Citizens' Committee of One Thousand which seemed to have the ear of the federal government. Along with vindictive anti-strike propaganda they were responsible for amendments to the Immigration Act which allowed for the deportation of all aliens on strike.

Bill Pritchard went to Winnipeg from Calgary and gave what the Strike Bulletin of June 13 described as an "electrifying address" to a mass meeting in Victoria Park.

"I was in Winnipeg about seven days, that's all. I made another speech on the Sunday night with Woodsworth and a fellow named Smith [A.E. Smith], who became a communist. They were both ex-Methodist ministers and I was in the middle. There were twelve thousand in that park and there were no mikes, yet they could hear every word. I left Winnipeg and started to come home. The strike was still going on. I had a meeting in Brandon – a good meeting on a big common there.

"I was to leave the next day and some young fellow came and said that they had already arrested these fellows in Winnipeg and they were going to pick me up that night. I wanted to be picked up but I wanted to get to Vancouver and be picked up there. He sent out and got two train tickets on the Canadian National that went up from Brandon and into Moose Jaw. The tickets were right to Vancouver.

"We got through to Moose Jaw and stayed in a little hotel on the main street. It was a warm night and the windows were open. We lay on the bed. Newsboys were running up and down the street talking about the strike leaders arrested. 'Pritchard still at large,' they were calling out. And I'm lying on the bed listening to this.

"I got as far as Calgary. If I'd followed my original plan we'd have been all right. My intention was to get off before we hit Calgary, round about Ogden. Then I could have got an automobile or something and got through to British Columbia. But I thought we were sailing through. There I was on the train in Calgary and this man came through, looking around. He didn't detect me, sitting quietly with my companion. He went through the train. He was a policeman and I knew he was looking for me. When he came back he stopped. He asked me if I was Pritchard. I said yes and he put the cuffs on me. However, I talked to him. Lingo, you know. I said: 'Where do you come from, sir?' He told me he was born in Solford. 'Well,' I said, 'if I wasn't tied up I'd shake hands with you. That's where I was born.'

"What a night I put in jail there in Calgary. Big, fat policemen and drunks and poor people howling for something to drink. And they'd take a pot of cold tea and pour it down through the bars all over them. I stood up all that night. Then they brought in some clean bedding for me. And they brought in food.

"I was a whole week in that jail. They didn't charge me with anything there. But they held a kangaroo court in that jail, in a little room. You have to appear. You can only go eight days. This fellow let out something that he was booking me on and I looked around the place and asked: 'Excuse me, is this a court? I don't see the flag.' That was a pitiful one.

"During that week an officer who was pretty high in the mounted police came in to see me and wanted to look through my valise. Afterwards he asked me: 'Is there anything you would like?' I told him I'd like to be able to go somewhere I could get a shave and a good bath. So he drove me out to the mounted police place. There were all these guys in a room playing cards. He said: 'There's the bathroom and there's your suitcase.'

"It was ironic. While I was in that Calgary jail I couldn't get a knife. What they gave you was a spoon which had little teeth on it. The fork had a shield so that the prongs only stuck out a little piece. That was so you wouldn't cut your throat. Now I was here in the mounted police place, I had a razor and they had the window wide open."

Bill Pritchard laughs hard as he remembers the details of this episode. "When I had my shave and my bath, I came out and told him I was ready. And he says to me: 'You're not in a hurry are you? Wouldn't you like a trip around the city?' And he took me on a trip around Calgary and then I went back.

"When I was to be taken to Winnipeg they sent a guy down from there to get me. He was an Irishman, very nice, and this time he didn't handcuff me. As we got on the train this big mob of labour people were outside waving to us. The first evening out we were eating supper, and he looked across the table at me and said: 'Eat up, kid, this is on the government.' So I had a pretty good meal.

"It was two days and a night into Winnipeg, I think. It was evening when we arrived. The rest of the fellows arrested as principals in the strike had now been bailed out of Stony Mountain. I figured they'd let me go too. I got out onto the platform and there was an escort waiting. One man on either side of me and a very important Bill, an Englishman by his lingo. He had a bowler hat. They trundled me down to the Immigration Office. I could see I wasn't going to be let go, but I didn't know where I was going to be put. Along came a car. They took me where I wouldn't be seen too much and shoo – off to Stony Mountain.

"It was nine o'clock in the evening when I got to Stony Mountain and the warden, Graham, came out. 'Again?' he said, 'This has never happened in my experience.' You see, this was a federal jail and it was a provincial indictment. You go to jail after you're convicted, not before. But there they stood and they had the order.

"That was an experience. They opened one gate and then it went *clang* and you went down a long corridor to another gate that opened and closed *clang*. There were several gates and they all went *clang* and finally, I'm inside there. And right inside. There were a few of the fellows from North Winnipeg there. All of them foreigners, and almost all of them social democrats. All supporters of the strike but nothing whatever to do with it. Just thrown in there for coloration. They wanted to go on a hunger strike. I told them it wouldn't help them any. I was there about a week before I was bailed out and they were still in there when I left.

"One night I'd gone to bed. It was Friday, I think, and all at once I could hear the pattering of feet. And keys. And somebody out of breath. Running. Calling out to me: 'Mr. Pritchard. Mr. Pritchard. You're going to be taken out.' He was all excited, poor fellow. They had brought the bail. The rest were all on $10,000. I was on $20,000!"

After six weeks the Winnipeg General Strike is finally broken. They have been weeks the like of which Canada has never known. Federal

Winnipeg General Strike – strikers' meeting in Victoria Park. Photo: courtesy of Foote Collection, Manitoba Archives

"Loyalist" veterans demonstrate against the strikers. Photo: courtesy of Public Archives Canada C-48334

Headquarters of the Citizens' Committee of One Thousand at the Winnipeg Board of Trade building. Photo: courtesy of Foote Collection, Manitoba Archives

Police "specials", armed with clubs, advance on crowds, June 10, 1919.
Photo: courtesy of Public Archives Canada WS-348

Silent parade called by returned soldiers to protest arrest of strike leaders culminates in Winnipeg's "Bloody Saturday," July 21, 1919. Photo: courtesy of Foote Collection, Manitoba Archives

Mounties with clubs and drawn revolvers charge demonstrators, July 21, 1919. Photo: courtesy Manitoba Archives

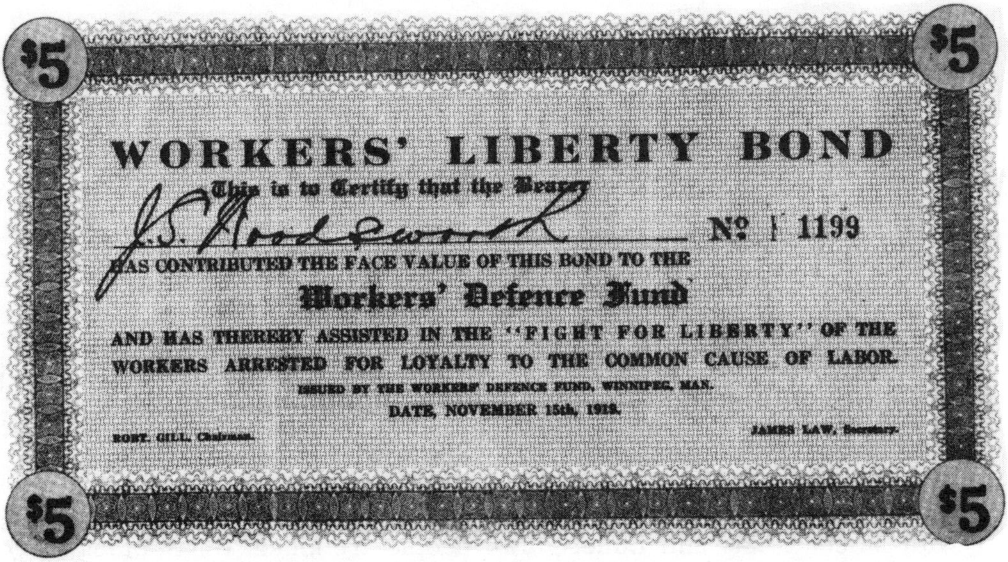

$5 $5

WORKERS' LIBERTY BOND

This is to Certify that the Bearer

J.S. Woodsworth

№ 1199

HAS CONTRIBUTED THE FACE VALUE OF THIS BOND TO THE

Workers' Defence Fund

AND HAS THEREBY ASSISTED IN THE "FIGHT FOR LIBERTY" OF THE WORKERS ARRESTED FOR LOYALTY TO THE COMMON CAUSE OF LABOR.

ISSUED BY THE WORKERS' DEFENCE FUND, WINNIPEG, MAN.

DATE, NOVEMBER 15th, 1919.

ROBT. GILL, Chairman.

JAMES LAW, Secretary.

$5 $5

Workers' Liberty Bond issued in support of the Workers' Defence Fund. Photo: courtesy of Public Archives Canada C-9293

Strike leaders at Stony Mountain penitentiary. Back row, left to right: R.E. Bray, G. Armstrong, J. Queen, R.B. Russell, R.J. Johns, W.A. Pritchard. Front row, left to right: Wm. Ivens, A.A. Heaps. Photo: courtesy of Manitoba Archives

cabinet ministers come from Ottawa but never meet with the central strike committee. The entire Winnipeg police force is dismissed for refusing to sign a contract prohibiting union membership. It is the opening the Citizens' Committee needs to move into the "law and order" arena with the recruitment of "specials."

Strike leaders are arrested and attempts are made to deport them under the new amendments to the Immigration Act. A silent parade is called by returned soldiers to protest the arrest of the strike leaders. The parade culminates in Winnipeg's "Bloody Saturday" as RNWMP and police "specials" attack the crowd of demonstrators and onlookers with baseball bats and bullets. Two people are killed, thirty others injured. Five days later the Winnipeg General Strike is over.

Eight men are charged with seditious conspiracy: R.B. Russell, R.J. Johns, William Ivens, John Queen, A.A. Heaps, George Armstrong, R.E. Bray and W.A. Pritchard. In addition, F.J. Dixon and J.S. Woodsworth are accused of seditious libel.

"Long before that time I had written an aphorism: Only fools try to make revolutions, wise men conform to them. And here I was now charged with conspiracy. I went back home and we had a number of meetings.

"It must have been a month or two we had to wait before we had the preliminary trial after I came out on bail. My wife stayed in the house with the axe behind the door, looking after the kids. Then she went to stay with someone and they looked after her. My wife wasn't afraid though. She wasn't built that way. She was a fighter, too. But Gilbert was only twelve months and Arthur four or five.

"It was then they made the raids all through the country. You never saw so many volumes of Marx's *Capital* as came into that courtroom. They went into my house and took everything I had. In those days I had a library that would have run into thousands of dollars. They took everything and I never got it back.

"After the preliminary hearing they put us in jail. They wouldn't give us bail. Then there was one heck of a row all through the country. And when the lawyer came to see us in Stony Mountain he told us: 'You men will be on the high seas within twenty-four hours and your families will be shipped later.' And Armstrong, he was comical, he says: 'Hey, but what are you going to do with me? Are you going to send me to Alaska?' He'd been born in Yorktown – Toronto. That was a poser. So that and the general revolt of the labour population of Canada, that saved us. But they weren't going to give us a jury trial. They just gave us a farce.

"When the trial was called they split Russell off from the rest of us. He was the only man indicted that had anything actually to do with the strike. We had to sit through his trial and then when our turn came we made several motions. One was to disqualify the judge on the grounds that he was the trial judge for Russell and that the evidence would be much the same, and therefore, he was already prejudiced. You know what his answer was to that? He was doing his best to get rid of it!

"More jurymen had been selected for that one trial than had been called for an entire assizes. Ivens made the motion that we could take the first twelve names out of a hat. Well, there was nothing in the law to provide for that. It was a ploy. Then Andrews, the legal counsel for the prosecution, got up and made a motion to the court that he be allowed to extend the veniremen indefinitely. And he already had 270 called. They'd all been canvassed by policemen selling sewing machines in the middle of winter out on the prairies.

"In our first meeting with Bonnar, the chief lawyer, he told us what we were going to do. They decided that Ivens would defend himself. And Queen said he would defend himself. And they all agreed I should. Holland was appointed to take care of Johns and someone took care of Bray. We were all tried together, so we could put our motions together. The defence all worked together as a team. Some of the lawyers weren't too bright. Bonnar, of course, was marvellous.

"The Citizens' Committee of One Thousand was topped by a collection of lawyers. Out of this collection they got all those people who were part of the prosecution's legal counsel in the trial. Alfred J. Andrews, who headed up the committee, was the chief. Of course, he had already got himself appointed federal deputy minister of justice!

"I feel a degree of amusement that Andrews could make a fortune out of that trial, doing it for the sake of his children and his property. You see, they were paid for overtime. We were there at ten o'clock in the morning. At twelve we went to lunch. Bingo – at one o'clock back again. Then we have one hour for supper and on again until ten o'clock. Anything beyond three or four o'clock, that's all overtime. And lawyer's fees are not longshoremen's.

"I wasn't being paid overtime. I was living away in North Winnipeg and I had to come on two streetcars to the city. That's where we were living. The wife was out there with me. It was the only place we could get. So it was very late when I got home and the last streetcar was lit by a little bit of an electric thing – whoo – at forty-odd below!

"My wife had insisted on coming to be with me during the trial. She brought our eldest and youngest sons. Our daughter we left with friends. In the court they had a big plug-ugly at the door. And he said something to her – insulted her. I don't know whether she slapped his face or not, but I imagine she would. In any case, Judge Metcalfe called me up about it. He said that my wife was a very loyal woman. 'How did she get into this?' I asked him. Then he told me. I said: 'If she bawled him out, and she would do that, he had it coming. You tell him to be a little bit more respectful to anyone entering your courtroom.'

"I was called to that bench many times – once when the judge got a letter from somebody threatening to blow his brains out. A returned soldier it was supposed to be. He was scared stiff. If ever I saw panic or fright in a man's eyes, I saw it then as he told me about this letter.

"There I am at the bench talking to him, sticking my chin up there on the shelf. 'What's this to do with me?' I ask him.

"'I judge it to be one of your people,' he says.

"'You must be very naive, my lord. Ever hear of agents provocateurs? This could be one of your people.'

"'Well, what do you think I should do?' he asks me.

"'If I was in your position, which I am not, I'd get a bodyguard.' And that night when he left there, he had two big carbon copies of the guy at the door. One on either side of him."

All that winter from late January, the Winnipeg State Trials dragged on. More than a thousand exhibits, most of them books and pamphlets confiscated in raids on houses and labour offices, were brought in as well as a host of witnesses. The object was to show the twelve farmers sitting as jury that the accused were dangerous criminals intent on overthrowing the government. William Pritchard laid his case to rest with a brilliant twenty-hour oration. The *Winnipeg Tribune* reported that he displayed "a knowledge of other cultural arts that would astound the average individual whose mental picture of a labour leader is a horny-handed, unread, ungrammatical toiler."

Though there was no evidence to support the conspiracy theory, Russell's sentence was two years. Pritchard, Ivens, Armstrong, Johns and Queen were sentenced to one year in prison. Bray got six months. Dixon and Heaps were acquitted and the Crown never proceeded with the charges against Woodsworth.

"Conditions in the jail were like all jails. We cleaned the darn thing out – scrubbed it from top to bottom. We all worked in there. When we went to the jail farm they were surprised by what we did. Dick Johns was a toolmaker and when the bearings wore out on the pump-car, he cut new bearings out of pieces of birch and he made that thing run. The governor had his place there and the roof leaked. He knew I'd been in construction in England. I went up to look at it and told him that his flashings had been put on upside down, so the water would run in instead of running down and out. I fixed it for him.

"Meantime, he'd taken us out to a big field – ten acres loaded with stumps. The timber had been taken off. First, we had to put a fence around it. That fence ran straight alongside the railroad track for the better part of five furlongs and we had to take tamarack and point them. We cut the poles and piled them up, and when we came to dig there was ice all about. So we had to break it all up with a crowbar, build a fire and boil water, pour it in and drive them in that way. I remember I did the surveying for it. I stood at that main post sighting that thing all the way down, meantime writing an epic poem that I've lost now. When the governor came and saw this long straight line, he was quite satisfied. But he did say: 'We got the idea you fellows didn't do any work – labour leaders getting paid.' Very few of them were getting paid in the labour movement in those days.

"When we got that fence finished and the rails on it, they brought down a stallion and a long cable with a hook on it. The stallion was fastened onto this to turn round and round. The cable would pull at the roots after they had been chopped. And that was Dick Johns' job. My job was handling the cable. We got a whole circle cleaned out. But the stump puller wasn't too good. In fact, pulling one time it slipped out and hit the big fellow that was helping us and broke his leg. He was a fireman that had been sent to jail for six months for something to do with the strike. I got another cable and extended it. I wrapped it one by one a half inch around each root. Then we could move the whole contraption and pull all those stumps out."

"We earned no money for the work we did on the jail farm. But jail wasn't that bad. You just had to keep busy. When we were there, the new wardeness had recently married the governor. The boys had been putting on shows and they were terrible. This woman had humour and she thought that maybe I could help clean this up somewhat. Here was a chance to get out of my cell. But what do I do?

"I came across a fellow, a young Scottish-Jewish fellow from Glasgow and he could play the trumpet. As we talked the whole thing developed and we decided to try and put on *Pinafore*. We had to knock a lot of it out, but I got out of my cell and was allowed to go around and test.

"There was a Jewish boy in there, a returned soldier. He was in there for drugs. A doctor in jail told us that they came out of the battle of the Marne and what not and were laid like cordwood while the few doctors and nurses shot dope into them. And now they'd come back and they were drug addicts. Anyway, this fellow was naturally comical. You'd teach him lines and when you'd come to do the thing in rehearsal and put it on, he'd alter them. So much so that it wasn't a matter of getting the bunch to put on an artificial laugh. It was spontaneous. You couldn't hold him down.

"We dressed him up and made him into Buttercup. We had to do that with all the female roles. The only lady in the thing, and I insisted on this, had to be one from the outside. She sang in the Christian Science church and was a very good soprano. Beautiful. And she played Josephine.

"I played the captain and I wrote the parodies. So it comes to the first performance and I speak to the governor. I hold the ace card. 'Every prisoner who is on good behaviour should come to the concert,'

I told him. 'But one thing. Those special policemen that worked in the Winnipeg strike who were caught later stealing and doing second-storey work (we had all kinds of them in jail), send them to Coventry.' The rest of the prisoners wouldn't even give a library book to these people. So they couldn't come. And they didn't come. But everyone else did. And the women were up in the women's gallery.

"When the election came that year we were all nominated while we were in jail. And I was not even a Winnipeg resident! They even took the papers after the date for filing. They came down in an airplane to the jail farm. The only thing we had were sheets and we tied them all together to make a mark on the field. They landed at a place about two miles down the line and came back up on the railroad. They got us to sign these papers; then we were on the ballot.

"Armstrong was carried in. So were Ivens and Dixon. And I was so close. Just think, I might have been elected to the Manitoba legislature and the whole thing would have been illegal! And why didn't they object? Why didn't they object that our papers weren't filed on time? They were scared. And there's nothing worse than a scared politician. He's worse than a crooked one.

"At the end I was in the jail hospital for a month. An epidemic went through the jail and it swept me on with it. I was unconscious for two weeks. They were the most beautiful two weeks I spent there. When I woke up it was almost coming out time. They'd told me, the fellows inside there, that when the time comes for you to leave you get very restless. I didn't believe it. But I did get restless. You can do nothing.

"I was spokesman for our crowd in jail. When we were to be let out, I went in to see the governor. I told him that it would be advisable to let us out immediately after midnight. 'The usual time is ten o'clock in the morning,' he said. I told him that by ten o'clock in the morning the place would be surrounded by thousands of people. It took some arguing but he saw the point. He went outside just after midnight, but there were maybe fifty, sixty or a hundred people. So he had to close the door. He tried the back door. They were at the back door, too. After a while I told this jailer to go out and open the back door. All the people went round to the back door and we went out the front.

"There was snow on the ground, all packed down. I had to get those two streetcars out to where my wife was. It was about a quarter to two when I tapped on the door. The lady she rented the place from came down and I said: 'Do you mind telling Mrs. Pritchard that her husband has come home.' She opened the door all excited. She'd never met me."

Bill Pritchard's eyes look far away into a past I can only glimpse through his stories. He shakes his head. "Oh, it would take me the rest of my life to clean up on the myths that have been created on this thing! About Woodsworth, for instance. They still insist that he was sent to Stony Mountain. He never went to Stony Mountain. He went to the Winnipeg jail. He was there a few weeks but his trial never came up."

The Pritchard family went back to British Columbia to try to remake their lives. A stubborn idealist, Pritchard toured the province still fighting for the idea of the One Big Union. But power politics had already killed it.

"We never really got the OBU going. It was there, the votes were there, it was overwhelming. And immediately, international officers from the AF of L came from their headquarters into Canada, meeting with the government and with the business element. The employers, AFL officials and the government. An unholy trinity if ever there was one. When the men went back to work they were stopped at the gates. 'Give up your OBU card,' they were told. That's how it was. And this wasn't only in Winnipeg. This was everywhere. In Vancouver, it happened with the boilermakers. They had to give up that card. And even then, some of them never got back to work anyway.

"The thing was that with the OBU we reduced the hierarchy of the labour movement. In the Longshoremen's Union a secretary, or a president, could be elected for six months only. You could be reelected later on. But only for six months. Then you went back and worked on the waterfront. It kept you straight. And we were doing away with those huge fees for a worker to join a union when he hadn't the money to pay for initiation. But they broke it. And it was only just born. In Winnipeg, it hung on for a while. And finally, with the street railwaymen, they held."

The next year, a company union was brought in to replace the

"When I come out on to the street, I stood on the sidewalk. I still wasn't sure whether or not I was clear. This young cop he come up to me and said: 'We don't agree with people smashin' up furniture and materials. We think you were guilty.' So I said to 'im: 'What would you do if you were in a place where you couldn't breathe? You'd try to get out. And a single man can't get out of a place like that without takin' the works with 'im.' We said we were goin' to close the place up and it never opened after that.

"That was in March '34. We applied for relief and they started shippin' us to relief camps. I was sent up to Spences Bridge, a place up the railroad. I got there in the evening. The next morning I went to work on the roads. We were building new highways. Apparently, the superintendent or some of the men that were there went through my clothes. They found some working-class literature. So the next morning they kept me in. They didn't say anything. They just kept me in supposedly to do some work around the camp. About nine o'clock when everybody had gone to work they told me I was goin' to be shipped out of the camp. I was half-expectin' it would happen some time, but not so soon.

"It was true I was goin' to organize that camp. We had to organize the camps. It was our only hope. We couldn't see any future. It seemed we'd be in those camps for eight or ten years. We had our office in Vancouver at 52½ Cordova Street and from there we set up the Relief Camp Workers' Union. It was the only thing we could do.

"Anyone bein' shipped to a camp would come down to the Unemployed Hall and we'd take his name down and he would tell us what camp he was goin' to. If we had to send out an organizer to that camp, he was the contact. We used to have a system. If I was shipped out to a camp and I wasn't very good at organizing, I would come down and exchange my papers and give them to another, to a good organizer. And he would go in my place. They didn't know the difference. Everybody had a phony name anyway. I never did change my name at all.

"I come back down to Vancouver. I applied for relief and after three days I get blacklist relief. The broad arrow was on my card and I knew I was blacklisted. They wouldn't send me to a camp.

"We were gettin' $3.05 a week. Two dollars a meal-ticket and $1.05

for the bed. You'd go to the hotel with the chit for the bed. You'd give it to the clerk. When you walk in the room there's somebody in the same bed you were goin' to sleep in. You dunno who it is. Many times I slept on the floor. I wouldn't get in bed with anybody.

"When things got real bad we had a tactic. We'd walk into a restaurant and order a big meal. You'd need about thirty cents. That would be considered a big substantial meal. When they'd come and bring the coffee we'd give them a nickel to call the police. 'We can't pay you for the meal,' we'd tell 'em. 'And it's gone now.' Calling the police wouldn't do any good so usually they had to let us go.

"Part of the time I lived with Slim Evans and his family. We used to get up in the mornings and the mother would come and tell us she didn't have any milk for breakfast. So we'd get out of bed, dress up and hit the streets. We'd bum a dime, fifteen or twenty-five cents and we'd buy a couple of quarts of milk to take back for the youngster to have on her cereal so she could go to school.

"I recall one morning there was a show in the Rex Theatre downtown. It cost fifteen cents to get in. I didn't have fifteen cents but I had enough to get coffee and toast for my breakfast. I went into the restaurant and had my coffee and toast. That was a nickel. Then I headed down the street to try to bum enough to make the show. All I wanted was fifteen cents.

"They were all office workers around that area. I met this one individual and I hit him up for the fifteen cents. He asked me if I had any breakfast. 'Of course I didn't have any breakfast. That's what I want the money for,' I told him. 'Come right in with me,' he said. 'I'm going to have breakfast now.'

"I go in with him and he got fried eggs and bacon for me and potatoes and toast. I was loaded when I come out. I hadn't had a breakfast like that for a couple of years. So I met a second one and he says the same thing. But I had to quit. I had to say: 'I haven't eaten in so long my stomach is painin'. I'll be able to eat again around noon.' So he give me the fifteen cents. I went out on the street and down in the alley. I put my fingers down my throat and puked up everything I had eaten. But I got two bits for the show anyway.

"Little stunts like that we used to pull when we got hungry. Even the people with jobs understood. They were very good. They knew that anytime they might be where we were, too. They didn't know what was goin' to happen.

"It was a bad situation. You take a family of four. Man and wife and two children. If the boy was sixteen years old and the girl was around fifteen, they would eat in three days all the relief that the family had for a week. The father would take a gunnysack and go up to the Relief Office and get his document, come down to the store and he could carry all that for a week home on his back.

"One day I remember this man come to me and ask if there was room for his son in the organization. 'How old is he?' I ask. 'He's sixteen,' he tells me. 'This is too rough for a sixteen-year-old,' I say. 'Well, he has to go some place. He's eatin' up all the relief. He's growin' and growin'. A kid sixteen is all the time hungry and there's no increase in the relief.'

"I suggested he send him to the Salvation Army. 'Yeah, and they'll tell 'im all the lies from here to Kalamazoo,' he says. Finally, I let him send his son down to us. Before long we had three hundred youth in our organization. The kids had never worked for wages. They'd never had a job. So they thought that this was it. This was the way they were goin' to live forever. And they did continue that way until 19 and 39.

"There were about two thousand men in relief camps in British Columbia in 1935. The provincial government couldn't take care of this. They didn't have the money to operate the camps. So the federal government took over the camps and placed them under the jurisdiction of the Department of National Defence. The men were supplied with army boots and clothing. They had a surplus of this stuff and it didn't cost them anything to dish it out. One first-aid person took care of a whole camp. Not a doctor – just a trained orderly or something like that.

"There was no hesitation on the part of the men to join our organization. Take a single, unemployed man of twenty-one or twenty-two years of age. He was lookin' at his future in the camp. Twenty cents a day. How long was it goin' to last? He paid his dues to join the union. Five cents a month. We had plenty of working-class literature so we organized study sessions. There was a camp newspaper, too. And we'd put forward grievances if conditions were not up to scratch.

"We did what we could. There didn't seem to be any end to it. Only the war brought an end to it. I know businessmen right here in Vancouver who went down on their knees and thanked God for Hitler. He put them on their feet.

"The government took the position that it didn't have any money for a public works programme. That was the excuse right up to 19 and 39 in September when Canada declared war on Germany and Italy. Then they appropriated $600 million to produce war materials. But twenty-four hours previous to that they didn't have any money for a public works programme. They did as little as they could for the unemployed during that period.

"Young guys were always ridin' the freight during the summertime. Huntin' a job if they could find one. They would go on the prairies and do the harvest. You would get a couple of hundred dollars for that. Sometimes, in some places, the police would harass you and you'd be given a floater out of town. Or they'd put you in jail for thirty days on a charge of vagrancy.

"They didn't want us on the streets of Vancouver though or any other city. So they built the relief camps to get rid of the youth of the country. Put 'em out in the woods so that nobody would see 'em and they wouldn't be any trouble in town.

"In March 1935 we held a conference in Kamloops. The delegates reported on the conditions of the workers in the various camps. We decided to pull the camps in April. We would come out on strike because it was the only answer we had. Work and wages – that's what we were lookin' for. The idea was that if we all went together there'd be a chance.

"Princeton was supposed to be a tough district. They sent two of us in February out to stay in Princeton to contact the men in the camps. We had a couple of organizers in there.

"I lived in town in a shack. I couldn't go out. I didn't want to get locked up. The camp organizers would come in at nights. It was seventy miles from town to the camps. They'd get a ride in a truck and we'd lay down the plans for the strike. There was to be no disturbance in the camps until April. That was when we'd go out on strike.

"About five days before the strike I went out to the camps. I got a truck-ride part of the way, the rest I walked. I was supposed to be a prospector goin' out to my gold claim. The boys came out to meet me and they took me into the camp. The top camp. That whole highway was built on slave labour. They were all billeted on the roads about ten or twelve miles apart all in a line.

"I slept there that night and we pulled the camp in the morning. We took over whatever trucks were available to take in the baggage. Then we walked into Princeton. There was 450 of us. It took us a couple of days. We didn't have any food. At night we'd build fires and we'd get around the warmth as much as we could.

"The feeling among the men was that they were prepared for anything to get out of those camps. Anything at all. Once we got to Princeton we hopped a freight to Vancouver. Then we tried to get a place to sleep. And there was the question of meals. How long can a person go without eating?

"The finance committee of the men that were in had a few hundred dollars in the kitty. They dished it out, as far as it would go. Then we got help from the City Hall. Not very much but we forced it on them. We didn't get any help from the government in Victoria.

"We brought in all together around fifteen hundred men from different areas. That was a lot of people when they were hungry and there was no relief. Everybody was out watchin' us. They likened it to Cox's army marchin' on Washington. If I had been out workin' myself with a job, I would have been out watchin' them myself. I wouldn't have been able to understand it. But the fact that I was with 'em, I understood it quite well. There was a few still workin'. Not very many.

"We applied to the city for a permit to hold a tag day. They refused to give us a permit to collect money to supply meals and beds for the men. So we put on the tag day anyway. We had 2,000 tin canners out on the corners of the streets. We sent 25 collectors to New Westminster. They threw 'em in jail. We sent 50. They threw 'em in jail. Then we got on the phone to the chief of police over there and we told 'im we were sending 300. He let the others go. He turned 'em loose and we did tag in New Westminster.

"When it was finished we had $5,000. That would be equal to about

May Day Parade, Vancouver, 1935. Photo: courtesy of Vancouver Public Library

An unemployed youth demonstrates during the Depression. Many such men were shunted off the relief camps. Photo: courtesy of the Toronto Star

The soup kitchen/bread lines of the Depression years. Photo: courtesy of CBC

Harrison Mills Relief Camp in British Columbia. Photo: courtesy of Vancouver Public Library

On to Ottawa Trek, 1935. The unemployed on their way through Calgary.
Photo: courtesy of Saskatchewan Archives

Riot in Market Square, Regina, July 1, 1935. Photo: courtesy of Saskatchewan Archives

$50,000 now. We got it up in the Unemployed Hall and what are we goin' to do with it? We had to put guards on it at night. So we phoned the police station and asked 'em for two police to come down and guard the money from the tag day until the next morning. They come down and stayed all night guardin' the money.

"We went into Spencer's and Woodward's and Hudson's Bay and disrupted the activity of the big stores. People comin' in and buyin' things, they would stop and look at us with our placards. We were goin' around and around. The police come and they tried to coax us to get out of the store. There was no trouble. Only at Hudson's Bay. The guys didn't want to get out on to the street."

The Hudson's Bay episode started off in much the same way as the marches on the other big department stores. The relief camp workers marched in formation to the main floor of the downtown store and held a kind of rally there. A couple of their spokesmen explained to the shoppers why they were there and what they hoped to achieve. For about half an hour it was a peaceful demonstration until suddenly about a hundred policemen armed with clubs invaded the store and tried forcibly to evict the marchers. Though the striking workers were unarmed a bloody battle ensued. A number of people were injured and some of the strikers were arrested.

But the real action was taking place out in the street. News of the attack spread like wildfire. All over the city contingents of unemployed workers and sympathetic citizens converged on Victory Square where they were confronted by the Vancouver city police out now in full array with the added forces of the RCMP and a large number of provincial police as well.

A delegation of the striking camp workers was quickly elected and sent to meet with Mayor Gerry McGeer who had made no secret of his anti-labour sentiments. There was little dialogue with his Lordship. The entire delegation was arrested and charged with vagrancy and the mayor went immediately to the Cenotaph in Victory Square and read the Riot Act.

The police finally agreed to allow the strikers to march back to their headquarters. Vancouver settled back again into a wary truce. But the day's events left the relief camp workers even more determined to fight for what they knew were their just demands. They became more and more inventive.

"My division was No. 2. What we'd do to forestall the stool pigeon or the informer if we had any special action planned was this. In the middle of the meeting the chairman, he would say, 'Let's go.' And nobody would know where they were goin'. Only him. The police informer had to get in with the bunch and go, or stand on the sidewalk.

"Our division didn't take over the Vancouver city museum. I think that was Division 1. But we knew it was goin' to happen. They got in there, all the employees left, and they took over the place. The chief of police got a hold of myself and Mike McCauley and he took us up to the museum. It was upstairs over the public library. When the strikers see us they let us in and the chief come with us. We told them not to disturb anything in the museum that belonged to the people. It didn't belong to any group of individuals or any individual. So leave it as you come into it, we told 'em. Clean up if you make a mess.

"Outside on the street, people were sendin' up oodles of food and they held the museum for twenty-four hours. The authorities were nervous. They didn't know what to make of us. They'd never witnessed anything like that before.

"There was an enquiry while we were still in Vancouver. An investigation into the relief camps. The MacDonald Commission they called it. But nothing come of it. One of the commissioners, McHattie his name was, he was vice-president of the company that supplied the camp clothes. It was all just a cover-up. We knew that."

Though the Relief Camp Workers' Union had little faith in the MacDonald Commission they sent the Commission a formal list of their demands:

1. That work with wages be instituted at a minimum rate of 50 cents per hour for unskilled workers, and trade union rates for all skilled work, on the basis of a six-hour day, five-day week, with a minimum of twenty work days per month.
2. That all workers in relief camps be covered by the Compensation Act, and that adequate first-aid supplies be carried on the job at all times.
3. That the National Defence and all military control, with

their system of blacklisting, where men are cut off from all means of livelihood, be abolished.

4. That democratically elected committees be recognized in every camp.

5. That there be instituted a system of noncontributory unemployment insurance, based on the "workers" bill of social and unemployment insurance.

6. That all workers be given their democratic right to work.

7. That section 98 of the Criminal Code, sections 41-42 of the Immigration Act, vagrancy laws, and all anti-working-class laws be repealed.

However, the union was informed that the demands did not generally fall within the scope of the Commission's authority.

"Finally we had exhausted all help here in Vancouver. There was nothing left to do. We couldn't stay on strike any longer. Stan Lowe was in the Young Communist League and at a meeting of the party members he suggested the Trek to Ottawa. Once it had penetrated they were all for it.

"It made a lot of sense. The government was passin' the buck all the way through. The provincial government would say it was a federal proposition. They said it had nothing to do with them. The same with the city. And we couldn't open negotiations with the federal government. They were in Ottawa and we were here. So the only way we could get to 'em was to go down there.

"We decided to leave right away. The longshoremen, they were on the verge of bein' locked out in Vancouver and we didn't want to be there. We didn't want to handicap them in their struggle against the Shipping Federation. Work and wages – that's what we were goin' to Ottawa to ask the government for. Fifty cents an hour for common labour and trade union rates for skilled labour. So the Trek got underway.

"We all lined up. The CPR freight stopped at the foot of Gore Street and the first 800 got on. I was in that group. And the next CN freight, when she stopped there, another 800 got on. All the empties were sealed so we got on top of the boxcars. We could have broken the seals and got in but we didn't do that. The railroad companies didn't try to stop us. There were too many of us.

"It was very cold on those boxcars, on the top, over the Rockies particularly. But nobody got hurt ridin' the freights. You slept on the roof of the car with a blanket that you'd wrap around your head and just doze off. There was one long tunnel in the Rockies give us some trouble. We didn't know if we'd be able to breathe. But we come through all right.

"A few thousand come to see us off. There was a feeling of joy. Nobody tried to stop us. They were glad to get rid of us. We come into Kamloops, for instance, and the conductor of the freight held up the train so we could get back on after we had a meal there. So we could go farther east.

"I myself at that time didn't think it would succeed. I thought the men would just scatter when we got on the freights. I thought every division point we stopped they would get off and disappear and the thing would fizzle out. But after Kamloops, the first stop we made, I changed my mind.

"Until we got to Kamloops there was no provision made to feed the two thousand men. So we organized a committee there. We got one meal anyway. From then on we sent a committee ahead of us to organize as we went.

"In Golden, I'll never forget that. We got off the freight at four o'clock in the morning. I was so cold when I come off the roof of that boxcar I thought I was goin' to fall down. It was in June but it was cold at night up there in the Rockies.

"The committee had gone ahead of us to organize our incoming. They were gettin' everything ready for us. We walked up through the little park there and this one woman, Mrs. Sorley, a grey-haired woman well on in years, she's over a bathtub filled with food. She's got a stick about three feet long and she's stirrin' the stew.

"I just stood back there and my eyes must have popped out. She turned around and looked at me and she told me to line up the men over near the park. 'There's some tables there. We'll give 'em a hot meal,' she said. I'll never forget that bathtub. That was the best we had all the way.

"It had to be strict discipline. Any disruption in the ranks and we would expel 'em from the Trek. Just get 'em out all together. In Calgary we took up a tag day and we stayed there three days. We held a meeting and we invited all the people who sympathized with labour to voice their opinion at the meeting.

"I was chairman of that meeting and this woman come in with a note. She handed the note up to me to read. It said that it was too bad the boys were lonesome for women. She would endeavour to provide a woman for every man on the Trek. I read it out to the audience and there was bedlam. Of course we turned it down. We couldn't have anything like that.

"We were pickin' up people on the way. We knew there were 3,000 waitin' to join us in Winnipeg. We figured we would have 50,000 by the time we got to Ottawa. When we would go through towns the people were all with us. They were very sympathetic. We never had any trouble. I thought we were makin' history. No doubt about that.

"When we come to Regina what a welcome there was for us. They were down to the railroad to meet us – about 1,500 of them. But the orders had come through from Ottawa to the Royal Canadian Mounted Police to stop the Trek there. We weren't to go any farther either by train or on the highway.

"They put us in the stadium. There was lots of straw on the floor so we had a good bed and the city of Regina gave us three meals a day. Gardiner was the premier of Saskatchewan and his attorney-general was Davis. We got to know 'em pretty well, by havin' meetings with 'em.

"Then after about a week the government in Ottawa sent two representatives to Regina to negotiate with the leadership of the Trek. Dr. Manion, a cabinet minister, and Weir, the minister of agriculture, met with us in the Saskatchewan Hotel. They put it to us that we would send a delegation to Ottawa to discuss our problems with the government. They'd negotiate our demands.

"They had us across a barrel. We couldn't turn it down. Our central slogan from the time we come out of the camps was to negotiate with the federal government. If we refused them the newspapers would come out with banner headlines just slammin' hell out of us for refusing this when we had suggested it all along. But we didn't trust them. We thought it was an excuse to get the leadership away and arrest them. We figured they thought the organization would fall apart then. But it didn't work out that way.

"We were about 2,500 men now in Regina. We chose the delegation according to the position in the organization. I was the leader of Division 2. Then there was somebody else from each of the other divisions. We were eight people. Arthur Evans, Tony Martin, myself, Doc Savage, Mike McCauley, Pete Neilsen, Paddy O'Neill and John Cosgrove.

"They gave us first-class passage and meals. When we arrived in Ottawa around three o'clock in the mornin', there was an RCMP policeman to meet us. Nobody else. He took us to the hotel where we were goin' to stay. It was a hotel that had been closed and they opened it up for us. There was nobody there but us. The next morning we were to meet the government at 11:30 for a half-hour meeting. We were in there an hour and a half.

"We met Bennett, the Tory prime minister, and his cabinet. There were ten or eleven. Weir was there and Dr. Manion and there was one individual in the cabinet, Sir George Perley, a little shrivelled-up guy, and Evans wanted to know who he was. What was he doin' with the rest of 'em there?

"We met in one of the cabinet offices. A red carpet on the floor. A big, long table it was and Bennett was sittin' right in the centre. His secretary was on the corner of the table with his pad and pencil and he was takin' down notes. Bennett wanted to know first of all where we were from, where we grew up.

"Evans was the only one born and raised in Canada. I told him I was from Ireland. My forefathers had come from Galway but I wasn't born in no Ireland. I didn't care. I knew we weren't goin' to get anything from the federal government.

"Bennett had on a swallowtail coat, the collar with the wings and a dotted tie. He was so stiff and starchy, he would squeak when he moved. I had on overalls. So did Evans – he was the speaker for our group. He had on a pair of combination overalls and under that was his underwear. That was all he had. We looked like eight tramps in there.

"Evans was ready to jump right on top of Bennett's neck. He was sittin' there across the table and when he found out that none of us was born in the country, only Evans, he asked him: 'Are you sure, Mr. Evans?'

"'Yes,' says Evans, 'I wonder if I can say the same about you?'

"'You have been in jail in Westminster penitentiary, Mr. Evans,' says Bennett then.

"'No, I have never been in jail in Westminster penitentiary,' replies Evans.

"'You were also charged with theft in Alberta, in Drumheller. You were arrested, charged with theft and done time.'

"Evans got up, walked over and put his hands on the table and looked at him, eyeball to eyeball. 'You're a liar, Mr. Bennett. There's a file on me here in Ottawa, there's a file on me in Alberta, and there's also a file on me in British Columbia. I was never in jail in Westminster penitentiary and I was never arrested for theft. You're a lawyer, Mr. Bennett, you should know that. But you're lying just as you were lying to the people in 1930 when you were elected. You're the prime minister of a country with a fairly intelligent people. You're not qualified to be the prime minister of a Hottentot village in Africa.'

"I nudged McCauley and said: 'Here we go.' The RCMP was all around and the newspaper reporters was up on the transom of the door trying to get everything they could. There was only two or three spoke. They spoke against us. They took the position that the camps were not work camps. They were a place for single, unemployed men because they were loose. They didn't want them in the cities so they sent them out to the camps. They weren't adapted for work and wages.

"Bennett was very hostile. On the way out he told us: 'You're creating trouble. We will send the necessary forces north, south, east and west to stop agitators like you.' That was the end of the show. We left and come back to Regina.

"We called a meeting for the people of Regina to tell them what happened in Ottawa. It was an open-air meeting held on Market

Square on the holiday, the first of July. There was around a thousand there. Just citizens of Regina, some of 'em with baby carriages. We'd told the Trekkers to stay away. It wasn't for us at all. Only Evans was there as the speaker to tell what happened in Ottawa. But he never got a chance to speak.

"They just got the meeting goin' and then the police attacked and started clubbin' everybody that got in their way. There were shots fired. And there were over a hundred hurt. One was killed. He was a plainclothes detective. He was dressed in civilian clothes and we think the police mistook him and killed him thinking it was Evans. He was the same height, the same build. Slim and tall.

"I was in the Unemployed Hall preparing a press release with two or three others. It was a couple of blocks from where the meeting was bein' held. Then this individual come in and told us the meeting was attacked by the police. I went out and it was in full bloom right then. I see people runnin' in every direction. The police were runnin' too. There was smoke and dust and glass. Scarth Street where the meeting was held on Market Square – it looked like a tank had went through it.

"I got up on a garbage can to try to rally what was around there to get them back to the stadium where we were stayin'. Over my head from the concrete wall, the dust was goin' down my neck. They were firin' bullets. I went right down in that garbage can and tried to get under cover. It went on from about eight o'clock in the evening until midnight.

"Across the highway from the stadium they were buildin' the Grain Exchange. When we come out the next morning, there were policemen up on that with rifles and machine guns. They were all over the place. We had a meeting with the premier that morning at ten o'clock. We had to go through the police to get to the meeting. When we did get there we suggested ourselves goin' back to Vancouver, organized as we'd come into Regina. There was nobody goin' to split the organization.

"We suggested two trains and food on each train sufficient to take care of the men until we got to the coast. And they agreed on that. Those who wished to go east to their families, they would ride on the cushions and have a second-class ticket. Some of 'em did take advantage of that and went as far as Nova Scotia. But most of 'em come back to Vancouver.

"The men felt kind of let down. They blamed the government. Some of 'em got on the highway and tried to trek to Brandon, Manitoba. But they were stopped by the police. They had to come back. About a hundred of our people were arrested. There was a warrant out for me. McCauley come and told me the federal government had a warrant out for my arrest. They said if I gave myself up to the attorney-general in Saskatchewan that would quash the federal warrant. I said no. If they want me they can come and get me. I'm not goin' to give myself up at all. A federal warrant would overstep any provincial warrant, I knew that. But they arrested Evans, Cosgrove and George Black. They were three leaders of the Trek. Then they arrested a lot of rank and file. They were really after Evans. They didn't get 'im that time though. He was only in jail about three months."

Arthur "Slim" Evans became something of a legend in western Canada. As early as 1911 he was organizing coal and hard-rock miners into industrial unions through the famous "Wobblies" – the Industrial Workers of the World. Evans left the IWW and joined the Communist party when it was first formed. By the Thirties he was an organizer for the Workers' Unity League. When the Depression struck, Evans very naturally became a leader of the unemployed movement and eventually its chief spokesman.

"Evans' tactic in any organization was to get up there and fight with the police. He was all right though. A real leader.

"We come back to Vancouver on a passenger train. I was on this one train with about eight hundred and we were supposed to pick up coffee in Kamloops. But before we got there somebody found a newspaper – the *Kamloops Sentinel* I think it was. It said there that an attempt would be made to take us off the train.

"I went through the train and told the men: 'If the switch is pulled and the track is lined up for a siding, we're gonna cut the engine from the train.' But when we got to the switch-off, the switch was lined up for the station. So we stayed put.

"When the train stopped, I got out with McCauley, went into the station and picked up a couple of telegrams from the union. The two pots of coffee were right there. We took them out. There's a plainclothesman on one side of the door and there's a policeman on the other side. This policeman asks: 'Where's the men?' I told him they were in the cars riding on the cushions. First bed they'd had in four or five years. They'd been laying on concrete. 'I thought they'd come out,' he said. I told him there was nothing to come out for. We were riding right through to Vancouver.

"We had food. The government had given us over $800 worth of food on that train. There was no need for the men to come out. I had picket lines at every entrance with orders not to let any cop in the train at all.

"So we come right through to the coast. We turned over what food we had left on the train to the longshoremen. We stayed around town for a while but we had used up all our resources. The people couldn't continue to support us so we went back to the camps.

"In the fall of that year there was an election and R.B. Bennett was thrown out. That business in Regina, that was what brought them down. Mackenzie King defeated him and he changed the camps to work camps. The individual could go to work for the CPR railroad or the CN on extra gangs. When he worked he got forty cents an hour. After three months he'd be laid off and sent to Vancouver to use up that money and buy new clothes for himself. He lived a whole lot more decent. That situation carried on until the war started. Then everybody went to work."

This story carries a sombre postscript. By the time Canada went to war in 1939 very many of the relief camp workers already were war veterans. They had responded to a call for help by the Republican government of Spain, democratically elected and fighting for its life in a bloody civil war.

Volunteers who had been active in the relief camps made up close to half of the Mackenzie-Papineau Battalion, the Canadian unit that went to fight fascism. Of the 1,200 Canadians who went to Spain, 600 remain buried there. Red Walsh went to Spain. He was one of the lucky ones who came back.

"The Spanish government had appealed to all democratic countries to help them beat Franco. We didn't know then we would have to defeat Mussolini and Hitler, too. Or that Spain would be the testing ground for the machinery they were going to use in the Second World War.

"It wasn't legal to go. The Canadian government had decided that. On the back of my passport it said: This passport not valid for Spain.

"I was wounded in the last action of the Spanish war. I picked up shrapnel in the guts. After a while in hospital I left Spain with the prisoners, the last to be released. This was in February 1939. Six of us walked over the border and into France.

"Spain was the most important thing in my life. That was where you put your life on the line for your beliefs. You can't go further than that."

3

GEORGE MacEACHERN

Organizing Sydney's Steelworkers in the Thirties

Among Cape Breton miners, union tradition goes back a whole century. But for the Sydney steelworkers, the struggle to establish a union was long and difficult. The first attempt came in 1904 when the miners' union, the Provincial Workmen's Association tried to bring the unorganized steelworkers into their fold. The attempt failed. The provincial government called in federal troops to force the PWA out of the Sydney plant. For the miners it was a slap in the face. For the steelworkers it was a bitter defeat, the first of many to come.

While the Cape Breton steelworkers went unorganized, other workers across the continent were forming unions on a craft basis. Most of the organized workers at that time were master craftsmen – bricklayers, electricians, plumbers, carpenters, painters, machinists, steamfitters, printers. Many of them had come originally from Great Britain and Europe bringing their trade union traditions with them. They belonged to the Trades and Labour Congress of Canada and to its fraternal body – the American Federation of Labour.

But after the First World War the make-up of the labour force changed as Canada's economy took a different turn. Millions of dollars were poured into manufacturing industries. Thousands of rural workers moved to the cities to find jobs in plants and factories. Immigrants, eager to make a new life here, turned to industry for their livelihood.

The TLC had little interest in organizing these industrial workers. Like the AF of L it was set up to help skilled workers improve their immediate position. Moreover, Canada's central labour body, like its American counterpart, had no interest in seriously challenging the economic or political status quo. Radical unionism was seen as a threat to the established order.

Already the "Wobblies" – the Industrial Workers of the World – and the One Big Union had come and gone, unable to take hold against the combined forces of big business and craft unionism. But in 1935 a new militant labour cry was heard across North America as the Committee for Industrial Organization was born. The CIO brought fresh hope to hundreds of thousands of unorganized industrial workers.

In 1936, Cape Breton steelworker George MacEachern laid the basis for a CIO union in the Sydney plant. Barely a year after the CIO was formed the steelworkers received their charter for Lodge 1064 of the Steel Workers Organizing Committee (CIO). For George MacEachern it was a personal victory. In Cape Breton they still talk about him as the father of the steelworkers' union.

George MacEachern is retired now but is active still among the union's pensioners. He has been part of the labour scene in Cape Breton for close to sixty years and he looks back calmly on both the good times and the bad.

"When you're a radical in a big town you have quite a large circle of friends and things are much easier," he explains as we drive through the old part of Sydney down near the coke ovens and Whitney Pier. "But when you're a radical in a small town then you go through things like the McCarthy period and the Cold War days where people are afraid to be seen talking to you. They're afraid to come to your house. Afterwards they're good friends and all that sort of thing. But they're just not goin' to get involved. So we had to go through situations here that are not common to most people."

MacEachern still follows with interest the doings of the big steel local in the city, well aware of what it means to have a strong union in the Sydney plant. When he began to work there it was a different story.

"I started to work in the steel plant in September of 1922. I was eighteen. I got on as an apprentice-machinist and started at fifteen cents an hour. As an apprentice you were cheap labour doing far more work than you were paid for. There was no training schedule. No instructors. You learned solely from your fellow workers.

"My apprenticeship was supposed to be four years – 12,000 hours. But because of strikes and layoffs it took me over five years to learn the trade. Two of these years were night shift where I worked twelve hours a night to get in hours on my time and to get a little extra money, too. Twelve hours a night, six days a week.

"The seventy-two-hour week was common and then if you were fortunate enough to be allowed to work Sunday you worked. This was the way it went. Nothing extra for holidays. On the seventy-two-hour week if you worked the full week you were allowed to go home early on Sunday morning. A half hour early without loss of pay. On the day shift you worked sixty hours but you were allowed to go home a half hour early on Saturday. There were no such things as vacations.

"It was dirty in the plant. Dirty as hell. The smoke and the dirt. We'd put on clean clothes, and we didn't do that too often, and they'd be dirty before the day was over. But then you'd keep them on for a week. And there was always this smell in the air. It wasn't only a smell. You could eat your lunch while you were in this atmosphere but suppose you were to take your lunch out and try to eat it afterwards, you couldn't. It would just seep right into it.

"There was total disregard for the dignity of humans, especially people that weren't highly skilled and hard to replace. Bosses were aggressive and domineering. They could fire you out of hand and nothing would be done about it. Get off the lot – and that was it. Most workers were resigned to this. It was a condition you understood shortly after you got on if you didn't know it beforehand. It was all part of the work scene so you went along with it and tried to make the best of it. There was a lot of good humour among people. It's part of the business of being poor collectively. It helps you to bear it.

"You'd think these would have been ideal conditions to build a union. But the steelworkers hadn't been on strike since 1904. The coal miners – they were the United Mine Workers then – were on strike pretty often. We were considered to be on the weak side.

"Coal mining is the old, old occupation in Cape Breton. The coal mines were operating a century before the steel mill. But there was no railroad in those days and what shipments of coal there were would be shipped by schooner. Then in 1900, or thereabouts, an American firm headed by financier H.M. Whitney saw a great opportunity to get cheap coal for his enterprises in Massachusetts. He had a gas works and he had coal sales. He came down here and with government help bought into the coal mines. He was able to ship the coal up there cheaper than he could buy it in the United States by virtue of the fact that he owned it and sold it to himself. It was he, too, who started the steel plant.

"Whitney didn't stay here very long. He moved out but the thing kept on. They were really exploiters and wasters. They imported most of their labour. A few, a very few, came from the United States, from Alabama. There were Newfoundlanders. Then there were English that pretty generally got small-boss jobs, and big-boss jobs too. There were the Europeans. The Italians. The Ukrainians came a bit later. And the Barbadians – black people. The Polish came. And the Hungarians.

"We had communities of these people. Sort of ghettos. They stayed together because of language problems. I think that a variety of people were taken in for the purpose of keeping the workers separated. This was a common practice in steel plants throughout North America. The foreign-born had little chance of getting ahead with the exception of the odd one that would be responsible for the rest.

"The steel plant was a big operation. About four thousand were employed. In those days there was a lot of manual labour to do work later done by machines. The coke ovens, for instance, were done with a fork.

"When I went to the plant first I was shocked to see people who commanded some respect from their families and in the community being used as though they were just nothings. But it was part of the scene. Still there was a protest there even though it was a very quiet one. The workers had ways of showing their feelings toward the boss.

"I remember Lord Bessborough visited the plant one time. I don't know what his position was in English society but he was a pretty big wheel. They had the workers go down on a slight hill overlooking No. 1 gate. The gate was all festooned with boughs and that sort of thing. His Lordship arrived. H.F. Kelly, an American who was then general manager, he was a few strides ahead of his Lordship and he urged they all give his Lordship the big hand. But there was no big hand at all. However, waddling along quite a bit behind the parade was one of the foremen of the plant. He was a very corpulent guy and the butt of very many jokes. His own people used to say of him: 'The same high, the same thick.' The crowd put up three cheers for old Bruno. It was to show their disdain for the official group.

"Life was pretty grim for workers. The base rate in the plant was thirty cents. It would be a very fortunate worker that would have the luxury of a basement in his house and electric lights and running water. The cost of living was going up daily with no increase in wages.

"In February 1923, an effort was made to organize a local or a lodge as they called it of the Amalgamated Association of Iron, Steel and Tin Workers. It was a AF of L affiliate. The company resisted right from the start and one of the leading people was fired. The union responded by calling everybody out. They got a good response but the strike lasted only one day. It petered out and people drifted back."

Just a few years before in 1920 the British Steel Corporation had taken over the plant. Besco's president, Roy "The Wolf" Wolvin, stepped up the union-smashing activity. He even tried unsuccessfully to organize a company union. However, once the union had demonstrated it could take the workers out Wolvin pulled no punches. He stated bluntly to his directors that trade unionism was wrong in principle and would not be tolerated.

With full government help, Wolvin declared open season on all union activists. The company offered the workers a 10 percent raise but at the same time raided their houses. Firings and beatings were commonplace and militant workers were controlled by an elaborate spy system set up between intelligence forces of the army, the RCMP and the provincial police. But the vicious repression helped polarize the workers.

"Only about four hundred belonged to the union at the time of the

February strike. But we resented the strike police and the soldiers that came in. There were quite a number joined the union between February and June.

"In June that same year the steelworkers struck again. They didn't all come out but the majority was out. Then afterwards the strikers used to raid the plant and try to drive out the others. That's why they brought in the police. The city police didn't take a very active part. These were strike police that were recruited by the provincial government. Some were local men but very, very few. They were uniformed and had beautiful horses. And they were armed.

"Anybody that was foreign-born and had shown an interest in the labour movement was subject to these attacks. The papers would be full of them. It was ridiculous. They'd find a shotgun in a person's house and that would make him a revolutionary. When the truth was that pretty near every working-class family had a shotgun because they depended on meat from the woods to keep them going.

"Then there was the big clash at Whitney Pier. The mounted police who behaved themselves uptown often charged down the streets through the coke ovens with sabres and long nightsticks. It was a terrorist tactic. But one Sunday night they went down there drunk. There was quite a crowd coming from church. The police charged into them and beat them right and left. It wasn't a picket line that they were beating. They were just ordinary citizens – men, women and children – but there could have been quite a few strikers among them. The charge at Whitney Pier brought the miners out. J.B. McLachlan called out the miners to support us."

James Bryson McLachlan had been a leader in Cape Breton almost since he had arrived from Scotland in 1902. In 1909 when District 26 of the United Mine Workers of America was formed McLachlan was elected secretary-treasurer. His passionate conviction that working people could overcome exploitation and indignity through a strong aggressive trade union made him a ready target for a nervous government. Now he was arrested and charged with sedition.

The new Nova Scotia government of Ernest H. Armstrong had already declared that trade unionism and working-class solidarity were not to be tolerated. But no one expected the international union to line up its position right behind the government. In a surprise move, John L. Lewis, president of the international UMWA, suspended McLachlan from office and expelled him from the union.

Lewis and McLachlan had crossed swords a number of times before this. Just a few months earlier, when McLachlan led the miners out on strike and cut the company's production by at least a third, Lewis publicly denounced the miners for striking. Furthermore, Lewis was categorically opposed to McLachlan's openly professed communist politics."

"They all wanted him out of their hair – the heads of the union down in the States, governments and all. I liked Jim McLachlan. A lot of us that associated with him in those days figured Jim had all the answers. He was a wonderful platform speaker, never stuck for a phrase. If he had to make it up it was still good. But he was more or less retiring outside of that. You didn't get very close to McLachlan.

"He had been, according to his wife, pretty religious before the socialist bug hit him. But he was a very good fella. He called the miners out on strike in violation of the contract. But he called them out in support of the steelworkers.

"They charged Jim McLachlan with sedition and sentenced him to two years in the Dorchester Penitentiary. It was really Lewis who sent him to prison. By taking the support from under him he left him vulnerable.

"Jim told me himself that when he was on trial they put a policeman on the stand who had been in on the business at Whitney Pier beating up the people. Jim's lawyer asked this man if the policemen were drinking at that time. He answered yes. Would you say that they were drunk? Yes, he said. They moved then that the case be dismissed. That was the charge against McLachlan, that he'd said the policemen were drunk. This was the sedition.

"But the judge then explained what sedition was. He explained it this way. If the Prince of Wales was to come down Barrington Street staggering and somebody said he was drunk, and the prince wasn't drunk but was staggering for some other reason, this would be slander. But if he was drunk, it would be sedition. Imagine! McLachlan was sent to the Dorchester Penitentiary.

"Lewis deposed the executive of District 26 of the UMWA and ordered the miners back to work. And they went. He notified the steel management of this by telegram. According to Duane Curtis, one of the strike leaders, they were in the steel office discussing recognition of the union and the telegram from Lewis came. Lewis informed the management of the steel plant before the workers themselves knew that this was taking place. The bottom fell out of the whole thing. The strike just fell apart. Once the miners went we had nothing left.

"There weren't any great wage demands in our strike. Recognition was the main thing. But like the February walkout, it petered out. It broke the union completely. The workers were subdued. Some were blacklisted and went away. The company was pretty well satisfied. There was no danger of unions for a while.

"People that had taken an actual part in the strike, they were angry. And then shortly after that the company set up a plant council. It was like a company union. Some of the leaders of the strike joined that. They ran as delegates to it. I didn't want anything to do with it. It was so obviously phony. They had a pretty good set of constitution bylaws but the company wasn't obliged to live up to them because, well, if they didn't what could the workers do about it?

"Besco later became Dosco – Dominion Steel and Coal. They owned the coal mines, too. Here in Sydney workers depended almost entirely on work at the steel plant. There were other smaller industries that folded up one after the other. People would say at the time that Dosco didn't want any other employers around here; that they wanted to have a monopoly on the labour market; that they wanted to be able to pick and choose. So Dosco was the big thing. It was a pretty ruthless outfit.

"When production got low and there were layoffs, then the public outcry would be for a government-financed rail order for the CNR or whatever. If you got a million-dollar order in those days you were set for a long while. It provided a backlog and other operations in the mill could go on and produce at a lower rate because of the volume. It was a political thing that they could arrange to have things at a low ebb coming on election. Then they'd holler for a rail order. They'd get the rail order and this represented votes.

"It was all politics. My God, it was almost unbelievable that governments could be so controlled by industry. But they were. The company would just have to call on the government and the government would act."

The plant council at the Sydney mill met weekly over lunch for the next few years. As the militants expected, it was totally ineffectual. Management delegates made sure that when any of the workers' representatives stepped out of line they were quickly dispensed with and fired. Twelve- or thirteen-hour shifts, seven days a week, were still the order of the day at the Sydney plant.

By the middle of 1932, Dosco had cut wages by 15 percent. When production came to a standstill early the following year the plant closed down. City landlords were generally sympathetic about rents owing, but Dosco insisted upon deducting back-rent for all company houses when the men were eventually rehired. Living conditions for steelworkers were deplorable and with each new injustice, resentment against the company flared up anew. Again and again, militant workers would devise new schemes to organize.

"When the Amalgamated Association failed, the OBU had made an effort to organize. It was around 1928 but it didn't get off the ground at all. People were still fearful. In 1930 there was a man named Rannie that had come here from the Halifax shipyards. He'd been active in the old Workers' party, the forerunner of the Communist party. He came into the plant and immediately he went onto the plant council, the first election.

"He had quite a personality and he did know a thing or two that the rest of us didn't. He knew something about Marx. And he wanted a machinists' union. We agreed the union would be a good thing. We held a meeting and I was elected recording secretary. But the day we got our charter, all our executive and quite a number of the others were fired.

"Of course we protested. The company got busy and moved all the work out of the shop so that if the Department of Labour sent somebody in they'd see that there was no work and that's why we'd been laid off.

"The day after I was laid off from the plant I went out to Glace Bay

J.B. McLachlan, an early leader of the United Mine Workers of America in Cape Breton. Photo: courtesy of Beaton Institute, College of Cape Breton

Sydney steel union executive in 1942. George MacEachern, president, second from left in front row (partially obscured). Photo: courtesy of Beaton Institute, College of Cape Breton

where they were building the Seaboard Power Plant. I went out on the first tram car in the morning and applied for a job. I was signed up and the fella that was signing me up, the superintendent or whatever, asked where I worked last. I told him the Sydney steel plant and he just tore up the papers and said: 'I'm sorry I can't hire you.'

"I don't know if that was a personal blacklist or an arrangement that the company had with them because they were intending to take back some of the workers and they didn't want to lose them. At the same time, they wanted to get rid of those they considered ringleaders.

"I went down to Lunenberg and worked there for a while. I only had a couple of months there, then I had seven days on the highway before the election, and another week at Atlantic Spring. In ten months that was the only income we had.

"We had it pretty tough. We were damn good and hungry at times. There was no unemployment insurance in those days. We ate canned beans or whatever we could get. I remember once we were living on canned pineapple that we got for ten cents a tin. Generally the things that we'd eat would be just what would fill you. Make you feel half-satisfied. Still we got by.

"On the advice of some friends I met in the bootlegger's, I went to see Mr. Fraser, the general superintendent of the Sydney plant. You see, even when you can't get enough to eat, people will invite you to have a drink. They told me things were picking up and that I should be trying to get my job back. So I walked to Mr. Fraser's house and I was surprised at the reception I got. He might have been drinking, too. He said he was amazed I wasn't back to work. He wound up telling me that he'd tell the master mechanic the very next day to put me back to work.

"I worked fairly steady for almost a year or more. Then the Depression started to take hold here. Again we were out of work. Mind you, our living conditions had always been such that the Depression didn't cause any of us to jump out windows because it represented so little in the way of change. Most of the time we didn't have a dime. We went hungry. Oh Jesus, yes. But what the hell. We never had anything anyway.

"Only a very, very small number were working. Just maintenance mainly. Parts of the plant you couldn't close down. You couldn't close down the coke ovens, the blast furnace, or those mills that operate by heat without warping them.

"I joined the Unemployed Union and was active in that. Then through the Unemployed I got word of the Canadian Labour Defence League that the Rev. A.E. Smith had organized. I joined that too and the class consciousness was growing all the time.

"The CLDL's job was to defend working people who were arrested during the Depression years. And there were around ten thousand arrested in that period. For their opinions mainly. The formal charge would be vagrancy or whatever. Anyone trying to organize would be the tallest tree that lightning strikes first. Organization was always a menace to the powers that be. But they didn't confine themselves to that. They'd arrest anyone that would take part in a demonstration whether you were a leader or not.

"Some workers were deported. I remember Hans Kist. He was taken from Upper Canada and deported through Halifax to Nazi Germany where he was immediately killed by weights dropped on him, starting at his feet, the story went. He was deported for being a radical, I suppose. They could do this with impunity. There was no work for them anyway, they used to say, so they might as well be out of here. But people in the labour movement knew why they were being deported.

"There were some deported back to Scotland and England, too. That was a surprise to most people that heard it. These workers that had considered themselves part of Canada couldn't be considered to be Canadians no matter how long they were here. It was always a danger if you were a radical in the labour movement.

"In the Canadian Labour Defence League I met with Earl McNeill. Earl had been around quite a bit in unemployed demonstrations. He was a communist. Then after that, Sam Scarlett came to town. Sam had quite a record in the IWW and in the peace movement in the States. He was an organizer for the Workers' Unity League.

"We used to have little study meetings at Bill Clark's store in the evenings. Bill didn't have a regular store. He used to sell Rawleigh's products and he used to have them there. A fella came in called Phil

Luck. I don't know if that was his real name. People in those days used to adopt what they'd call revolutionary names. Phil asked if I'd ever thought of joining the Communist party. I told him I had but I didn't know where the Communist party was. I knew of McLachlan and that was all. So he signed me up. This must have been '34.

"There was a new idea afoot around this time that militants should use the company-sponsored plant council to build a real union. You were given a great deal of freedom if you were on the council. So I ran for plant council and was elected. After some months I got the council interested enough in the wage question to warrant a visit from the president of Besco. His name was Sir Newton Moore. He lived in England. He came to our meeting and told us that it wasn't a question of more wages but how long they could pay the wages they were paying and continue to operate. He told us of the hard time he had getting along.

"After the meeting I got a few of the plant councillors together – just a few, it was all I could. I asked them if they were prepared to go back and tell the workers it was hopeless. What else could we do, they wanted to know. I told them that at least we could put the alternative as follows: It's hopeless under this set-up but it wouldn't be under a union.

"I asked them to come to my house that night. Five of them came. Three were plant councillors. Two were militant workers. The only decision we could come to was to go back and ask the workers if they wanted a union, then meet the following Thursday night and decide what the next step would be.

"The next Thursday night came and only one arrived. He wasn't a man in the best position to organize a union. He didn't have a great deal of education. He was brought up in one of the Newfoundland outports. He knew what side he was on though, that can be said. He had a big family to feed and he was a cripple. He'd had a thigh broken in the Drumheller mines in Alberta. It hadn't been set properly and he had a very bad limp. Harry Davis was his name.

"We waited, Harry and I, until nine o'clock. Nobody else showed up. They were afraid to come. The only thing to do was try and build a union from scratch. We decided to start out with what we had. We elected Harry president of the new union, myself as secretary. The next day I took the day off and went to Glace Bay to a printers and got union cards and stamps made.

"When we got all this material we called a meeting and got a pretty good response. After our second meeting the plant council was called in and given a 10 percent increase in wages. Wages by that time had dropped to twenty-eight cents an hour so that 10 percent would be only three cents.

"We had the makings of a fairly good union. There would have been about 3,000 working in the steel mill at this stage. We had signed up 660. The Independent Steelworkers of Nova Scotia it was called. The dues were very low – something like ten cents a month.

"There was a move at that time to form these independent unions. One was started in Hamilton at Stelco, in Sault Ste. Marie at Algoma, and in Trenton, Nova Scotia, another part of the Dosco empire. There were independent steelworkers all over. We didn't know where to affiliate. The AF of L didn't offer anything for industrial unions. The old AF of L Amalgamated Iron Steel and Tin Workers had almost fallen apart.

"Later that same year there were two more wage increases of 7½ percent. Our meetings fell off. Then there was an election where R.B. Bennett came out with his eight-point programme for social progress. One of the points was the eight-hour day.

"The workers in the plant wanted the eight-hour day without any reduction in pay naturally. It was an opportunity to work up some enthusiasm for the union again. Not too many places down this way had the eight-hour day. It was a good issue, made to order.

"One Thursday we got a meeting with Mr. Kelly, the general manager. I wasn't on the plant council at this time. I'd just stayed on it for one term until I got the independent union going. But there were a couple of members of the plant council there. Kelly told us they'd give us the eight-hour day when they were good and ready and in the meantime he wasn't talking to any goddamn bunch of gate-crashers.

"That Saturday night we arranged a big meeting at the Temperance Hall. We had written to Finlay MacDonald, the Conservative member of Parliament, and asked him to speak at our meeting. When he didn't show up we sent a man out to see if he could find him. But MacDonald wasn't anywhere to be found. However, our messenger happened to go by the radio station where he found Bob Stewart waiting outside. Bob was one of the left-wing leaders of the miners. He told our man that Jim McLachlan and Annie Buller, the well-known union organizer who had come to Cape Breton to manage McLachlan's electoral campaign, were upstairs at the radio station giving an election address. The messenger came back to the meeting where we had a good crowd and we asked if they wanted to hear McLachlan and Annie Buller. The crowd said yes so they came and spoke. It was quite a night.

"The following night there was a meeting at the Strand Theatre. It was packed and Bob Stewart and I sent a joint telegram to R.B. Bennett from the Amalgamated Mine Workers and the Steelworkers unions. We told him we wanted the eight-hour day and we wanted it immediately. We didn't want to wait for an election.

"This really frightened the company. We had so much support and there was so much talk about it. They had their staff out on Sunday night. The lights were all on at the general office. Then the first thing Monday morning they called in the plant council and announced when each department would get the eight-hour day. It had been all worked out on the Sunday night. That was quite a change from Thursday to Monday. But they wanted to head off trouble.

"All this was very encouraging but it still didn't increase the membership of the union. It had really dropped off. Our meetings were few and far between. The Independent Steelworkers of Nova Scotia was dying of extreme independence. We didn't have an affiliation anywhere."

It was at this time that the great debate over the issue of whether or not to organize workers in mass industries became very central. While a few union leaders like John L. Lewis supported the idea of industrial unions, the old craft unions were still vehemently opposed.

However, in 1935 a number of large AF of L unions, including Lewis' United Mine Workers of America, at odds with the Federation's growing conservatism defiantly set up the Committee for Industrial Organization. Its aim was to organize on an industry basis regardless of trade or craft.

The CIO was a powerful new organizing tool for hundreds of thousands of industrial workers across North America. For George MacEachern and the steelworkers at the Sydney plant it offered a new way to struggle against the exploitation of the powerful Dominion Steel and Coal Corporation. Now, with the CIO, the Cape Breton steelworkers would no longer be an isolated union trying to go it alone against Dosco and the government.

"I wrote to Van A. Bittner, the director of organization for the CIO, and got credentials to organize. You had to have ten members to get a charter. Carl Neville agreed to act as president. I got ten executive members at a dollar apiece, sent the names away and got our charter. We became Lodge 1064 of the Steel Workers Organizing Committee (CIO).

"Then Carl and I went to the district convention of the United Mine Workers and got a pledge of support there. They said they'd support us to the point of strike to see that we were recognized and organized. The miners asked the international office to appoint Silby Barrett, at that time an international board member of UMW, responsible for the organization of the steelworkers.

"Our relationship with Barrett was pretty good. He was a Newfoundlander, a coal miner, and he walked in the shadow of John L. Lewis. If John L. Lewis was to the left, Barrett automatically went to the left. He didn't even have to think about it. If John L. Lewis turned away from the left, Barrett turned away too. But in the early days Lewis was quite happy to use communists to organize in the CIO. He knew we were dedicated and we were willing to work free.

"We didn't get a cent from the international. We didn't need it. There was a little bit of money left over from the independent union. We hired halls all over the city wherever we could get them. We arranged meetings one after the other and did practically all the work ourselves. Silby Barrett came to one or two meetings, that was all.

"It was moral support we needed. People in those days were looking in the direction of Roosevelt as though he were the representative of the Second Coming and with pretty good reason. He wasn't the worst president the U.S. ever had by any means. Even here in Canada people were looking in that direction and were connecting up the CIO successes with the Roosevelt liberalism. We still had a few people who'd been hurt in 1923 and who were against international unions but by and large everyone supported the CIO.

"There was terrible animosity between the CIO and the TLC in Canada. We ran into some pretty poisonous people. I think the worst of them I had anything to do with was the president of the Halifax Longshoremen's Union. Just to mention the word CIO would set him off. Even the very fact that we existed. We went down there to meet the government one time and somebody brought him up to our room in the hotel. Oh boy, was he an angry man! We were nothing but a bunch of bloody 'reds.'

"However, that wasn't the main argument against the CIO. It was the fact that people were being organized industrially and presenting a danger to the little empires that were being set up by the craft unions. They felt that all of us industrial workers should stay unorganized unless we were in select groups and could be controlled.

"But they couldn't stop us. The CIO was magic. It was carrying on great big struggles all over the continent and the people were able to identify with them.

"The thirteenth day of December was our first meeting. By March 1937 we had three thousand members in the union. The big attraction was that we were joining a big organization on the go. Dues at that time for the Steel Workers Organizing Committee were only twenty-five cents a month. You might say anybody'd give you a quarter to get rid of you. But that wasn't the picture at all. We had an office on the main street. On payday there'd be a line-up down the stairs, down the street. People waiting to pay their quarter.

"Still the company wouldn't recognize us. They said they had a union in the plant council. Carl and I went down and asked the council to disband. They wouldn't do it. We were actually timid about going on strike because the international office had no funds. They had big strikes in the States and there was nothing to send down here.

They even told us one time they needed our cheques to pay the office staff in Pittsburgh."

The situation looked grim. Then the steelworkers found a friend in an unexpected quarter. Angus L. Macdonald, the Liberal premier of Nova Scotia, happened to be making a visit to Sydney where his brother Stanley was a priest. Could they reach the premier through his brother? The steelworkers decided to try.

"Carl Neville approached Stanley Macdonald to set up a meeting with Angus L., which he did in the Isle Royale hotel. We met him and he agreed to help us. He said he couldn't promise us a Trade Union Act because there was nothing like it in Canada at the time.

"We had a bill drawn up. It was based on the Wagner Act in the United States. The premier promised us before he left that it would come before the House if he had to introduce it himself. But he said: 'Don't expect too much because I have no workers in my cabinet, let alone trade unionists, and I'm bound to have a lot of opposition. Get as much support for your bill as you can around here. That'll help me greatly.'

"We got out petitions. We got out resolutions. We got a wonderful response. There was no organization except the Sydney Board of Trade that refused to endorse the bill. Pretty near the end of the session of the legislature we went up to go before the Law Amendments Committee. The result was that we got the Trade Union Act. It became law on April 17, 1937.

"The act gave us the right to organize. It enforced recognition and the checkoff of union dues. As far as I know it was the first Trade Union Act in Canada.

"The plant council disbanded once the act was passed and the company had to meet with us. I remember well that when we had our first meeting with the boss after the CIO was established our first demand, and it wasn't a written demand or part of any negotiations, was that the workers be treated with respect.

"Mr. Fraser, the general superintendent at the time, was kind of taken aback by this. His idea of respect was different from ours. He thought respect meant you touched your cap to people or you pulled your hairlock or something like this. He said: 'I suppose you want the boss to call them *sir.*' But we told him it wasn't necessary. If they'd just stop abusing the workers, that's all we wanted.

"It had a very good effect. It had such an effect that some bosses who thought before that the role of a boss was to bully and badger found that when they weren't allowed to do that, life was more livable. They got just as much work done and they felt better themselves about things. In fact, one fella even got to be kind of popular as a result.

"This was the spring of 1937. We didn't start right away to negotiate a contract. Some of us weren't all that fussy about contracts. There were so many things that needed straightening out, we figured they'd be better straightened out by direct action. For years we'd been hearing that the contracts in the mines hadn't been that good. So we didn't press for one ourselves. We were afraid it would tie us down. We had recognition and we'd go down with our grievances. We were kept busy. There were a lot of steel departmental strikes going on. The workers found this was the only way they could get problems solved.

"It wasn't until around 1940 that Silby Barrett pushed us to go for a contract. There weren't any clear-cut demands. We negotiated for what we could get which was nothing. The international office sent a man up to help us. He wasn't much help. He was a United Mine Workers man and a state senator, Senator Sneed. He suggested a cut for some of the men in the Wire and Nail Mill. The local executive just walked out of that meeting.

"We'd been offered a raise of one cent for these men but Sneed thought they were getting more money than they'd earned. The rate had been set when the place was full of acid fumes. The fumes were no longer there and he felt there wasn't any reason why they should get the extra money. But we weren't cutting anybody's wages.

"I was part of the negotiating team. We felt like Mr. In-between. We had the international office on one side and the company on the other. Both of them were trying to do a job on us. We weren't very happy. The international policy was to get things the easiest way possible. They were a business union. They wanted to get a contract and they'd go to any length to get it.

"In the days when John L. Lewis headed up the thing the whole organization was militant. But by this time Lewis had got fed up and he copped out. He was the kind of guy that had to have his own way or he'd take his ball and bat and go home. He stayed head of the United Mine Workers and Philip Murray was in strict control of Steel.

"Murray had made it known he wouldn't support us in the case of a strike. He didn't have to give a reason. I suppose he had no money for one thing. He had already told Carl Neville that they'd been waiting for our cheque, ours and Trenton's, to pay the office staff in Pittsburgh. There was no money in the States. They had all those big strikes. The workers accepted this. I was surprised they did. I also wonder what the alternative would have been. It wouldn't have been good at all. It would have meant a short, sharp struggle if anything. It would have meant discouragement. It was a pretty hard pill to take but they took it.

"We put it to a vote. Some of us were pretty rebellious but reason had to take over. All our work would have gone down the drain and we would have had nothing. We had to wait for another day to fight. We knew very well that Murray would never just wash his hands of us. He'd be actively opposed to us. It'd be a great chance for him to clean house and put in an administration.

"These negotiations failed and we got a conciliation board which was possible in those days with the government paying the full shot. Father Boyle who was active in the People's School of the St. Francis Xavier Extension Department was our representative on the board.

"After meeting for months and months between here and Montreal they came down with the recommendation of less than two cents an hour increase. It was an odd fraction and the company found it easier bookkeeping to give two cents an hour. The remarkable thing is that the workers accepted it."

Finally, the Steel Workers Organizing Committee (CIO) had settled its first contract with Dosco. They won little in the way of economic gains and there were still tortuous times ahead. The real satisfaction lay in the fact that the principle of collective bargaining had been soundly established in the Sydney steel mill. It was a right they had won forever.

"Our people weren't pushed around much once we got the union going. We had power as a union group,"recalls George MacEachern.

Two years later, in 1942, Lodge 1064 of SWOC became Local 1064 of the United Steelworkers of America. Like the coal miners, the steelworkers in Cape Breton now had a weapon to use against the vagaries of Dosco whose policy was still to hire and fire workers according to the fluctuations of the market. Year after year production kept slipping as the Sydney plant continued to operate with obsolete technology. Profits made in Sydney were reinvested in Ontario and Quebec. Cape Breton steelworkers were forced to leave for Toronto and Montreal to find work.

The Sydney steelworkers had learned to fight the hard way and just as well. In October 1967, Dosco made a surprise announcement that it would phase out operations in the steel plant and close it down completely within six months. Local 1064 immediately went into action. They mobilized the entire region to save their plant. This time it was not just some jobs at stake. Now their entire livelihood was being taken away. They used all the militant tactics learned by Cape Breton workers since the turn of the century.

The public response was so strong that within weeks the government of Nova Scotia committed itself to take over the Sydney plant and run it as a Crown Corporation. Jubilant steelworkers were determined to show that given half a chance their industry could be successful. At the end of twelve months they had ejected over a million tons of steel and established a seventy-year production record. It was the beginning of a new phase in their long battle for survival.

4

RAY STEVENSON

Sudbury and Northern Ontario's Miners in the Forties

The militant, radical tradition of the Mine, Mill and Smelter Workers Union remains classic in trade union history. It reaches back to the early syndicalist struggles of the Industrial Workers of the World and to the rapid development of the Western Federation of Miners out of the appalling conditions that existed in mines in Canada and the United States.

By 1916, the union was well entrenched in the West and had gained a foothold in the silver mines of Cobalt, Ontario. But industrial trade unionism fell on bad times. By 1930, Mine-Mill had almost disappeared.

Then powerful, new forces came into play. In 1931, the communist-led Workers' Unity League began organizing industrial workers and a few years later, the wild enthusiasm generated by the Committee for Industrial Organization swept over the continent. Suddenly, sparked with fresh vitality, the Mine, Mill and Smelter Workers Union burst upon the scene again in the mining fields of northern Ontario.

At first, the big union drive was centred in Sudbury where the powerful International Nickel Company employed about eight thousand workers. But Inco fought back ferociously and finally in 1938 the main organizational activity was moved to Kirkland Lake and the goldfields. Gold was strong on the international market and the possibility of organizing in a community where there were ten individual companies seemed better than having to take on the giant Inco.

Mine-Mill then embarked on the most turbulent period of its history. Before it was finished Hitler, Mackenzie King, Senator Taft, the

U.S. State Department and the Canadian labour movement would all play a role in the unfolding drama.

Ray Stevenson was another player in the Mine-Mill story. After many years as an organizer in the mines of northern Ontario and Quebec he joined the national executive board of the union. Later, he became editor of the *Mine-Mill Herald*. When the Mine, Mill and Smelter Workers Union merged with the Steelworkers in 1962, Stevenson joined the public relations department of the United Steelworkers of America.

His years as a Mine-Mill organizer put Ray Stevenson in the thick of the union's struggle. In several meetings in Toronto he told me this story before leaving for a new job with the World Peace Council in Helsinki, Finland. His work there will deal with the activities of the multinational corporations and how trade unions around the world can protect their interests in the face of the vast power these corporations represent.

Ray Stevenson took up this new post in January 1979. But back in 1938, he was just another seventeen-year-old Manitoba farm boy who hopped a freight and came looking for work in the goldfields.

"I had thirteen cents when I arrived in Kirkland Lake. I was there about a month, living on handouts, mowing lawns, whatever I could do. I found a couple of fellows I had known out west. They grubstaked me once in a while and we managed. I finally got a job at this Upper Canada Mine and on the second day as I was putting my clothes on the hooks in the dry-out at the change-house, the fellow dressing next to me whispered: 'I want to see you after.' 'What about?' I asked him. 'The union,' he said. So down we went and I joined the union.

"It was still a very clandestine thing. To have proclaimed union membership would have been asking for trouble. There was a union office but it was watched. People going in and coming out were known. So a lot of people just didn't go there. The union was established in the sense that there were a number of people working as committee people very quietly, as quietly as you could in most of the mines.

"The production of gold had become quite important, particularly after 1933 when Roosevelt raised the price to $35 an ounce from something like $22. We had some large mines there – Lakeshore which was the Sir Harry Oakes' holding and Wright-Hargreaves which was the economic basis on which the *Globe and Mail* was established were two of the big ones. Bill Wright had used profits from the mine to bring about the amalgamation of the *Mail and Empire* and the *Globe* in Toronto. So the press was on their side.

"Kirkland Lake was a boom town in that there was employment. The wage rates of four dollars a day plus were rather high wages in those days. So you had a work force that was earning good wages. At the same time you had a constant influx of people into the area looking for work. There must have been about eighteen thousand people in Kirkland Lake at that time. There were a lot of miners who had come into the area before the 1930s from Cobalt because of the situation that developed when the bottom fell out of the silver market. In a sense they were the real founders of Kirkland Lake. They built homes, some sort of educational system, some kind of hospital care. All these things were there when I arrived.

"Taxes were very high because there were no municipal levies against the mining industry. It's the reason that to this day Kirkland Lake is not a municipality. It's a township. The gold mines always opposed the idea of becoming a municipality because the mines were right in and under the town and if it had been incorporated they would have been subject to certain tax levies. By maintaining it as a township they escaped that.

"Huge amounts of wealth were being mined and shipped out and the gold barons were prospering. Their political relationship with the government, particularly the government of Ontario, was a very interesting one. Mitchell Hepburn who was elected during that mid-Thirties period was the main anti-CIO warrior. He had very close ties with Bickell of McIntyre, with Oakes, Wright and so on. It was very much a Tory-Liberal-big business-dominated town.

"It was pretty hellish work. The hours first of all. You'd finish your job then you'd go home. Occasionally, maybe once or twice a week, you'd finish an hour or so ahead. So those days you didn't work eight hours underground. You worked seven. But most of the time men were staying down nine, ten hours in order to complete the particular job they were assigned.

"There was tremendous speed-up. One of the jobs that I had was called 'mucking in the drift.' This was with shovels. You'd approach a thirty- or thirty-five-ton pile of broken rock with a little car on rails. You shovelled that rock into that little car, then you pushed the car as far as you had to, dumped it and brought it back. Two of you would manhandle thirty-five or forty tons a day. You were in a constant state of near exhaustion, sweat, stripped-down.

"They had to leaven all this stuff so an incentive system for underground workers was set up so that you'd make another 50 cents a day. The really great bonus, as they used to call it, was a dollar a day. This was on top of the $4.20 basic rate for an underground labourer. The more advanced worker, the miner, would make $4.65. But this necessarily led to shortcuts on safety measures.

"Mining in itself is dangerous. You're dealing with steel, rock and explosives in the dark. In Kirkland Lake when I went there they were still using the old carbide lamps. They didn't have the modern up-to-date electric lamps. Somebody would blast down the way a piece and your light would go out. If you couldn't get it going again you were there in the dark. And that's pretty dark.

"We kept working at trying to build the union. At an organizational level it meant seeking out those people in the work force that you were with in each mine to get them to sign membership cards and agree to pay one dollar a month dues. We used to have regular meetings of the membership at a place called the Polish Hall built by the progressive Polish community. There we would discuss general strategy and tactics. But the main thing that had to be beaten was the fear – fear of reprisal by the company, fear of being fired, fear of not being able to provide for families. That was the essential thing. And from that point of view the people that we'd meet underground, or get out in a corner somewhere outside of the mine property to talk about the union, would be the most active and developed core. The idea was that if we got them organized there were a lot of other people who would follow them. We had to get into a position of challenging the absolute rights the company had. And in order to do that we had to bring these people together.

"The various companies were very well organized. There was a fascinating character by the name of Alec Harris who, during the days of the Workers' Unity League in Kirkland Lake pre-1936, had appeared at the Lakeshore mine. He was in charge of supplies and so on which meant he came in contact with a great many workers. And he was a great listening post. People began to suspect that he was reporting to the company although he appeared as just another worker.

"When the Mine-Mill-CIO chartered Local 240 Mr. Harris' true colours became apparent. He became secretary of the Kirkland Lake and District Mining Association. He made a huge jump from a tool clerk-keeper right up into the top echelons.

"Many and many a fired worker changed his name and went to another place to get a job. But very efficient lists of 'undesirables' were kept by all the companies and later there was some kind of centralized information that the companies shared with each other.

"There's no question that the blacklist thing operated and workers knew it. Companies didn't even go to too much trouble to hide it. They wanted workers to know they were being watched.

"Right at the beginning of the war the only difference up there was that the labour market in itself had changed. Now instead of people running around looking for jobs they ran away and joined the army. As a matter of fact Charlie Millard who was trying desperately at that time to get the directorship of the Mine, Mill and Smelter Workers came to Kirkland Lake in 1939 in order to make a speech at one of our meetings. He said that most of the people who had gone into the First Division were people from the unemployed rolls. Then he went up to Timmins to make the same speech and the Royal Canadian Mounted Police arrested him for carrying on antiwar activities. And poor old Charlie had to backwater like mad on that one.

"By 1940 we had made some progress in different mines and we had built up a membership particularly at one mine called Teck-Hughes. There was a bit of an abortive strike there in 1940. The tactic was wrong obviously. They couldn't hold out but they were out for two days and that to us was a great victory.

"The decision of the international executive board then was to intensify the organizational efforts in the Kirkland Lake area. And this flowed from a whole number of circumstances including the fact that the United States was not at war, that there seemed to be a bright future for gold production, and that not everybody was knowledgeable then about what was going to happen.

"So in 1940 the international sent in a chap by the name of Tom Maguire. Tom was from Montana. He was originally a smelter-man and his father had been a miner. He was a very ardent union guy except that he was Catholic and anticommunist. He had been sent in by the international to clean the reds out and then to intensify the organizing.

"Tom arrived there and all the main people around were left-wing, communists, whatever. I had joined the Communist party in 1939. I wasn't quite sure of what I was doing but I did. Anyway Tom decided he'd have to work with us for a while. We began to develop new tactics and finally got to the point of a couple of plant-gate rallies where we had about two hundred guys. But I think the biggest turning point was a Victory Loan parade.

"After a big debate we decided to participate as a union in this Victory Loan parade. We tried to get everybody out that we could. Everyone was on tenderhooks because we didn't know if we'd have 200 or what we'd have. As it turned out either because of the work we'd done or just plain cussedness or opposition to the company, there were about 3 or 4,000 of us. This was early in the spring of 1941. We knew then that we were succeeding and we called upon the companies to sit down and bargain.

"During that entire period there was nothing that said that even if you organized a mine 100 percent that the company had to sit down and bargain. The only way you could compel the recognition of the union was the strike weapon. There was the Industrial Disputes Investigation Act and some of these other acts but there was nothing that compelled a company to sit down and bargain collectively. That was what we were fighting.

"There was a special commission established with the man who later became Justice McTague to investigate the situation. We appeared in front of that. By this time a lot of attention was being focussed on

Kirkland Lake by labour circles in the rest of Canada. People saw it as the battleground for the whole struggle for union recognition. And of course the companies helped with that.

"When we finally submitted our list of ten demands to them, I think it was in June of '41, they responded that they'd be prepared to meet with committees of men to discuss nine of the points but they would not discuss point No. 1 which was for union recognition.

"The issue sharpened to the point where we had a strike vote in late September or early October that carried at eight of the ten mines. From there on it was all downhill. We were headed for a confrontation. In August, to test our strength we had pulled off a one-day holiday as we called it – a stoppage. This was before the strike vote. We closed all of the mines tight for twenty-four hours and at the same time offered that we'd work a Sunday to make up for production so they didn't come at us. Out of that one-day stoppage the confrontation situation continued to develop and so on November 22 we were out on strike. All eight of the ten mines.

"Two mines voted against the strike. They were smaller mines but important too – the Upper Canada Mine which was about fourteen or fifteen miles east of Kirkland Lake and the mine in Swastika. I think it was essentially because of the management-worker relationship. I worked myself for a time at the Upper Canada Mine before the strike and the management there was quite liberal. They'd sit down and talk with the boys. The same thing at this other small mine in Swastika. The vote there was very close but the majority was against it.

"I don't recall precisely how the vote went on an overall basis but in the eight mines that did carry out the strike there were something like 4,000 workers involved. When we set up the pickets, of that 4,000 I suppose there were at least 1,000 who didn't come out with us. They scabbed.

"A deliberate policy of the mining companies in northern Ontario in those days was to exclude local French Canadians from working in the mines and then utilize them in a strike as a scab force. These were augmented by new people who were brought in and lived on the mine sites. This was particularly true of the Wright-Hargreaves where they brought in as many as a hundred and more from rural Quebec. A great many of them from a place called Mud Lake, which is on the east side of Lake Temiskaming.

"These people didn't know what they were getting into. They were taken into the mine, housed and fed in there. They were virtually prisoners. It became a matter of debate during the course of the strike what our attitude to them should be. There were two opposing points of view. The official view prevailed that we should work with these people to try to persuade them to come out with us. The other point of view was that we should knock them on the head. Find ways and means of making it impossible for them.

"There was a lot of pretty rough stuff went on during that strike, mainly to scare the hell out of these people so that they would disappear and get out of our way. Many of them were beaten up. Not so much the French Canadians at the Wright-Hargreaves mine. They were maintained on the property. It was difficult even to get to them. The mine sites were under heavy guard.

"One inflammatory element that was introduced very early in the strike was the action of Hepburn and the Ontario government in sending in as many as four hundred Ontario provincial police who were very much in evidence. They came on a special train to Swastika. Then they were taken by bus to the outskirts of Kirkland Lake on the west end and marched through the town in military formation. That was their grand arrival and it was done to intimidate the strikers.

"As the strike developed it became almost like guerrilla warfare. We had to set up counter-squads. I was the captain of one of these clandestine squads myself. We worked out the strategy of trying to get those workers who were hoistmen and put them out of commission. You can't run a mine without hoistmen. There were many incidents of charges of intimidation. That was the charge they liked to lay against anyone who wore a union button. Even for no reason. But the other side of it is there were a few scabs who got it and got it good.

"Because the connections between the provincial government of Mitchell Hepburn and the gold-mining barons were very close, the government was moving hard to support the gold operators and prevent an amicable settlement of the situation. It wasn't just a passive role they played. The other confounding thing was that we were operating under the War Emergency Powers Act which created a very unclear situation as to the federal-provincial jurisdiction.

"George McCullogh, the publisher of the *Globe and Mail*, had organized what was known as the Leadership League. It was a neo-fascist organization and one of the elements that lay behind a paramilitary group known as the Frontiersmen. These were people who dressed almost the same as the mounted police – the broad, flat-brimmed hat, the breeches, the high boots – though they wore a blue serge jacket with silver epaulets. They were supposed to be a semi-civil-defence outfit but they appeared in those areas where labour organization was taking place.

"Composed mainly of mine managers and their underlings, they paraded around Kirkland Lake during the whole organizational period. Nothing ever came of it in terms of any open conflicts but it was a part of the whole psychological terrorist development that had its mainstream in industry but which was very assiduously cultivated by people like McCullogh and by the government itself.

"We were pretty sure that it would be a long and hard strike because we neither had the legal right to bargain nor did we have a lot of support that we could see. As it happened there was much more support than we thought and over the course of the strike the National Committee for Kirkland Lake was established amongst the trade unions.

"Money raising was the responsibility of the international union and Forrest Emerson was one of the people who was put on the road to go out and raise money. Other people did too. It was quite successful. A system of strike relief was established which for that time was very generous. We provided drugs for families on a need basis. Single strikers got around $3 a week, married people got $7 or $8 with additional for dependent children.

"One of the great enterprises we had was supplying firewood. We managed to get our hands on a bit of crown land where there was a good cut of timber. All the miners went out there to cut down timber but they got everything messed up and not very well organized. What they had to do was cut down the trees and saw them up into firewood lengths, get it on trucks and take it to the homes. But it wasn't work-

An assembly of strikebreaking Ontario provincial police during the Mine, Mill and Smelter Workers Union strike of November 1941 – February 1942. Photo: courtesy of Public Archives Canada PA 121252

ing very well. Joe Rankin was originally in charge of it. We had a meeting with the picket captains and decided that Rankin should drop that duty and we would muster all the Finnish guys to do it. They were excellent woodsmen. We put them out there in the woodlot and they pretty well stayed there for the duration. The woodlot ran like a charm.

"A mainstay of the strike that emerged early was an organization known as the Workers Co-op which was organized by the left-wing Ukrainian and Finnish people. They had stores in Timmins, in Kirkland Lake and Larder Lake. They said that as long as the strike continued, the food voucher provided by the union would be honoured by the co-op. This became extremely important because as the strike went on some of the smaller independent grocers and so on withdrew recognition of the union voucher. The Workers Co-op was the only store that was honouring it. In return we used to put people in there to work.

"There were two central issues in the strike that had to be solved. The first was compulsory collective bargaining and the fact that there was no legal right that existed for the unions to sit down and bargain. We had to use our collective strength through strikes and other actions to compel the companies to sit down. In this instance the companies refused to do that. The second issue was whether or not gold was an essential product as far as the war effort was concerned.

"Since the Hyde Park talks and the beginning of Lend-Lease and the agreements between Canada and the United States on the whole question of the war effort and extension of credit to finance it, gold had not held any position of importance. It seemed of no value at all in the total war effort. We sent many delegations to see Mackenzie King to have this defined. Our position was that if gold was not essential we should be granted the right to collective bargaining and then as miners and skilled workers we should be moved into the base metal areas. But he would never even meet with us.

"When we'd sent the fourth or fifth delegation to Ottawa to meet with King on precisely this question and he again refused to meet with them we felt there was no use going on. Reid Robinson, the international president, and Tom Maguire, who by this time was working very closely with the left, met with the strike committee. We were running out of money. It was a very tough situation. We decided to put it to the membership.

"We were a composite local even though we represented workers at so many mines and we operated on the basis of single meetings for the entire membership. Each mine had a right to vote up or down on any question, but the decisions of the local were binding on the whole. We didn't have a place big enough for everybody to meet but there was this theatre, the Uptown, which would seat about eight hundred. In order to have complete coverage we used to have two meetings – one at midday and the other a little later in the afternoon.

"We had the first meeting. Robinson, Maguire and the strike committee all stood up and said: 'It's no use going on. We recommend calling the strike off.' But before the second meeting could assemble a wire arrived from Ottawa. King had agreed under pressure to meet with our delegation. So of course the strike was on again.

"This was the high point of morale for the whole strike. It was a night for dancing in the streets. All through this thing the women had done a magnificent job. They'd set up sewing centres and soup kitchens and looked after the welfare. The women's auxiliary had grown to close to a thousand members. And that night I'll never forget them snake-dancing in the middle of the street because the strike was still on. It was really something.

"However, King refused point-blank to define the position of gold as an essential product or not in the war effort. We were no further ahead. The company by this time had mounted an even more vicious propaganda campaign against us and they had the support of the government and the police. Strikers were being intimidated, picked up and run in for no reason. We were not a mighty union in the sense that we had great funds or anything like that but we had a helluva lot of willpower. Still we couldn't hold out much longer.

"We were run into the ground. We were in a strike for a useless product. Deep questioning began to go on among people on the picket line, though at first they didn't want to talk about it. By mid-January things looked grim indeed.

"The National Committee for Kirkland Lake that had been set up within the Canadian Congress of Labour started debating whether or not to call for a general twenty-four-hour work stoppage across Canada in our support. This was debated too on the floor of meetings in Kirkland Lake and the unanimous position, even from those on the right politically, was that this was what we needed. Nobody wanted a general strike at that time because of the war effort but they were all ready to go with a twenty-four-hour work stoppage. But that never happened.

"The workers voted finally to end the strike and that was it. The strike was off and thereafter they were on their own. They had no jobs to return to, no legal bargaining status of any kind. They were blacklisted. Differences in the leadership emerged at that point. The position of the left was that every striker should try to get his job back and we should make a fight of that. Others claimed we couldn't do that, it was silly to even try it. So no real issue was ever made of the matter.

"It was heartbreaking to see many of the workers, proud men, who would go back to the gates and say: 'I'm so and so. I worked here and I want my job back.' The company knew that gold was not essential and that government policy was to drain those camps of workers. They'd reply: 'We don't need you right now. Come back in a couple of weeks.'

"More than a sense of defeat, there was a sense of rage. By July the population of Kirkland Lake had shrunk to about ten thousand. The conventional wisdom there blamed the strike but the fact was that Kirkland Lake was sacrificed by Mackenzie King and the mine operators. There was no production of gold that amounted to a hill of beans in that whole period.

"Sudbury grew fantastically then. As Kirkland Lake and the gold market went down, base metal in Noranda and Sudbury went up. The fight for union organization shifted to base metal. Following the strike, Bob Carlin, secretary of Local 240, was sent to Sudbury. I went there too. Committees were formed and we were on the verge of chartering a new local. However, International Nickel also had its plans. Six days after we called the strike off in Kirkland Lake they raided the union office on the main street of Sudbury.

"On February 24, 1942, eleven shift-bosses were organized by the company at the Frood mine. They went to work, punched their time cards, then got back into cars and were driven into town. In mid-afternoon, in broad daylight on the main street they rim-racked the union office. Smashed it completely. Forrest Emerson was there and he was severely beaten up and left with a very bad scalp wound. One of the other chaps that happened to be there was Jack Willahan. He was critically injured by these people.

"The office was upstairs in a building still on Durham Street called the Levine block. This was the old Levine block, a two-storey frame building that had outside stairs going up to our offices. It's interesting that Levine had the nerve and the courage to rent premises to the union at that time. In any event, these thugs had gone up the stairs and were in the office creating a ruckus. They threw typewriters onto the street, records, anything they could find. People naturally gathered to see what was going on but there were police at the bottom of the stairs to prevent anyone from going in on them. The names of all these people were published but no one was ever arrested.

"Inco was determined they were going to drive the union forever out of northern Ontario. They would maintain the open shop. But we were determined too. When they smashed the union offices we moved our offices out of the town. But Sudbury was still the concentration point.

"The essential thing about Inco production was that though nickel was their strategic weapon they had a tremendous quantity of other elements in that ore. They had copper, they had gold, silver, platinum – they were the largest producers of platinum in the Western World. And then they had many of the rare earths – columbium, ruthenium, all of these things. In that sense the Sudbury ore body is unique. There's no other ore body that carries this range of minerals.

"The iron content in that ore is so high that in 1937 strenuous efforts were made by the Hitlerite government of Germany to buy the slag pile in Sudbury. They had developed some process whereby they could easily separate the iron and Inco didn't have that process. Plans were very far advanced for the sale of the slag pile to Nazi Germany when it was discovered and a huge hue-and-cry went out. As a result the Canadian government stepped in. But Inco's interests went that far.

"The out-and-out terrorizing of workers by the company was incredible. I remember one example at the Frood mine where the union had established what amounted to illegal cells. People in these cells used to meet in groups of five or six but no more. When there got to be seven or eight a new cell was formed. People didn't know each other. They weren't permitted to give each other their names. No records were kept or very few. But these cells were operative. They were acting and organized.

"At the 2,400-foot level there was a Croatian fellow who was in one of these cells and he was operating for the union with about 120 men. They were making a few inroads. Of course they were very careful. Any hint of union and you were out of the gate. But the company got wind of it in some way. They knew that somebody was actively organizing on this particular level. But they couldn't put their finger on this fellow. So they fired the whole level. Just like that. One morning they all go to work. They go to punch their cards but instead of their punch cards they all find blue slips.

"One of the real violations in Sudbury was the way some of the supervisors, with the knowledge of the company, used to take advantage of miners' wives, miners' daughters. It was common knowledge. There was more than one suicide that we knew of that took place over this crazy situation.

"I couldn't get a job in Sudbury. I went back to Kirkland Lake and was asked by both the union and the Communist party to go to Noranda. I was there for a few months and got an active committee established. Then in June they asked me to leave there and proceed to Val d'Or and get a job in a base-metal mine called the Quebec Manitou. It was a new government-subsidized enterprise.

"I got there and started organizing but I didn't speak French and was very much of the opinion that we needed someone who did. So it was then that a chap from Timmins, a French Canadian and a communist, Pete Mongeon, came to Val d'Or to work with me. We were going great guns there and reached a point where we had decided to break open publicly the organizational effort. We got out a leaflet and hired a room in the basement of the Val d'Or hotel.

"The evening of the meeting I was walking west toward the hotel at about five o'clock. It was in the fall of the year and Val d'Or on the west side lies in a kind of a valley. As the sun sank behind that thing it was in my eyes and I couldn't believe what I thought I was seeing. I thought it was a bunch of mounted police at first. I could see the silhouette against the sun of these hats and this marching body of men. It was crazier than a Nelson Eddy movie! In any event as they got closer I saw it was a squad of Frontiersmen. They were organized in Val d'Or too. That night of the meeting they marched up the street then they'd turn around and march back again, back and forth, always in front of the hotel where we were having the meeting. Well, we got sixty people out anyway!

"Then Maguire and Carlin came in from Sudbury. We had a meeting in the Frontenac Hotel and they said they were pulling Mongeon out and putting him in Sudbury. That was the place that had to be cracked."

Sudbury finally was organized and the union officially recognized there in 1944 with unexpected assistance from the Canadian government.

"What none of us had known at the time of the Kirkland Lake strike was that Mackenzie King was going to implement some kind of legislation for compulsory collective bargaining. He didn't implement it, however, until the strike had faded sufficiently into the background. He didn't want his legislation to be connected with the struggle of the workers. It had to be something that was handed down from on high.

"Eighteen months after the end of the strike he brought in the implementation of order-in-council PC 1003. It granted under the War Emergency Powers the right to compulsory, collective bargaining. And it was on that basis that organized labour developed throughout industry in Canada.

"Two purposes were served by PC 1003. It kept production for the war effort high. But it had a political function too. They needed to mend some of the national divisions that had occurred around the question of conscription, for instance.

"From that political decision flowed the setting up of the labour courts here in Ontario under which Sudbury was first certified as a Mine-Mill union, Local 598. Of course when King froze everybody in their jobs that gave us a great assist. Nobody could be fired so they all joined the union. These workers had come out of nine or ten years of depression. They were sweat-shopped, they were exploited, they were misery-ridden and they were looking for a change. They needed it and they needed it very badly. They flooded into the union in the Sudbury area in the space of a few months. Suddenly the bloody road was open.

"The first collective agreement was signed by Inco in March 1944. It was an interesting situation bargaining-wise. We were still bound under a wage freeze. You couldn't bargain for money or time off. You couldn't bargain for very much at all. What's more, the companies were convinced they'd go back to the old open shop once the war was over. But they were wrong. The union was there to stay."

By the time the contract was signed in Sudbury, Ray Stevenson had volunteered for the army. He became a captain, chief educational officer for the Canadian Armoured Corps. But the war period was just a hiatus in the union struggle.

"In the fall of '45 Justice Ivan Rand set a precedent for the postwar period with his famous formula calling for compulsory checkoff; this was something that the mining industry was not prepared to accept. There had been no checkoff with the initial recognition. Nothing like that. Now companies had varying responses. If they thought we could hurt them economically by striking they'd grant it. But Inco didn't grant it immediately, and the gold bandits held out to the end. They were the very last to grant checkoff. I was forced to settle agreements in the gold-mining industry in 1956 without checkoff.

"Gold was still a fixed price – $35 an ounce. The international value of the Canadian dollar at that time took away a few dollars. An ounce of Canadian gold sold on the American market, where all of it went, for $32 or $33. The gold operators were crying poverty and the federal government came to their rescue with the Emergency Gold Mining Assistance Act. So they were able to hold out.

"We'd signed all these contracts from Val d'Or right through to Timmins. There must have been thirty or forty of them. But there was very little in them. We were still faced with the problem of trying to bring workers in the gold mines into line with the advances won by other workers. So we devised a tactic for northern Ontario and north-western Quebec. We said we'd let all the contracts with the gold-mining industry terminate at their different times and then confront the entire industry with the united strength of workers from Timmins to Val d'Or. We'd make a national issue. We'd make an international issue.

"The international union agreed with the tactic. We embarked on it somewhere in '47 and then all sorts of things began to happen. Reid Robinson who was formerly international president of the union was sent in to northern Ontario to help us. He was the logical guy for it. He knew the industry, was a very capable man, and very eloquent. He came in with a couple of organizers.

"Very soon after, Mr. Senator Taft, author of the Taft-Hartley Act which made it necessary for you to sign your name and say you were not a communist before you could run for union office, stood on the floor of the House of Congress and delivered himself of a speech concerning the problems of the communities of northern Ontario and north-western Quebec. The problem as he saw it was that this entire area had been invaded by American communists who were setting out to establish Lord-only-knows-what but probably the proletarian revolution.

"That was a signal. Somebody had made some decision including the State Department. In March of '48, Robinson and the two organizers were picked up and deported. The whole anticommunist hysteria came down on those communities with a fury I've never seen equalled anywhere else. Newspapers, church parades, specialists on communism being brought in to lecture to the masses, radio – a constant barrage went on.

"One infamous character, by the name of Professor Watson Kirkconnell, had distinguished himself earlier as an anticommunist red-baiter. He was brought into Timmins by some church organization to lecture at a theatre. We rallied our forces and told the people: 'This guy's an expert on communism. We also are experts on communism. Let's go down and talk to him.' The whole thing turned into a fantastic 'Hey Rube' and they had to call the meeting off with the result that his picture and mine appeared on the front page of the press.

"Certain sections of the trade union leadership played a significant role in this anticommunist campaign. They not only refused to stand with Mine-Mill but actively engaged in the red-baiting along with the rest. And this was the importation of the Cold War into Canada.

"When Robinson and the others were deported, the mass offensive that took place against us smashed the overall confrontation we were trying to conduct with the gold barons. The workers were being isolated from each other instead of using their collective strength in the struggle with the mine owners. Then in 1948, the Canadian Congress of Labour got into the whole damned campaign.

"First the CCL suspended us allegedly over a story that had appeared in the international Mine-Mill paper criticizing Aaron Mosher, the CCL president, for a rotten settlement that he'd made for the railroad workers. We were suspended for being indiscreet. As a result of that the international president of Mine-Mill, John Clark, came up from the States to the CCL convention in Ottawa. At our urging he got up and made abject apologies to the Congress. It didn't do any good. The following year they made a motion for our expulsion.

"They said we hadn't paid our per capita tax. It was true that some of our cheques hadn't been cashed but they were the ones who hadn't cashed them. The other reason given was that we had refused to carry out the directive of the CCL executive. That had come to us in '48. They said that the Mine, Mill and Smelter Workers Union should dissolve itself in Canada. All of the local unions that had been organized would affiliate directly with the Canadian Congress of Labour. Later they'd be handed over to a fitting jurisdiction. Our official response was 'go to hell.' We'd been a founding member of the CCL but they expelled us. Mine-Mill had become the outlawed 'communist' organization."

Once the union was expelled from the Canadian Congress of Labour it was fair game for the United Steelworkers of America which spent millions of dollars in a relentless raiding campaign that lasted thirteen years.

Throughout this savage, internecine warfare Mine-Mill held tenaciously to its principles and, where it could, to its jurisdiction. Then in 1962, in a particularly bitter battle, it lost the big Inco local by 15 votes. The die was cast.

The Mine, Mill and Smelter Workers Union merged with its powerful rival. It seemed the only thing left to do. Except for the Falconbridge local in Sudbury which continued as a separate independent union, Mine-Mill with all its bold militancy disappeared from the scene. It was the end of an era for Canadian labour.

5

GEORGE BURT

The UAW and the Ford Windsor Strike 1945

On September 10, 1939, Canadians grouped around their radios to hear Prime Minister Mackenzie King declare the nation to be at war with Germany. In that one moment life changed dramatically for most people. The hungry Depression years were over.

A division of armed men was assembled and sent quickly overseas. Production tripled as Canada, safe from the threat of bombings, became Britain's prime source of war production. Almost overnight there were jobs for all the men and women available. Workers lost their fear of organizing. Employers could no longer terrorize them with the threat of "two hundred others waiting outside to do your job."

Trade unionism came into its own again especially in the mass production industries organizing under the banner of the CIO, grown now from the Committee to the Congress of Industrial Organizations. Management resisted the militant wave of union activity. Workers were forced to wrest labour rights from the powerful industrialists.

The burgeoning automobile industry provided one of the most active battlegrounds for the new CIO. General Motors, Chrysler and Ford had all set up Canadian plants. In 1937, some four thousand General Motors workers in Oshawa had walked off the job to force recognition of their union, the United Automobile Workers of America (CIO). They made some gains with the contract they were able to negotiate, but no mention was made of the UAW.

It was left to the Canadian Ford workers to set the significant precedent of formal union recognition matched with some measure of union security. The fourteen thousand Ford workers in Windsor, Ontario, needed all of the war years to make their gains. And before they were through they had to take on the combined forces of the company, the federal and provincial governments, the RCMP and the provincial police. What they achieved by the end of 1945 laid the groundwork for many subsequent union victories.

By then the war was over. But in 1939, as Canada prepared for battle the United Automobile Workers of America (CIO) elected a thirty-five-year-old production worker from Oshawa's General Motors plant as their Canadian director. Through astute political manoeuvring George Burt edged out Charles Millard who had aligned himself too closely to the losing right-wing faction of the UAW in the United States.

George Burt retired in 1969 after thirty years as Canadian director of the UAW. Part of history now, he is philosophic about the labour leaders he has seen come and go. Today, from the glassed-in porch of his home in Kingsville on the shores of Lake Erie, George Burt watches the Canada geese migrate back and forth across the border.

On the face of it he seems a satisfied retiree, developing new machines to scoop the falling leaves from around his wooded lot, tooling a grandfather clock in his workshop, or discovering uncharted courses in local rivers and streams. But this constant activity masks very lightly the man's restlessness. He states unequivocally that he has still a great deal to offer the labour movement and wonders aloud that he is not asked to contribute more.

George Burt speaks with enthusiasm when he remembers back to the war years. "I moved the UAW national office from Toronto to Windsor. That's where all the action was. I used to go by the Ford plant and wonder however in the devil I'd get a union started there.

"Seventy percent of Ford of Canada production used to be exported to British Empire countries. But when the war started they lost this overseas market and went quickly into war production, making gun-carrier bodies for the 8th Army in Africa.

"The plant here was largely controlled from across the river and in Detroit they had a service department headed by a man named Harry Bennett. Henry Ford himself had picked up Bennett. He was a former marine sergeant, a very tough guy, and his job was to organize this service department.

"It consisted of groups of people in the plant working on the production line or in other places, and they were paid extra money to keep the union out. You never knew who they were. But if you talked too much to a member of the service department you were fired. Out you went right away.

"Already in Detroit the union had organized successfully and had agreements in both Chrysler and General Motors. We knew we had to tackle Ford and the place to do it first was in the U.S. The Ford family controlled the Canadian plant. We could never hope to organize here if they hadn't organized over the border. So we watched with some interest the union's activities in the United States.

"In 1940 the CIO decided to take a hand and they appointed Emil Mazey to take charge of the Ford drive. I had a number of meetings with Emil but our plant didn't show very many signs of becoming active except for a secret group.

"A lot of the fellas in the group were skilled tradesmen from the old country. They knew what trade unionism was about. They formed the Ford Club. The club's main recreation were contests for who could drink the most beer. But privately, they were talking to the workers in the plant.

"This was wartime and labour relations had been taken over entirely by the federal government. They'd passed an order-in-council 2685 which said clearly that: 'During the period of the war effort, employers should bargain collectively with employees through unions of their choice.'

"They'd even passed an amendment to the Criminal Code stating that 'no employer will discharge an employee or discriminate against him for the sole reason that such an employee is a member of a trade union or working on its behalf.' But the key word here was 'sole' – 'for the sole reason.' They fired you and said it was because you weren't doing a good job in the plant!

"Employers could do what they liked. We had no assurances of anything. Then all of a sudden in 1941, the Ford company capitulated and stopped their active opposition to the union through Bennett's service department in the big Rouge River plant. They had a total of some forty thousand workers and there was a bomber plant out there at the time too.

"It was the biggest organizational job the UAW had ever tackled. But they didn't have a majority. They were deathly afraid of that. So they put on a dues collection day. They put up a barricade around the plant with every car they could muster, then our UAW guys went out there and collected a dollar from each of the workers before they let them in. That way they got a majority and were ready for the Labour Relations Board.

"Ford agreed finally to bargain with the union. They did a complete back-flip and gave to the UAW what we had not won in any major plant in the U.S. or Canada – a union shop with checkoff. It made it a condition of employment for all employees of the Rouge to belong to the union and remain in good standing thereafter.

"Our Canadian guys got interested right away. And they became more interested. The little Ford Club blossomed forth and began to talk openly in the plant. With the agreement signed in the United States and the Canadian plant under American control, we felt there wasn't much reason to believe that the Ford Motor Company would start firing people.

"The workers had lost their fear of losing their jobs anyway. We'd been at war since 1939 and work was plentiful. They started to join the union. We applied for a charter and became Local 200 of the UAW. I rented two rooms in the Prince Edward Hotel and we had weekly meetings to try to organize leadership in the plant. After about six months the thing really took off. We had to get the Carpenters' Hall to hold the crowd and then the Market Building.

"At that stage, Wallace Campbell, the president of the company, took us on. He went around and harangued the people in the plant. We had no protection. There was no law against what he was doing.

"He bought up full-page ads in the *Windsor Star.* He bought up all the local radio time. I wanted to answer him but I couldn't get on radio. Finally I went over to Local 600 in Detroit. They had just organized their local under a union shop with forty thousand people. Their president, Paul Ste-Marie, was almost as big as the president of the U.S. himself. They said they'd buy me time on WWJ Detroit which was far stronger than the local Windsor station.

"Campbell came on radio that night saying: 'I'm going to have the last say about this matter.' About five minutes later I came on WWJ and countered: 'No, Mr. Campbell isn't going to have the last say.'

"He made a lot of mistakes. He went into the foundry where there was a bunch of black people working. That's where they usually worked. The rottenest, heaviest jobs were given to the blacks. He told them: 'We don't expect you guys here in the foundry to work like niggers.' That night all the blacks came up and joined the union.

"Campbell swore he'd never deal with the UAW. But we kept organizing. We had representatives in damn near every department. At that stage Ford was paying seventy-five cents an hour. It wasn't as good as General Motors and was ten cents under Chrysler. What's more, Ford had some really bad practices. They started you at seventy-five cents an hour. After six months you were entitled to an increase of ten cents. So they'd keep you for six months. Then they'd lay you off and rehire you again at seventy-five cents. This didn't go down very good. And none of the plants then paid overtime.

"Art Reaume was the mayor of Windsor. One of my staff members, Bob Stacey, met Art and brought him to meet me. We formed a friendship right away and Art became our champion in Ford. He'd come to our meetings to speak and the things he used to say about that company! It was a terrific shot in the arm for the union.

"Finally Campbell came out with an ad in the paper that had a proposal. He proposed to take a vote among the employees on the following ballot: 'Are you in favour of the company's offer? Yes or No.' The company's offer was to be a committee for collective bargaining purposes. No union as such. Not a word about the UAW. I became almost hysterical.

"We had the plant organized about 75 percent. So I called up R.J. Thomas in Detroit. He was the international president of UAW. He told me they were going in to see Harry Bennett that day and suggested I come over. Bennett was the big shot, Henry Ford's confidant. He had more power than anybody else in the company.

"I went over to the big Rotunda Building in the Rouge plant, and into Harry Bennett's beautiful private dining room. Harry had a couple of army officers there. He got through with them then turned to me and asked what he could do for me. I told him I'd come over to see R.J. Thomas because we were all in the one union. 'You're not gonna ask Thomas to close down the big Rouge plant to satisfy your demands in Windsor?' he asked. I'd never even thought of it. I told him I was simply going to ask that Thomas have all the materials shut off to the Windsor plant. That would accomplish the same thing. We depended entirely on the Rouge plant for parts.

"'That'd do it, wouldn't it?' he said. 'But you must promise not to close the Rouge plant.' He was nervous. They were having wildcat strikes over there almost every day. Then Bennett himself called the manager of the transportation department of the company and told him: 'Shut off all the materials going to Canada. If you've got any trucks or freight cars loaded, unload them and throw it all back in the plant until further notice.'

"Before I even got home, word had got into Windsor. Campbell accused me of treason because this was a war plant. The next day I got a call from the government in Ottawa from the minister of labour himself. He said: 'We're sending an RCAF plane after you. We want you down here in Ottawa. You and Mr. England.' Roy England was the president of Local 200. By the time we left for Ottawa the plant had closed down.

"The minister, who was the Windsor lawyer McLarty, started off giving me a lecture, a real song and dance. 'We depend on that plant. We've got a war going on and that plant is supplying the 8th Army. We have a ballot prepared here and we want your reaction to it.' He handed me the ballot and left the room.

"Roy and I looked at each other. The ballot read: 'Are you in favour of bargaining through (a) the company offer (b) the UAW-CIO.' Roy said there must be something wrong. But I knew we had moved the company through the government.

"The minister came back and asked what we thought of the ballot. 'It's all right as far as it goes,' I told him. 'But you're asking a question here of about thirteen thousand employees. Suppose they vote in favour of bargaining through the UAW-CIO. What compels the company to bargain?' He answered quickly: 'The government.'

"I told him then that I wanted something in writing signed by the minister to that effect because there was nothing in the law to compel the company to bargain and negotiate a collective agreement. We got that.

"We went back to Windsor, the election took place and we won it. For the first time in the history of Canada a large plant collective-bargaining election had been held under the auspices of the federal government. There was no legislation governing that kind of thing in any of the provinces.

"Over the river they had Roosevelt and the Labour Relations Act to become certified. Here, General Motors workers had a contract but it did not provide recognition of the union as such. We had a couple of little plants that recognized the union local but not the UAW, or that recognized the local UAW without the international union. There was always some form of omission in the name of the union in the recognition clause. The Ford ballot overcame that.

"We sat down with the company to bargain. This was early fall and we had an agreement before Christmas. We signed it on January 15, 1942. Ford was still an open shop. The union had to collect the dues. We built up our steward body. The stronger the steward body, the better our dues collection was going to be. And in Ford, unlike General Motors, the company agreed to steward recognition. We had a steward in every department.

"We didn't have all the 14,000 workers in the plant but because of the fever that we generated we had a very substantial membership. There were some tremendous meetings in the Market Building – the only place in town that would hold us all. We'd get about 8,000 of those guys and we'd have no chairs for them. They had to stand up. There's such an excitement in that kind of meeting. The union officers, we'd be on a raised platform. We'd have 1,500 workers behind us and the rest out there in front. Sometimes they didn't agree with what we were saying. We'd be in trouble and it was a very bad place to get into trouble.

"It gave such an impetus to the whole labour field in Canada to have Ford organized this way. Wallace Campbell was considered to be one of the biggest industrialists in the country. To beat him the way we did was a remarkable achievement."

The new Ford contract still did not put Canadian workers on an equal footing with their brothers across the river but it was a big step forward. Ironically, the Canadian government traditionally on the side of big business seemed to have softened its attitude to the working man. Labour was in short supply and war production had to be maintained. At long last the Canadian worker held the trump card and could begin to insist on a decent working existence. But nothing was easily won.

"Our relationship with Ford was very bad. The company tried in every way possible to make the contract fail. They seemed to delight in stirring up the guys. The result was that they had numerous walkouts in all their plants.

"In '44 we had this damn walkout because of the company's decision to hire 750 girls. They had a special order from the government for war work, and as they couldn't get men, so the women were going to do men's work on assembly. They'd already installed the necessary conveniences.

"The secretary of the War Labour Board recommended the company ask for 60 percent of the men's rate for the women. As soon as we heard that we went wild. We didn't mind if they hired the girls but we said they should get equal pay. We struck the plant. It was a strike that came between the contract terms and it wasn't authorized by the international but we carried it on anyway.

"We closed the powerhouse. The powerhouse in Ford was not a supplementary source of power like it is in other companies. It was the main source of power with Hydro as supplementary. If you closed the powerhouse you closed down the whole operation.

"The government sent in Mr. Justice O'Connor to help solve the dispute. Mr. Gregg, the company's secretary-treasurer, sat in for the company. I remember well that it was spring. Gregg sat at the window and wouldn't even look at us. I threw all kinds of remarks at him but he wouldn't even come to the table. So poor old O'Connor left Windsor without any success at all.

"The upshot was that Peter Heenan, minister of labour for Ontario, came to Windsor. He had his deputy, J.B. Metzler, with him and a guy from Nova Scotia. The company under Mr. Campbell led the negotiations. I represented the union along with Tommy MacLean, my assistant, England and the union committee.

"We sat up all Saturday night writing settlements to each other. They'd turn down ours, then we'd turn down theirs. On Sunday morning, Heenan called a meeting. Campbell was there and Wally Clark, Ford's industrial relations manager. I was there with England, MacLean, the committee and J.L. Cohen, the labour lawyer. He was hired by the local. Heenan said: 'I want you to know that I have the authority of both governments to settle this dispute. We're at war. I have a written settlement here. I'll give each of you a copy of it and fifteen minutes to accept it. There'll be no rejection.'

"As soon as I read it I realized it was what we had asked for. It said we had equal pay for equal work. Heenan knew what he'd done. He asked Campbell what he thought of the settlement. Campbell was a great big man over six feet tall. He drew himself up to his full height and said: 'Mr. Minister, the company does not like your settlement at all but under the circumstances we have no other course to pursue but to accept it.'

"The strike was over. But the company sent back the war order to the government. They never hired one single, solitary girl in their production operations for the whole period of the war."

Each new concession won was only a stopgap measure. Resentment continued to grow among Canadian Ford workers. Their wages were frozen under a wartime regulation, they had no insurance, the company could still fire a man rather than raise his wages, and they were slaves to that relentless assembly line.

The line had been old Henry Ford's gift to industrial America. A mechanized belt that kept production churning out at a steady rate, reducing the individual worker's contribution to a swift, mindless repetition of motions. All the company had to do was turn up the line and the workers would work faster. The belt never tired. It went at the same speed at seven in the evening as it did at six in the morning.

George Burt remembers still the old days on the production line at General Motors in Oshawa. Then a worker would do what he had to

Barricade erected as a strike action around the Ford Motor Company plant in Windsor, Ontario, November 1945. Photo: courtesy of the Toronto Star

Opposite Page: Strikers of the Ford Plant and veterans of both world wars march through downtown Windsor, November 1945. Photo: courtesy of the Toronto Star

The effects of the barricade on Windsor motorists. Photo: courtesy of the Toronto Star

SHOES
TIP TOP TAILORS
Tip Top Tailors
DIANE FROCKS
NOW

on an auto part and slide it along the floor for the next operation.

"Once the assembly line came in you had no time to rest. The first contract with General Motors we won a five-minute rest period. But in five minutes you can't even smoke a cigarette. With the first Ford contract we won a ten-minute rest period. They didn't even have that across the river.

"But the thing that continued to distress the guys most of all was that over the river they had an out-and-out union shop with checkoff and compulsory union membership as a condition of employment. Over here we didn't have anything. It was a hell of a job to try to maintain membership with an open shop. Yet the only battles being won were through the union."

Relations between Ford and its workers had grown steadily worse since the union effectively closed the plant in 1944 over the "equal pay for equal work" issue. When both parties sat down to negotiate their new contract a conciliator appointed by the Ontario government reported that the situation was very complicated and difficult. In his opinion an agreement was impossible.

Neither side would budge. For months the dispute dragged on with the company refusing to agree to the union's seven "contentious" demands: two-week vacations with pay, compensation for work on Sundays and statutory holidays, veterans' seniority, layoff pay, no reduction in take-home pay, and the two major issues of a union shop and checkoff.

By the fall of 1945 the general labour picture in Canada had changed drastically. The war was over. Veterans were coming home and wanting their old jobs back; production had dropped off with no more armaments needed. Workers were no closer to getting union security and thousands were being laid off.

In a final defiant gesture, Ford told the union that some 1,800 workers were to be laid off by the middle of September. It was the last straw. On September 12, Local 200 gave unanimous approval to its members to walk out.

"Everybody went out. We had about ten thousand on the picket line and the first thing was to raise money for the strike. We had no strike fund at that time. The international gave us a donation of some

$10,000 but it wasn't enough. We started sending out 'missionaries.' We sent them from one end of the country to the other. I sent them to Halifax to the mines, to Quebec and to Toronto. I sent them to British Columbia to the big unions on the coast – the woodworkers, the fishermen. We sent 'missionaries' everywhere to collect funds and they collected around $400,000.

"We got good press. People were down on the Ford Motor Company for not giving us the same conditions as Ford workers in the U.S. We had everybody behind us. Even the farmers from Essex county brought car-loads of potatoes and other produce for the picketers. We went to the Canadian Congress of Labour."

The CCL was the central labour body organized in 1940 after the craft-oriented TLC approved the expulsion of the industrial CIO unions. This came as a result of pressure from the AF of L which had already done the same thing in the United States. But the militant CIO unions were coming into their own. They merged with the All Canadian Congress of Labour to form a new labour congress. A.R. Mosher was named president. George Burt was a vice-president.

"I proposed that the Congress set up a National Ford Strike Committee to raise the tempo of the strike. They did it readily but I was later to rue the day I had suggested it.

"I went to Percy Bengough of the Trades and Labour Congress and he came out with a motion of support for the Ford strikers. It was the first time the TLC had supported the CIO since the expulsion in 1939.

"Statements in our support were made throughout the country. Even in Great Britain they knew of this terrific struggle going on in Canada for union security. All the building trades in Canada had union security then. You couldn't get into a building trade unless you were a member of a union. But the industrial workers were another matter. Steelworkers were in open shops. They let us take on the fight for union security and they didn't even give us much help. They were led by Charlie Millard and he took the position that this Ford strike was led by a bunch of communists.

"That was one of the things that dogged us all through the strike. But it was a lot of hooey and most of the people who were saying it didn't know communism from rheumatism. We needed everybody's help. I would have taken help from the Salvation Army, the Methodist church or anybody else. We were fighting one of the biggest companies in the country and we had to fight alone.

"We arranged a big meeting in Maple Leaf Gardens in Toronto. A motorcade drove from Windsor. It was a tremendous rally. David Lewis spoke, Charlie Millard of the Steelworkers and C.S. Jackson of the United Electrical Workers spoke. And of course Roy England and I spoke.

"The Gardens was filled. We raised about $15,000 that night. We had a special section on the ice surface reserved for the Ford workers. Several hundred of them marched in wearing their Local 200 coats and hats and got a standing ovation.

"It was getting cooler now and we decided to close the powerhouse down. We froze the plant right up. The Ford plant is a myriad of tunnels underneath the ground and they have to be pumped out. The powerhouse stopped the pumps, the tunnels filled with water and then froze. They were impassable. The plant was dead. Nobody tried to get into it. Management had their office in the Prince Edward Hotel.

"Now the government became interested again. They set up a meeting with the minister of labour, Humphrey Mitchell. We met in Queen's Park. The Ontario minister of labour was there, Louis Fine, the province's conciliation officer, and M.M. McLean, the chief conciliation officer for the federal government.

"Louis Fine said that there were four people in the room who could settle the strike: Mr. Burt, Mr. Campbell, Mr. Clark and Mr. England. He suggested we get together that evening in the hotel and talk it out. At that point the ministers of labour got into an argument about federal-provincial jurisdiction. Campbell and I looked at each other. 'I guess they've forgotten all about us,' he said.

"We met that night in Campbell's suite at the Royal York Hotel. The first thing he did was produce a silver flask of whisky which he said dated back to 1910. He gave us a very meagre little shot and said: 'What do I have to do to settle it?' I told him there was only one issue that was really important. Union security. 'I can't agree to it, Mr. Burt,' he said, 'I just can't. I would get in wrong with all my fellow employers across this country.' I asked him then why not when his parent company in the States had agreed to it. But he said he would never admit he didn't have control of the company.

"We got nowhere at all. It all started to drag. There was a lot of pressure on us, too. People were starting to lose their homes. We didn't have enough money. The international didn't have enough to help us out any more although the secretary-treasurer, George Addes, did the best he could for us.

"I sent 'missionaries' to Cleveland, to Detroit and Chicago and up to Flint to all the big locals. I personally went to Flint three or four times to the big Buick local. They had 20,000 members.

"Christmas was coming on too and we had to think of that. We organized a tremendous Christmas cheer for the Ford workers and their families. We had the names of all the kids and packed 10,000 parcels or more with the help of the Red Cross. It was a real production line.

"We weren't talking to the company at all at this stage. There was nothing to talk about. We'd cut down our mass pickets. It was really cold. The radiators in the plant were all froze up. Machines were heaved off their bases with the frost. The company claimed we were damaging the plant.

"Then the Ford Motor Company of Dearborn, Michigan, sued the Ford Motor Company of Canada over certain equipment and machines they claimed were being held illegally. They sent the sheriff in to get it out. But it was just a ruse. They never got a thing.

"Finally the company decided to open up the powerhouse one Monday. They asked for the police to be sent in. Art Reaume, the mayor, was chairman of the Police Commission. He refused to call them in. But then the provincial government got into the act and ordered the provincial police to Windsor.

"I don't know how they intended opening the powerhouse. The powerhouse workers were members of our union and were legally on strike. This was the main power plant and the bosses couldn't have run the boilers. You had to be experienced.

"We heard then that they were sending in the army from military district No. 1 in London. I closed down all the plants then in Local

195. This was an amalgamated local of 10,000 workers with forty plants in the city. I closed them all down and broke their contracts. To hell with it. Now we had 20,000 pickets available. We told them all to come.

"I asked Tommy MacLean if he remembered the barricade for dues on Millar Road in the States. 'Put up a Millar Road around the plant,' I told him. 'Get all the cars. The committee men and the officers first. My car will be in front of the Plant No. 1 office tomorrow morning at seven o'clock. Build her up!'

"They had the provincial police quartered in the naval barracks. A bunch of young naval guys came home. They lined them up at the Windsor Station and marched them up to the naval barracks to wait on the police. To serve them their meals and cook for them and God knows what else. Some of these guys' fathers were on the picket line.

"A bunch of the young sailors came down and joined the picket line that Sunday night. I was walking with a sailor who told me: 'Don't worry, the police won't attack you tomorrow. We put Feen-a-Mints in their coffee tonight!'

"That barricade was formidable. We put hundreds of cars on her. Damn near the whole town was on strike now. We had Chrysler down too. Several thousand Chrysler workers marched up to the line.

"Bus drivers drove their city buses right into the barricade and parked them. People were mad. A lot of them were American businessmen who lived out along the lake. As a matter of fact I didn't take my car to work that morning. I hitchhiked down with an American. God forgive me, I let him drive right into the barricade then said: 'Thanks for the ride. This is as far as I go.'

"The barricade was there a week. We made one mistake though. We had a fish truck full of fish. We let him drive into the barricade and he was there for the whole time. You could smell fish all over Windsor.

"The guys were excited. Nothing like this had ever happened before. They took pictures of it from the air and sent them all over the United States and Canada. The press said it was no longer a strike, it was an insurrection.

"We were called down to the RCMP office downtown in the Canada building. A sergeant who had just come down from Kirkland

Lake from a big strike there said that they had heard the pickets were armed. 'Nonsense,' I told him. 'One guy came down one night with a World War I rifle and a bayonet on it. We had a hell of a time getting him to take it home. And sure the guys expect violence and sit up nights making little short clubs out of a piece of hose with lead poured in the end to weight it. But it is not the policy of this union to arm pickets.'

"I told him that people weren't armed generally though it was impossible to know what some of them might carry. Everyone was pretty worked up and I couldn't vouch for what might happen if the police interfered with the picket line.

"At that moment, the guy sitting next to me dropped his tobacco pouch. As he reached down to get it a billy fell out of the pocket of his windbreaker. He picked it up and the cop never saw it. We were lucky.

"I never gave much thought to the possibility of violence. If there had been any I'd have been right in the middle of it. There were no charges made on the Ford picket line in that strike, even though we might have broken the law or stretched it a bit on numerous occasions. We guaranteed all those people who had their cars in the barricade they would not suffer any loss by theft. And we only had to pay out for one radio!

"While the barricade was still up the coal pile caught fire. Spontaneous combustion. Coal piled up like that needs to have holes drilled in it every so often. The plant was right on the river and what the company didn't know was that we were stealing coal from the back of that big pile for the picket fires.

"It was getting cold by then. Starting to freeze. This was the reason they were trying to open the plant by force. The company talked of two million dollars worth of damage. But nobody got in. As a matter of fact, the plant protection people at the gate (we let them work for insurance reasons) had two cats in the Plant No. 1 office that were afraid to go into the plant. There were too many rats. There was no heat, no anything, and the rats just took over.

"Neither the army nor the police ever attacked us. They didn't even show up. I was there on a sound truck telling the guys what to expect and telling them we were going to fight to the last man. We had this great space for our pickets, thousands of them. But the army never arrived and the police just kept to the barracks. Finally they left town."

The barricade had served its purpose well. News pictures appeared in the press across the country. Editorials urged the government to intervene and bring about a settlement. But the strike was no nearer a solution than it had been in the beginning. Ford of Canada refused categorically to negotiate a union shop and checkoff. Some of the workers felt that more drastic tactics had to be used.

The joint policy committee of Locals 195 and 200 called on all unions affiliated with the CCL to stage a one-day walkout in support of the Ford strikers. The CCL's National Ford Strike Committee were divided on the question and the whole idea eventually petered out with only a few thousand workers in Kitchener and Sarnia walking off their jobs.

"Finally Pat Conroy appeared in Windsor. Pat was the secretary-treasurer of the CCL. He wanted to see me privately. 'I've got this on damn good authority,' he told me, 'but you'll have to take it on faith. The government wants the strike settled. If you will accept arbitration they have guaranteed to me they'll name an arbitrator that will give you what you want.' I asked him if he'd put it in writing. He said no. 'You'll have to take my word for it.'

"We talked it out. I was attracted. I felt that Pat wouldn't appear unless he had the authority of the government. But I had a problem. I had to tell ten thousand people at a meeting that they should accept arbitration without being able to tell them they'd get what they wanted.

"I called in Roy England and Tommy MacLean to see what they'd say. England agreed. MacLean was violently opposed to it. He was a fighter. It was the only way he knew to act. Then we had to consult this damn Ford Strike Committee of the CCL. It was composed of Millard, C.S. Jackson, Conroy and Alec McAusland from the Railway Brotherhood out west.

"Jackson was a super-militant leftie and he opposed it. When Millard found out that Jackson was opposed, he was in favour of it.

McAusland went along with it because he and Pat Conroy were pretty close.

"I told them it was going to be hard to influence our membership on the question. I felt I'd like to have unanimous consent. So Jackson said: 'If the rest of the gang go along with it and it's what you want, George, I'm not going to raise a fuss about it. After all, you're the head of the union.'

"This was a Sunday afternoon. The next day in the *Toronto Daily Star* the headlines were enormous: 'Ford Strike End Near – Millard.' Then in the *London Free Press* was another story: 'Millard Is Selling the Ford Workers Down the River.' George Harris of the UE had been in telephone communication with Jackson who had told him what was brewing. Harris then went to a Labour-Progressive party meeting – that was the Communist party during the war – and they'd given the story to the London press.

"Pat Conroy was so damn mad, it's a wonder he didn't have a fit. The government denied any involvement in it whatsoever. We were left holding the bag. The CCL Ford Strike Committee was still in town on Monday afternoon and I called them together and told them: 'I hereby dissolve this goddamn committee forever. Don't show your faces in Windsor again.'

"We stayed out another couple of weeks, then I had another call from Conroy. He came up from Ottawa and said that the government was still interested in getting the settlement and on the same terms. I told him I was willing to go to the membership if Roy England would go too. George Addes of the international union came over to help us sell it to the membership. It didn't work though.

"Some of our negotiating committee were against it and a small percentage of the membership voted us down. The whole country was looking at us. I had faith in Conroy. I knew the government wanted a settlement.

"Finally our own committee people that were opposed to the arbitration idea decided they would go along with it. There was nothing else to do and they were at their wit's end. We put it to the membership again and this time they voted for it overwhelmingly."

On December 19, 1945, it was announced that the union membership had agreed to accept the government's offer of arbitration. The men were recalled to the plant and Humphrey Mitchell made public the appointment of Ivan C. Rand of the Supreme Court of Canada as arbitrator.

For a month Rand toured the plant, held hearings, accepted submissions before bringing down his decision which was to be binding on both parties.

"Rand was very clever. He started to ask questions. He started at the company. 'Your relationship with the union hasn't been very good?' The company admitted it had been very bad. 'But you do believe in collective bargaining?' he asked. They said yes. 'Would you rather have a good strong union or a weak one?' he went on. The company didn't think it was any of their business. 'It should be,' said Rand. 'It's the union you have to deal with. But if you don't care, why are you so resistant to giving them the union shop?'

"Mr. Campbell had suffered a stroke just two or three weeks before and Gregg and Clark were there for the company. 'We don't think employees should be forced to join any organization,' they told Rand. 'Then you don't know much about my union,' said Rand. 'Lawyers here have to belong to the Law Society of Upper Canada or we can't practise.'

"I was really enjoying it. 'If you believe in collective bargaining,' he went on, 'you should believe in the financial stability of the union. I've gone over your contract and I've seen some very important phrases. It's expensive for the union. They have expenses to pay for lost time, for committee men, for training they must do. Don't you think every employee should help to pay for that, for the benefits they receive?'

"Then he started on me. 'Mr. Burt, according to the record you've had a great many wildcat strikes. Do you think it right to close down part of a company's operations like this without the proper negotiations?' He made the sweat run down my neck for a while, too.

"In the end he came out with his Rand Formula. It required everybody to pay the dues formally levied against the members by the union according to the constitution, and by checkoff. However, it did not require workers to join the union. In addition, he ruled that in the event the company did not institute a proper insurance programme including life and sickness and accident insurance within ninety days, the union would be entitled to underwrite a proper insurance plan which they would manage. The company would then be required to check off the necessary premiums."

It was not everything they had asked for but the Rand Formula did give Ford workers a modified union shop. Though workers did not have to belong to the union, everyone covered by the agreement had to pay union dues. Rand gave the company a measure of security too. Individual workers could be fined and the union lose checkoff privileges for any "illegal" or "wildcat" strikes.

"We were satisfied. The Rand Formula set a precedent. It was very easy to negotiate. We applied it in General Motors. It spread all over Canada. It jumped the border and spread over the United States. They didn't have union security like that. Only in Ford and that was a most unusual thing.

"I remember seeing Wallace Campbell at the airport one day after the strike was settled. He was walking with a cane and was still partly paralyzed. 'You beat me,' he said. 'I wouldn't put it that way,' I told him, 'we got an agreement and both parties are apparently satisfied.' 'Oh no, you beat me,' he insisted. 'Very well,' I told him, 'if you want it that way. We beat you and we beat the hell out of you too.'"

6

MADELEINE PARENT

Valleyfield's Textile Workers 1946

Once war was declared in 1939, mobilization for the war effort catapulted Quebec into a new industrial era. Production was booming, work plentiful and workers less fearful about losing their jobs.

Here, too, the CIO was taking its first militant steps to organize industrial workers. But the two entrenched trade union federations were the Quebec Federation of Labour composed mainly of AF of L affiliates who made a big drive now to organize the new work force involved in defence industries, and the Confederation of Catholic Workers of Canada founded in 1921.

The nationalism of the CCWC where a worker could speak in his own language had a strong appeal for Quebec's workers. But the Confederation was still dominated by extremely conservative elements within the Catholic church.

Kent Rowley, a twenty-five-year-old organizer with the Montreal Trades and Labour Council suggested that the time was ripe to unionize the highly exploited workers in Quebec's domestic industries. R. Kent Rowley had volunteered into the army at the beginning of the war. After an honourable discharge he denounced the federal government for reneging on their promise that there would be no conscription in Quebec. Within a day or two, Rowley was picked up by the RCMP and held in Petawawa and then in the Hull jail. There were no charges, no trial. The War Measures Act was in force and Kent

Rowley was simply interned for two and a half years.

Now he was free again and his idea was to start organizing Quebec's cotton mill workers. They had shown enormous courage in sporadic attempts to organize over some fifty or sixty years but had always been beaten down by the anti-labour Anglo industrialists who ran the textile industry.

The AF of L traditionalists in Montreal's central labour council had ready arguments for Kent Rowley's proposals. The cotton companies were tough and powerful and the mills full of women and children. How could he ever hope to organize them? But Rowley was not easily put off. He took an assignment to help organize munitions workers at Nitro, the big Defence Industries Limited plant just outside of Valleyfield about forty-five miles southwest of Montreal. Most of the Nitro workers lived in Valleyfield, largely a one-industry town with the biggest cotton mill in the country employing over three thousand workers. The mill was operated by Montreal Cottons, a firm with very close links to Dominion Textile Company, Canada's largest cotton corporation.

When Kent Rowley first went to Valleyfield, the Montreal Trades and Labour Council had a twenty-four-year-old secretary named Madeleine Parent. Today, Parent is a passionate, uncompromising trade union organizer who has made history in a field where women long suffered discrimination and neglect. She and Kent Rowley shared a dream of a militant, autonomous Canadian labour movement. Together for thirty-six years until his death in 1978 they were untiring in their efforts to make it come true.

Madeleine Parent remembers how in 1942 Rowley finally convinced the reluctant Trades and Labour Council that they should put their resources behind the cotton mill workers.

"When Kent was able to report back to the organizing committee that he had a fair group of contacts from the cotton mill in Valleyfield and that they were determined to organize, it was much more difficult for the antagonistic AF of L elements to refuse them admission. He was told he could go on.

"From that moment he concentrated mainly in organizing the cotton mill workers, even though he still assisted in the DIL campaign.

As secretary to the committee I would attend all the meetings, take minutes and do whatever work had to be done. If I watched myself I could even speak up!

"In the remarkable period of three or four months, Kent had signed up a majority of the cotton mill workers in that huge mill. So we applied for certification. Under wartime regulation this had to be done through the federal government. Judge Savard who sat as the government commissioner to verify that we had the majority recommended that the company negotiate and sign a contract with us. This was virtual certification under wartime conditions.

"The company would have nothing to do with it. We expected this. We expected they would refuse to accept the government's recommendation. But the law itself didn't have that much teeth. It was obvious that it was necessary to spread the base of rank and file membership. Then at a later time if it were necessary to have a confrontation we would have a stronger base with which to do it. We had to choose another cotton mill where we could organize.

"We had some contacts in the cotton mill at St. Henri – Merchants Cotton Mill along the Lachine Canal – which had about thirteen hundred workers. It was another Dominion Textile plant. Kent asked if I would come on as full-time organizer. To be an organizer was what I had wanted to do for a long time and it appealed to me very strongly that it should be in an industry where there were a large number of women and young people. So on the first of February I went to work as full-time organizer for the union which Kent by then was leading – the United Textile Workers of America, AF of L.

"When Kent had started to organize we had tried to persuade the Trades and Labour Congress of Canada with headquarters in Ottawa to give us a Canadian charter so that we would not be obliged to go to the AF of L. This was denied us and the main artisan of this denial in Canada was Arthur Daoust, the secretary-treasurer of the Congress at that time, who belonged to the elitest papermakers' union. He insisted we would have to go to Washington to Frank Fenton, the director of organization of the AF of L who would turn us over to the United Textile Workers of America, AF of L.

"For us to organize into a Canadian union which we very much wanted to do would have meant cutting ourselves off from our companions and associates in the Montreal Trades and Labour Council – the plumbers and steamfitters, the tobacco workers, the RCA Victor electrical workers and the others who were really our brothers and sisters in this kind of struggle to organize. And we didn't think we could do it at that time. Not wedged in between the AF of L unions on the one hand, the company unions dominated by the company bureaucrats and the Catholic syndicates on the third side. Let alone the Catholic church, the Duplessis government and the Dominion Textile Company – the most formidable of all adversaries.

"While Kent continued to organize in Valleyfield which was the largest base, I started at the Merchants mill. We got a majority there before springtime and applied for certification again.

"Next to the mill was a small shop of about sixty-five men. It was the general machine shop of the Dominion Textile mills mainly for the Montreal sector. They organized very readily and we obtained the first contract for them.

"After attempting to divert them from organizing, the company chose in its wisdom to give them a contract hoping they would consider themselves an elite and stand apart from the other cotton mill workers. There was talk about: 'Let's have a separate union. We're maintenance. We're tradesmen.' But we insisted that this was an industrial union. At least it was in Canada. 'Your brothers and sisters in the cotton mill are in your local,' we told them. So by springtime when we had the majority both in the general machine shop and in the cotton mill, we applied under the wartime regulations of the federal government for accreditation.

"While this was being processed, the company were resisting as they still were in Valleyfield. We went on to organize the Mount Royal cotton mill – another Dominion Textile plant on the south side of the Lachine Canal. We got that organized by late summer and then we moved to the large Hochelaga plant on Notre Dame Street East. This was one of the oldest plants in the country. We started organizing there around August or September and within a couple of months we had the majority in all three Montreal plants, besides the general machine shop.

"That was in '43. We had over six thousand workers organized in various degrees of accreditation. If it had not been wartime and we had not been tied by the 'no-strike' pledge of the AF of L and the Trades and Labour Congress of Canada we would have struck. We could have gone on to organize the whole industry very easily. But since we were part of the AF of L it was difficult to go against a general decision even if we didn't agree with it. We would have been denounced and stabbed in the back by our own associates within the movement and to take our troops into battle with an exposed rear would have been very serious.

"The cotton mills were in demand. They were getting orders. They were producing all they could possibly produce. The manager of the Valleyfield mill told Kent that the Valleyfield mill alone clothed the whole of the Canadian army at least three or four times over and he didn't know where the rest went.

"People were working day and night. Men and women worked ten hours a regular day. They worked from seven to twelve, knocked off from twelve to one when a large number of them went to their homes to eat. They lived in and around the Lachine Canal belt in Montreal and in Valleyfield in houses all around the mill. They'd work again from one to six. They worked the ten hours from Monday to Friday and on Saturday from seven to twelve.

"Wages went from 18 and 21 cents an hour for women and children to a high of 45–48, 50–53 cents for highly skilled loom-fixers and mechanics. Labour was cheap. There were no coffee breaks. At night the women and children worked ten hours with a break from midnight to one A.M. Men worked eleven or even up to twelve hours. This would mean that some men would go into work at six o'clock and come out at seven the next morning.

"Quebec law was very loose about children. It stated that a child should not go to work before the age of fourteen unless the parents certified that they needed the income of that child. Cotton mill workers were poorly paid. Many of them had large families so they were forced by economic circumstances to certify that a child of twelve or thirteen had to go to work. Sometimes the parents would give the birth certificate of an older child to apply to a younger brother or sister and say he or she was fourteen.

"I remember seeing children of ten and eleven years old coming off the night shift at midnight to go back to work at one o'clock. For mothers and fathers, who themselves were cotton mill workers getting very low pay, bringing a child to work was also a form of babysitting. There was no place for them and if the child was over thirteen they might as well teach him or her how to work and at the same time keep an eye on them as have them out on the streets while the parents were working.

"There were accidents – children who were badly maimed, people minus a finger or with bad skin conditions on their arms and legs. I remember one woman who used to have headaches constantly. She had had her hair pulled off into a machine in the card room. She had survived but she had migraine headaches for all the years I knew her.

"The workers couldn't see any way out. In 1937 they had staged a general strike. They had shown tremendous courage and still they had been smashed. Our biggest job – Kent's in Valleyfield and mine in Montreal – was to convince them we could change things together. We did it by visiting house to house until we developed a big enough base. Then individual workers could convince their fellow workers and have them join. They'd come to secret meetings or meetings after work that we could arrange in small restaurants or lunch counters close to the mills or at the union office.

"When it was realized that our organizing drive was serious, the Catholic church elements in the area of Valleyfield immediately sided with the company against the union. There were terrible attacks against us. We were called communists. We were called foreign agents, Russian spies – everything. Kent's internment in Petawawa was dragged out against him and there were calls to send him back to jail.

"The campaign was bitter and vitriolic. It promoted all kinds of gossip and whispering campaigns. I had to go around with my birth certificate showing that I was born in Montreal, christened in St. Louis de France church, of French-speaking parents to prove that I was not a Russian come over by submarine and landed on the shores.

"It took us four years of a consistent organizing drive in all those plants in Valleyfield and Montreal until we finally won the first real contracts in the cotton mill industry in Quebec. When you go for years without a contract you have to keep reorganizing all the time. At one moment in a plant of 3,000 you might have 1,850 supporting you and then it will narrow down to 300 in the face of attacks. With those 300 you might build it up to another 1,800 again. Then you're smashed and left with only a few hundred. This had to be started over and over again.

"In the process I went out to live in Valleyfield with a family of workers where both husband and wife had worked in the cotton mills. No cotton mill worker could afford to have me as a *pensionnaire* because they'd be blacklisted. The husband in this family now worked in a plant that was producing for the war and his wife had three small children and was at home. So I could live there.

"As our campaign to reorganize was peaking again there was a riot against us, engineered and developed by Monseigneur Paul-Emile Léger who was then the auxiliary to the bishop of Valleyfield. Catholic Action groups along with the Knights of Columbus secretly organized a meeting in the basement of the Valleyfield cathedral. From there they marched off to our union hall which they sacked and then came on to the City Hall where we were holding a public meeting. They surrounded the building.

"We let our members get away and we just stood our ground there, about twelve of us, until the riot spent itself around two or three o'clock in the morning and we were able to get out. They wanted to get rid of us completely. Their slogan was: 'Drive them out on flatcars.' They were talking about Kent Rowley and Madeleine Parent.

"In the midst of this riot, Monseigneur Léger came out in the street somewhere around midnight. We could hear him from inside the City Hall building where we were entrenched. He congratulated the rioters for the great show of patriotism, of love of family, of faith, of country.

"Most of the cotton mill workers were Catholic. Kent and I would speak to them about the need to organize, the need to fight, the conditions, the injustices of the government and of the company. But Trefflé Leduc, the president of the local, would speak as the Roman Catholic, a sort of brother and father of the flock.

"Trefflé had worked for that company from the age of about nine years old. He had been hired as a child to help dig the moat around the cotton mill. It was a huge stone building with mediaeval like turrets. The company had had a moat dug to make it all the more impressive and there was a bridge that you had to go across to get in through the main gate. Trefflé had gone on to work as a loom-fixer. He had been vice-president of the Catholic syndicates local in the general strike in 1937 and had been blacklisted for a couple of years because of his criticisms of the terms of settlement. Now, as president of our local he would speak to the workers about their feelings with respect to their faith and the attitude of the church. There was a tremendous response to him.

"We withstood the attacks and continued to organize all through the war years. At the end of the war we had to go back under provincial legislation again and Duplessis chose to say that the wartime accreditation didn't count any more and we had to start all over again.

"The Valleyfield workers said no. We were accredited. We had been through all the proceedings. We'd had a Royal Commission or whatever it was. We'd had everything. But in Montreal we decided to test it. We started all over again with the general machine shop. We got our accreditation. We got our contract. Then we started with the Merchants Cotton Mill. We got our accreditation and when the negotiations broke down had Judge Charles E. Guérin named as chairman of a board of conciliation.

"We got an accreditation at the Mount Royal mill of Dominion Textiles further west in Montreal but we weren't under the conciliation board yet. And we were still fighting for accreditation at the Hochelaga mill. We were at different levels of organization in each of the mills. It was not a strong bargaining position. If we had to strike we felt we wouldn't be able to. We counducted a tactical strike in Montreal on a Saturday morning in the fall of 1945.

"I led the strike at the Montreal mills. Kent led a delegation to Quebec City. With Deputy Minister of Labour Gérard Tremblay they worked out a settlement of the strike whereby if we went back to work, all of the government proceedings in Quebec around the Montreal mills would come under Judge Charles E. Guérin's final decision, whatever that would be. They would be separate units but he would adjudicate on all.

"Guérin was an old conservative who was part of the Union Nationale party. But he had independent financial means and he never bowed to Duplessis when it came to us. So he adjudicated. He worked out a first full collective agreement text and he recommended to the company that they sign it with us. The contract would apply to all the mills.

"It was open guerrilla warfare in the cotton mills from the time we went back right through the period when we waited for the conciliation board's decision. The company was exceedingly hostile, trying at every turn to eliminate leading activists among the workers. There were lockouts, sit-downs, slowdowns. We fought every way we could. When Guérin brought down his simple collective agreement and the company refused to sign it, the workers in all the mills went out on strike. It was June 1946.

"After a couple of months we had about 300 scabs in Montreal out of a total of 3,000-odd workers. They were mainly in the Hochelaga plant with a few in the Merchants plant in St. Henri. Our people were having a rough time. We were attacked by police constantly. The city police in Montreal, apart from the company's private police system, would phone workers, frighten them, intimidate them, announce they'd have to go back to work otherwise they'd lose their jobs.

"They would go with huge trucks which were protected with heavy screens and tarpaulins at the back. The uniformed company guards would go to the houses of workers, pick up those whom they could persuade, put them into these closed trucks and drive them through picket lines with city-police escort. These guards would be standing at the back of the truck in front of the tarpaulin which shielded the scabs. They carried chains with which they'd hit picketers as they went through the picket lines.

"The company was willing to discuss negotiations in Montreal but was absolutely unwilling to discuss them in Valleyfield. Our local bargaining committees – Kent, myself and our union – were not accepted as such in Canada but we allowed intermediaries to go and meet the company with the assistance of the provincial labour department. Antonio Barrette was the minister under Duplessis. They negotiated the terms of a collective agreement for Montreal.

"Most of these intermediaries, if they were acceptable to the Dominion Textile Company, were very treacherous as far as the workers were concerned. One was Lloyd Klenert, the secretary-treasurer of the international union who came in from Washington. He was really a friend of the company.

"Another person was Philip Cutler, then a representative of the Trades and Labour Congress of Canada. He was well accepted by the company and was promoted by Maurice Duplessis. Max Swerdlow was another one we had to be very careful about. He was also a representative of the Trades and Labour Congress.

"The fourth one was really our friend. His name was Elphège Beaudoin. He was president of the Quebec Federation of Labour and because of his presence in that committee of four we could be assured that everything would be reported to us.

"With the assistance of the Quebec government and some of these intermediaries, the company conceived of the notion of offering a contract for Montreal. It would not pertain to the workers in Valleyfield. The technical argument was that since we had gone through all the legal proceedings twice in Montreal – once before the federal government, once before the provincial government – that strike was legal. But because in Valleyfield we had gone through all the proceedings only once, before the federal government, that strike was unlawful.

"We considered this very carefully. We knew it was a trap set by the Dominion Textile Company to divide our members and then with the assistance of Lloyd Klenert from Washington to get rid of the union leaders and make it into a good business union that would cooperate with the company. On the other hand, it was very difficult to turn down the offer of a first genuine union contract for the Montreal mills in view of the number of scabs we had – a number which might grow.

"The 3,000 workers in Montreal and the 3,000 in their sister union in Valleyfield had gone on strike together and pledged solidarity in their common fight. When the offer was presented to us at the joint strike committee meeting of the Valleyfield and the Montreal workers, we decided that we would put the question to the Valleyfield workers first. We'd report to them what was available to the Montreal workers and ask them if they would free their fellow workers in Montreal and allow them to accept, with the understanding that solidarity would continue but in a different form. We also wanted them to understand the difficulties we faced if we all held out together.

"At a dramatic and very serious meeting we put the question to the Valleyfield strikers. There were some 5,000 people at the meeting held in the City Hall, spilling out into the marketplace and down the street into Sauvé Park. Our union meetings were always big public things. They were family affairs. There were always a great many women because many women worked in the plant. There were men and there were youths who came to the meetings as workers. But wives of members and mothers of members were welcome too. Very welcome. You always had to be careful about voting, that only members voted. But everybody felt part of the union.

"We had an excellent loudspeaking system. One of the local electronics merchants was a very good friend and supporter of ours. It was his pride and joy to supply the best system for the union that was available anywhere in those parts.

"So it was put to our members in Valleyfield and they, with heavy hearts but trying to understand the circumstances, agreed that the Montreal workers would be relieved of their pledge. This meant that the Valleyfield workers would continue the struggle alone.

"The next day we had a meeting of the Montreal workers at L'Assistance Publique Hall on Lagauchetière Street. We told them of the decision of the Valleyfield strikers. We reported on the offer of the company and they voted to accept. That first contract was signed and they went back to work around the first of August. It was for those days a good contract and the first real one in the cotton mills.

"The strike continued in Valleyfield. The textile workers here were concentrated in one mill known to be the finest in Canada with the greatest range of production equipment. It was totally self-contained right from bringing in the cotton bales up to any kind of production.

Madeleine Parent, under arrest for her part in a strike in Lachute, Quebec, May 1947. Photo: courtesy of Public Archives Canada 47-86-1

Everything you could imagine could be made by Valleyfield – Jacquard, corsetry, bathtowels, sheeting, army equipment, clothing – all dyed, bleached, finished.

"Almost immediately after the settlement in Montreal we felt that the climate in Valleyfield was beginning to change. The company was pressing hard. The company police additions to the provincial police detachment were all very noticeable. Duplessis, of course, was still declaring that the workers in Valleyfield would be forced to go back without any contract and their union would be destroyed.

"The work emanating from the church was mounting. A group of cloistered nuns in Valleyfield were in novena under the spiritual direction of Monseigneur Léger for the defeat of the union, and children in school were ordered to pray for me to be thrown out of Valleyfield. There were four parishes in the town and at one point a leaflet was put out stating: 'Let the faithful go to church every morning. When we will be numerous enough after Mass not to be afraid to go through the picket lines, we will have help to go through those lines.'

"Somewhere around the second week of August, after Mass on weekdays, a young vicar would escort the faithful, who had gone to Mass for purposes of scabbing, toward the mill gates. The company guards would pick them up where the vicar would leave them. Then with the assistance of the provincial police they would take them through the lines. They might have had a few less than 10 percent of the workers who were scabbing in this way.

"Then around August 13 the provincial police sent in a great detachment – the biggest ever. The company had recruited its guards, put uniforms on them, and those people who had gone to Mass were led down toward the plant by one of the priests and then left by him as the company guards took over. The company guards were particularly arrogant and spiteful and threatening to our picketers as they came through the lines that morning. The provincial police were in top aggressive form as well.

"Our people had been preparing for a showdown and this was the day. That forenoon after the scabs had gone through the plant gates, women in their houses all over town were passing the word around. Everybody on wheels or with a horse and wagon was going from door to door or store to store all over town saying: 'The fight is going to be at the cotton mill gates at noon today. Everybody at the gates.' By eleven o'clock or so virtually the whole of the population of Valleyfield found themselves at those mill gates.

"Even scabs in those days used to be expected to leave for the twelve to one o'clock lunch period. This day they came out of the plant doors but they remained on the company grounds quite a distance from the actual gate. When they saw the streets filled with crowds of workers they stayed there under orders from the company guards. The provincial police were at the forefront at the gates, and our smaller picket line was marching up and down. At one moment Kent alone was standing there with his pipe in his mouth and one of the workers just stood back to back with him.

"The crowd was all over the street on both sides. The provincial police fired tear gas. Our people picked up stones, tore up the streets, the pavement, the sidewalks and at one command there were literally five thousand bits of pavement or rocks thrown in the direction of the police. Then it was quiet again. The police fired another volley and the same thing happened.

"That kind of battle carried on for hours at both the main gates where crowds were concentrated. At the Dufferin Street gate there was a large, long, old stone guardhouse, two storeys high. The police were firing out on the crowd in Dufferin Park across the way. Some of the strikers picked up the burning tear gas and pitched it back onto the police.

"Our people were outside crying. They had pails of cold water, handkerchiefs and cloths to help them. But the police inside were in much worse condition. They had to go upstairs to continue firing. At one point the captain of the provincial police, Norbert L'Abbé, put out a white handkerchief. Obviously they wanted to talk. So Kent and one of the organizers went in together. But our people said: 'You will not go in alone.' And two of the women from the ladies' auxiliary – wives and mothers in their forties – insisted they would go in as their guards.

"The demand of the strikers that Kent relayed to Captain L'Abbé was to send the company guards out of town. They were the most obnoxious and the most aggressive group of all. There was some discussion and L'Abbé said he couldn't do that.

"These guards had been brought in from all over town. Their leader Claude, that was his family name, had been chief of police at Valleyfield years before. The city council had had to send him away because he was so detested by the population. He was known in those days as an agent of the company who would trap workers for petty thievery and have them fired or blacklisted. So he'd been hired by Dominion Textile as head of their guards and he had marched back into the city with a whole contingent of extras. The people wanted him out.

"There was no agreement. Our people came back out. The cops continued firing tear gas. Our people responded with stones and after a further period of that kind of exchange the white handkerchief came out again. The same foursome went in to negotiate. This time L'Abbé agreed that the company guards would be ordered out of town. On our behalf Kent agreed that as soon as the guards were forced out we would help escort the scabs out so that they'd be unharmed by the crowds. They would be escorted out to go to their homes provided L'Abbé agreed the plant gates would be closed again and there would be no scabbing.

"Our people came out. They waited. The company police came out in their cars. Then the scabs were marched out with one organizer in a police sidecar at the front of the parade and another at the end. The plant was shut down and there were no scabs there from that moment on until the strike was settled. However, within a week or so after that day Kent was arrested and taken to jail. Another organizer was arrested with him. The charge was incitement to riot. He was denied bail and we knew this was to try to break the strike.

"While there were no scabs we were negotiating indirectly through the deputy minister of labour who in turn was negotiating with the company. And the settlement terms which we finally agreed to on the hundredth day or so were contained in a telegram to the union from Antonio Barrette, the minister of labour. It said that if we returned to work and if we agreed to the taking of a secret-ballot vote between our union and the scab union then the company would agree upon a contract at Valleyfield whose terms would be comparable to those of Dominion Textile's contract in Montreal.

"The scab union had no recognition whatsoever and if we agreed to the secret vote it would simply be a concession to the church and to the company. We took twenty-four hours to think about that one. We had one meeting scheduled again with five thousand people. We said we had an important telegram from the minister. We had received one every week and they were never satisfactory. But this one was a little bit closer to what we needed.

"We told our members that we hadn't had time to discuss it but the strike committee would meet and the next evening we'd have a report and a recommendation to make, one way or the other. The meeting was adjourned quickly and that night the strike committee sat up all night as we discussed those terms. We finished at around six or seven in the morning and decided we'd recommend adoption of those terms. We recognized that the condition of our submitting to a secret-ballot vote conducted by the government was a dangerous and treacherous one but we figured that so long as we were very vigilant we could pull through and win.

"At the next meeting the following evening we read the telegram, explained the significance, pointed out the challenges that it contained for our people and said we were confident we could meet them all.

"They marched back into work after that meeting with a little union button that had been hurriedly done. VICTOIRE. The interesting part was that all of our enemies, the scabs and the company people, were asking what we were saying VICTOIRE about. 'You've won nothing,' they said. But our people didn't feel that way. And subsequent events proved that our people were right.

"People had lived very poorly throughout this strike. We had very modest relief, probably something like ten or twelve dollars a week. But people stood together and made do in spite of the difficulties. The ladies' auxiliary, and believe me they were no tea-party crowd – they were out there pitching rocks like everybody else when it was time, but they went around to the bakeries and got free bread from the previous day. They argued with the butcher to give them a bone and a little bit of meat. And anybody – the picketers or their children – could sit down to a plate of soup or very thin stew or a slice or two of bread at the strike canteen. People took the sacrifices because they believed in the causes. There was a humorous story years after about strike babies being born. It was a way of saying that families were closer together in that period than they had ever been.

"Sometime after the workers returned to work, Kent was released from jail. But he was not allowed under orders from the judge to go out to Valleyfield. Soon after that the vote was scheduled to be held. On the day before the vote, Laurence McCall, the government representative, went into Valleyfield. He was to meet with the union committee and with the company, and the vote was to be taken the next morning starting about six o'clock.

"In addition to the fact that Kent was not allowed to go to Valleyfield, there was a warrant out for my arrest that morning. Our lawyers asked the head of the provincial police what the warrant was about so that they could try to see a judge and arrange for bail if I appeared. But Hilaire Beauregard refused to admit that there was a warrant out even though the police were searching homes all over Valleyfield.

"In order to help our committee to continue the discussions with the government representatives and to be able to advise them, I went into hiding that morning in one of the workers' houses there in Valleyfield. By good fortune in spite of the fact that they searched many, many houses they didn't come upon that one.

"Meanwhile, Laurence McCall was telling our committee what the conditions for the vote were going to be. It was all stacked in favour of the company and against the worker. At the same time our lawyers were working at the courts to try to find out in Montreal what the charge against me was and to try to arrange bail. That night we had a big public meeting scheduled. Our final meeting before the vote.

"In the course of the day the message came through to me around four in the afternoon that the provincial police had been obliged to admit that there were charges against me. Our lawyers had seen a judge and he was willing to grant $500 bail if I went to him to turn myself in. So I was whisked in from Valleyfield to Montreal without the police getting to know and I appeared before the judge. I was put into the cells briefly and was granted bail. I sped back to Valleyfield in time to arrive in the middle of the meeting.

"It was a great victory for the workers because the police were still searching the houses in Valleyfield. The charge was a very nasty one. I was charged with attempting to bribe three children in Kent's trial which was pending at the time. It was a totally false charge. It was intended to cripple us in the preparations for the vote and to turn the public against us. In fact the company police had bribed those children to lie. I happened to realize what was going on and I had reached the children and warned them not to tell lies in court because they would go to jail.

"In any case, at the meeting there was a feeling of strength. It was decided that we could not let the government representatives steal our votes. The charges against me and what had happened in the course of the day was proof enough that Duplessis intended to rob that vote. We would have to be on a *pied de guerre* throughout until those votes were counted.

"After the meeting I called up Laurence McCall who with his dozen or so government representatives was at the local hotel. I told him I was going to meet him to renegotiate the terms. This was about ten o'clock at night. He said he had put in for the night. He would not see anybody. I said to him: 'You'd better get down in the lobby because I'm going to be down with one of our associates in ten minutes.'

"I arrived at the hotel with one of the workers and he had his twelve men posted at a respectful distance in the lobby. As we sat there talking, about three hundred women marched from the meeting and were serenading us with union songs outside the hotel lobby. It was just to make sure he sat there and negotiated.

"And he did. We were able to reorganize the whole setup for the vote. The next day the vote was held from six o'clock until approximately seven o'clock at night. We had two scrutineers at every poll and after the experience of the strike and the arrest and detention of Kent, my arrest and the attempt to steal the votes, every one of those scrutineers watched the government and the company just like hawks.

"All the scrutineers – company, union, scab union and government

– took the boxes to the old courthouse in Valleyfield for counting. We had called another public meeting for that night to announce the results of the vote and we must have had about 2 or 3,000 people outside the union hall awaiting the results.

"I got a call from the mayor of Valleyfield saying Laurence McCall was cooped up in the courthouse and didn't dare leave because there were about 1,500 workers on bicycles waiting, surrounding the courthouse. I told him we had to know the results before we would ask our people to leave. And those results had better be honest. There were calls back and forth and the mayor finally phoned and said: 'I have the results from Mr. McCall. It was about 2 to 1 in favour of the union. You have my solemn word, that is it.'

"We sent messages to our people that we had won the vote. They could let McCall leave town. Everybody came down to the meeting and we announced the result. That was still in September. After the vote Kent was finally granted permission to go to Valleyfield or anywhere he wanted as a free man.

"He conducted the negotiations with the management of the Valleyfield plant in fulfillment of the promise in that telegram from the minister of labour. In November that first contract was signed. It was the first one which we negotiated without intermediaries. It was not identical to the Montreal contract. In Valleyfield our people preferred to take more money rather than the eight-hour day. And that had to do with the fact that we had a somewhat larger proportion of men in Valleyfield. It was more of a one-industry town so that more of the workers there were the main support of their families. And they felt they preferred to have it that way. But for the rest the conditions were not inferior in any way.

"The battle then for enforcement and respect of those contracts started in both cities from that moment on. And in Valleyfield it was a consistent, stubborn battle carried out in a very courageous way by our shop stewards and department people. Time after time when the company arrogantly violated the contract there'd be a wildcat strike in a department and nothing moved until one of us went down. The manager would meet the whole department with his foreman and superintendents, our battery of stewards and shop chairmen, the local president and either Kent or myself. Sometimes in six- or seven-hour sessions there in the management's office, we'd hammer out a settlement and then they'd go back to work.

"Klenert and Valente from the international union were in collusion with the company. We didn't call on them. The company was obliged finally to deal with us directly in Valleyfield. So it was a more complete victory even though it took longer in coming.

"We would have liked to have made a break with the international union but those government accreditations with the Quebec government and those contracts were with our union as an international union. It would have created a tremendous number of technical and legal difficulties, and knowing that Duplessis and the company wanted to get us anyway we were fearful they would take advantage of those legal difficulties to decertify us once again. So that in a sense we'd have to start over.

"From 1943 on we'd had an annual district conference of our union. And every year the officers were elected by the Canadian workers. Kent was elected president, I was elected secretary-treasurer. We made it very clear to the international that when the workers would elect other people we would no longer be on the payroll of the international. What's more, our district conventions were held outside the provisions of the constitution of the international. They didn't like it.

"We built up our autonomy and made our own decisions all the time. Paying the per capita tax to Washington was something like paying a tax to be left alone. They never contributed anything to our strikes. We would send them so much money a month and expect them to send a certain portion of it back in salaries to organizers. But there was an armed truce between them and us all the time."

Madeleine Parent, Kent Rowley and the workers at the Dominion Textile cotton mills maintained their vigilant autonomy until 1950. They consistently resisted attacks from the anti-labour Duplessis regime, red-baiting McCarthy tactics from the United States, raiding by a rival CIO union, and corruption from their own international.

Then the company paid a final blow. In the next round of negotiations, management insisted on major changes in the wages clause. Workers would no longer have any guarantees against increasing workloads or cuts in the piecework rate.

Most of the textile workers were on piecework. They had built up those guarantees in contracts from year to year since 1946 and they were not going to give them up without a fight. The Montreal and Valleyfield workers all went out on strike.

Lloyd Klenert came to Montreal. He insisted that the union sign the contract the company wanted. Kent Rowley argued that only the strikers themselves could decide that. So Klenert fired Rowley, Parent and the entire Canadian staff.

"It was a desperate battle," remembers Madeleine Parent. "The next morning there was an announcement in the newspapers that Kent and his entire Canadian staff were fired because we were communists. Klenert said he'd appointed Sam Baron as Canadian director. Up to then Baron had been the leader of a rival union, the Textile Workers of America (CIO). He'd come up from the United States to found the Canadian section of the CIO textile union with the main purpose of destroying us. He was a personal advisor to the Dominion Textile Company and now he'd jumped from the other union. Roger Provost, the Quebec Federation of Labour president, another friend of the company, was named Quebec director.

"For another six weeks the strike carried on without benefit of accreditation because the accreditation went with the international. And for another six weeks they were unable to get a single scab in any one of those mills. Our funds were confiscated, frozen by court order. They were subsequently released in our favour but that was years after the strike had been lost.

"Our headquarters were sacked in the night with benefit of police assistance. Our local organizer, Conrad Leblanc, was arrested. His arm was smashed. As he was led up into the building where he was to be incarcerated, a couple of policemen on either side of him, they just turned his arm up behind to his shoulder and tore all the ligaments. They were never able to repay that. Even today he shakes hands with you with a stiff arm.

"The fateful morning when the break came, Paul Benoit was in charge of the provincial police corps in Valleyfield. All of our people were outside. There was not a single scab. Benoit came up to Kent and just hit him very hard with a blackjack on the head. I think that was the original cause of the strokes he had many years after. He fell bleeding and unconscious. They threw him into the paddy wagon and bounced him around. Some of the women there jumped up and tried to man the picket line but they were dragged off into another paddy wagon. People were just ordered into work.

"In Montreal we had police on horseback and in every possible conveyance who were pushing people and ordering them into work, while the radio was announcing that the strike was settled. There'd been a phony vote conducted by the government supposedly by secret ballot but the strikers were never allowed to have a scrutineer in that vote. So with the cooked results they announced that the workers had voted for a settlement and the contract was signed.

"There was a reign of fear. There were jobs for 3,000 workers whereas 6,000 had hit the picket lines. They literally doubled the workload. A considerable number of people in Valleyfield were blacklisted, including Trefflé Leduc, the union president. The company was running everything including the union.

"We conducted some rearguard defensive action for a while but we were never able to reorganize the whole thing. The fear was too great, the control was too absolute."

The battle was lost but even today Madeleine Parent refuses to concede defeat.

"Every labour battle," she argues, "teaches a worker how to fight. Nothing is ever completely lost."

Lloyd Klenert, secretary-treasurer of the United Textile Workers of America, AF of L, was thrown out of the union in 1957 when the U.S. Senate Select Committee on Improper Activities found that he and his friend, president Tony Valenti, had embezzled $65,000 of the union's funds.

Rowley and Parent remained active in a small national textile union – the Canadian Textile and Chemical Union. In 1969 they founded the Confederation of Canadian Unions, a central labour body for Canadian unions with no affiliation with an international. Today, ten years later, the CCU counts only 30,000 members. However, its very existence has helped keep open the question of an independent Canadian labour movement.

7

HARRY DAVIS AND BUD DOUCETTE

The Canadian Seamen's Strike 1949

The fight for independence in Canadian unionism reached a peak in 1949 with the desperate struggle for survival of the Canadian Seamen's Union. The CSU had been founded in 1936 and given a direct charter by the Trades and Labour Congress. It was one of a growing number of national unions without affiliation with an international in the United States – a bold position for a trade union in Canada to assume.

Just how bold became obvious in 1944 when the American Federation of Labour granted the Seafarers' International Union jurisdiction over seamen and fishermen in all waters of North America. The Trades and Labour Congress under president Percy Bengough made strong protest to the American Federation and insisted on the right of the Canadian Seamen's Union to retain their jurisdiction in Canada.

When the Second World War started the CSU like other TLC affiliates took a no-strike pledge. Canadian seamen manned ships on treacherous voyages delivering cargoes to the theatres of war. But when the war was over the CSU took on the shipping companies in the Great Lakes to win an eight-hour day for seamen working the lake vessels.

The campaign was carefully planned and well publicized but big companies like the Canada Steamship Lines resisted and resorted to violence. Gangs of armed thugs were hired to break up picket lines, and steam hoses were turned on seamen going through the locks of the lake canals. The strike lasted only a few weeks before the government stepped in and legislated a work settlement. An arbitrator was appointed and though the principle of the eight-hour, three-watch day was won many of the companies refused to comply with the government settlement.

While the union fought for justice on the ships, the TLC continued the fight with the AF of L for Canadian trade union autonomy. The Congress held its ground against the "roadmen" – full-time Canadian vice-presidents of the international unions – under the leadership of Frank Hall of the Brotherhood of Railway and Steamship Clerks, who carried out a series of concerted attacks against the CSU. In the spirit of the times it was all done in the name of anticommunism. However, at the TLC's 1948 convention in Victoria the delegates voted overwhelmingly to suspend the BRSC and affirmed the sovereign status of the Canadian Congress with the celebrated slogan "Cooperation Yes, Domination No!"

That same year, Pat Sullivan, president of the CSU and secretary-treasurer of the TLC, resigned from both positions and in a flurry of publicity set up the Canadian Lake Seamen's Union in direct opposition to the CSU. As tension mounted the deep-sea shipping companies stepped into the picture. They announced wage cuts of up to fifty dollars a month and plans to abolish the union hiring hall. Under the hiring-hall system the union maintained a list of seamen available for employment on a first-in, first-out basis. When shipowners needed a crew member they had to get him through the union hiring hall.

Harry Davis took over as president of the CSU when Pat Sullivan defected. Davis was widely respected among seamen for his gentle, rational manner. Like almost all of the CSU's elected officers he had been a seaman himself. Just two months after the outbreak of the Second World War he started sailing on an Imperial Oil tanker. Today, Davis is a businessman living with his family in a Montreal suburb. After thirty years he is still convinced that the union had no real alternative in 1949 but to call a worldwide strike.

"In 1948, negotiations for new contracts had begun on the deep-sea and the shipowners not only wouldn't go along with our demands but they insisted on a reduction in wages. We would have settled for the same terms as in the previous contract with no wage cuts but we didn't want to go backward. And one of the things they wanted to do was to get away from the union hiring hall.

"We knew their reason for this. The shipowners had always been inclined to blacklist union-conscious seamen and the hiring hall protected members against the whims of anti-union officers and shipping companies.

"We didn't have a deep-sea fleet in Canada for years and years. The only vessels we had were the government CN ships, some of the 'Lady' boats – passenger and cargo vessels running down to the West Indies, a couple of coastal vessels – Department of Transport ships, two or three cable ships running out of Halifax, plus the seven-ship deep-sea Imperial Oil fleet.

"The only thing we had really were the inland waterways which is unusual. We were a large exporting nation and as a result of not having a fleet of our own it was costing us more to ship our goods abroad. We had to pay foreign flag vessels. Plus the fact that a deep-sea industry would create employment for shoreside workers as well as seamen. One of the major CSU objectives was that an ocean-going fleet be built and maintained.

"By 1943 the deep-sea ships were starting to become a fair-sized operation. We were building ships under a Crown corporation – Park Steamship Company. They were mainly dry cargo vessels of 4,700 tons with a few 10,000-tonners. Most of them were on the north Atlantic run, some went to South Africa and Australia. They travelled around quite a bit. The odd one went to Russia. But after the war the government started to sell the ships at a very low price with the understanding that they'd be maintained under a Canadian flag.

"They were sold mainly to foreign shipowners. People from Italy and Greece in the main were getting those ships for so much on the dollar which was very cheap compared to what the Canadian taxpayer had paid for them. Soon even the promise that they'd be maintained under the Canadian flag was going by the board. Registries were being transferred to Panama or the U.K. – 'flags of convenience' to escape paying decent wages and taxes, too.

"For a while in the immediate period after the war employment wasn't too bad. But following that it started to drop off as a result of some of the ships being sold from under our feet. We saw that we were losing a lot of jobs and our big concern was to save the fleet. Shipowners were even starting to make out-and-out sales. Our ships were being transferred, one by one, to foreign flags, manned by foreign crews.

"The government was hostile to the CSU. We had a particular bad thing going against us. When negotiations bogged down with the Shipping Federation of Canada – this was the association of deep-sea shipowners – a conciliation board was set up to deal with the situation. The report was unanimous. Even the labour nominee, a fellow by the name of John Kerry, voted that we accept the wage cuts and the changes in the hiring-hall system. We couldn't accept that. The hiring hall is one of the basic tenets of any maritime industry. It means more union security. And we were worried about the weakening of the union through the hiring of foreign seamen.

"After the conciliation board ruling we didn't go on strike but tried to continue negotiations and win changes, particularly in those clauses involving the hiring hall. We didn't want to strike. The union was weak financially. The CSU was never a rich union but we were constantly going before the courts to defend seamen as well as organizers under the Canada Shipping Act. This is an old piece of legislation based on the British Shipping Act which Lord Nelson as head of the navy wrote in 1797 after a mutiny at the Nore. It has been amended here and there but basically it provides a kind of feudal law on board ship.

"It restricted the rights of the union, of organizing and even carrying out ordinary union activities. Because where the captain said you can't come aboard the ship and you went aboard the ship anyway, they could lay charges against you. And they did. Dozens of our members were charged and jailed for 'boarding without the Master's consent.'

"Season after season we'd been fighting battles. We were tired. So as a last straw our secretary-treasurer Gerry McManus and I went to meet with MacNamara, the deputy minister of labour, to see if we could come to some settlement.

"'I'll see what I can do,' he told us. And with that he went out of the room, allegedly to phone some of these shipowners. Before long he was back saying very cynically: 'I'm sorry, boys, it's too late. They've signed an agreement with the SIU.'

"It was a thunderbolt. We had no idea that things were that far advanced. We knew after the TLC Victoria convention that we were going to have battles with the SIU continuously. Already they'd been putting pressure on the shipowners by threatening not to unload Canadian ships in American ports unless they got rid of the CSU. There was a lot of anti-red sentiment around and they were smearing us with this. There were radical leaders within the CSU but they were smearing the whole union. We knew they were out to throw the book at us and smash us. It was increasingly clear that the whole establishment in Canada was against us as well. We were acting as a spark plug for the Canadian labour movement. We were a thorn in their side.

"However, the CSU was still the certified bargaining agent. We still had the support of the seamen. The SIU had no certification. They had no members here. They should have been certified before getting a contract. Both morally and legally they violated the labour laws of Canada. They'd just signed a back-door agreement.

"The SIU were known as red-baiting racketeers. As it turned out we didn't have all of the information which came out subsequently. People like Hal Banks who they sent up here to act as a strikebreaker had a notorious reputation in the States. He'd been arrested for criminal activities there and shouldn't even have been allowed into Canada. Yet he was brought in by the Liberal government in cahoots with the shipowners.

"I reacted with anger to MacNamara's news. We were prepared to make all kinds of concessions but once he presented us with this *fait accompli* I knew we had no choice. Before we left his office I intimated that we'd have to go on strike. But they knew that. They even hoped for it.

"We had authorization from the seamen for a strike quite some time before. So it didn't take too much to consult the members of the national executive to decide what to do. We all agreed we had no choice. We had to take strike action. We called a strike almost immediately. Within about twenty-four hours.

"Right from the beginning there were vicious tactics used against us. Shortly after the strike started I had occasion to go down to Halifax. There were a couple of ships tied up at that time. We got urgent calls during the night to come down to the waterfront. A CN train was coming in, a freight train loaded with thugs armed with crowbars and baseball bats. They did a job on a few CSU pickets. There were even guns fired. CSU members were wounded. One young kid lost an eye.

"These thugs were to escort scabbing seamen through the picket lines. What they wanted to do was to get these ships moving, if they had to do it with half a crew. In many cases the ships were not even meeting the requirements of the backward Canada Shipping Act and they'd still sail them out. Our men tried to fight back as best they could but the RCMP were also used to escort scabs aboard the vessels and were quite obviously in support of the shipowners by acting as scab-herders.

"There were incidents everywhere – in Halifax, Montreal, Sydney, Saint John, Vancouver. Every time we'd hear of an attempt to bring in scabs there'd be a whole mobilization of the membership. We'd always try to enlist support of the dockers. Sometimes we got it. There was some initial support from the dockers in Saint John, New Brunswick, until the other counterpart of the SIU, the International Longshoremen's Association, also a gangster-led union in the States, brought pressure to bear on the dockers' leadership in Saint John not to support the CSU, to work the ships or else. They couldn't resist that pressure and eventually they worked the ships there just as they did in Montreal and Halifax.

"Whatever ships were in Canadian ports all responded to the strike call. We wired all the ships that we knew were in foreign ports that the strike was on and to go out at the first friendly port. The seamen were on their own. They were isolated. It's the big difference between a seamen's union and a shoreside trade union.

"While the deep-sea membership was fairly new in comparison to the length of time we'd been organizing on the Great Lakes, they were a much more militant bunch of men than lake seamen. For a number of reasons. Many of the Great Lakes seamen were seasonal workers. A lot of them came off the farms, out of small towns in Ontario around

Georgian Bay. They went sailing, then they went back to shore to the farms again. Some of them came from the same hometowns as their captains. So there was a much closer relationship between most of the officers and the men.

"On the deep-sea ships by and large the officers were British and they were more aloof, more difficult to get on with, greater enforcers of discipline. So that life on a ship with British officers was like life on a British ship and to Canadians that was irritating, to say the least. Even petty matters became confrontation issues. There was very little effort made to accommodate.

"When we'd bring out the union agreement and point out that the agreement provides this and this, they would point out we'd made a separate agreement as individuals with the master. It was called the Ship's Articles and if we had grievances we should raise them when the voyage was over back in the home port. In the meantime what the captain said was law.

"We filed many grievances. When fellows got to the home port, they'd go to the manning pool and the port committee would take up the grievance but they might be gone again before it was settled and back to the same routine and the same old problems.

"The structure of the ship's discipline made it very difficult on long voyages for there to be any close relationship between officers and crew, particularly if there was an old Lord Nelson approach to discipline. And that was fairly common. The deep-sea seamen would often be out and away for months at a time. And among these men who lived together and worked together there was a remarkable camaraderie. They built up an *esprit de corps* that was quite unique.

"During the strike young men of seventeen and eighteen years old with no particular experience in trade union affairs really came to the fore. They put out bulletins, printed papers, got support, found people to give them money and food. Some of them were thousands of miles away in South Africa, some in Australia, in New Zealand, in British Guyana.

"Initially we generated a lot of support among the trade union movement internationally, from the World Federation of Trade Unions and even from the reactionary International Confederation of

Free Trade Unions. Several months before the strike started I went over to a meeting of the ICFTU national executive in London. I explained our situation and they pledged their support. Then after the strike broke out they backed off their pledge by saying that this was just a jurisdictional dispute and not a bona fide strike. They were instructing their members, which meant any dockers' union they might represent in any country of the world, to continue working the Canadian ships but not to man them. This was as far as their trade union solidarity was prepared to go.

"This was a bad blow. If we'd had the support of dockers in all the countries where we had ships it would have been a tremendous amount of pressure in our favour. It would have been almost as effective, perhaps even more so, as if we'd had the dockers here.

"In Australia there was very good support by the dockers, and the seamen were there for weeks. They got good support from most of the shoreside unions there. The same thing in New Zealand where charges were laid against the seamen under the Canada Shipping Act. They were arrested and the authorities tried to browbeat them into taking the ships out.

"There was a ship on strike at anchor in Cuba. This was pre-Castro Cuba. The seamen resisted attempts of the police that came in launches to drive them off. They took fire hoses and repelled them with water. They wouldn't let anyone board the ship. The authorities tried to starve them out but people used to come in little boats to bring them supplies – water, food and so on. This went on for weeks until finally the military surrounded the ship with gunboats, opened fire and then boarded it with bayonets drawn."

The Canadian Seamen's Union strike reverberated around the world. In England, the king signed special legislation to deal with it. A state of emergency was proclaimed as the port of London became a key area in the strike activities.

As soon as it seemed likely a strike would take place, the CSU assessed the situation in the Canadian ports. It was not a promising picture. The union had to face the fact that the seamen would get no support from Canadian longshoremen, in eastern ports, who were members of the International Longshoremen's Association – an AF of

L affiliate. A decision was made then to set up a strong crew on a ship which would tie up at the London docks and be the pivot for the activities in Europe should a strike need to be called.

Bud Doucette was a young man in his early twenties working out of Montreal as a union dispatcher. A veteran seaman, he had spent some time in Europe and knew England fairly well. With the union's blessing he dispatched himself out as quartermaster on the D.E.V. *Beaverbrae*, a diesel electric vessel and the largest ship in the Canadian merchant fleet.

The *Beaverbrae* had been a German submarine supply ship. It was captured by a British destroyer off the Norwegian coast toward the end of the war and was handed over to the Canadian Pacific Steamship Company as reparations for wartime losses.

That winter while the CSU tried to settle their differences with the shipping companies, Doucette sailed on the *Beaverbrae* carrying general cargo to the United Kingdom. Each time on the homeward-bound journey the ship would call at Bremerhaven, Germany, to pick up eight hundred displaced persons from refugee camps and bring them back to Canada. This was done under charter from the International Refugee Organization.

Toward the end of March 1949, the *Beaverbrae* set out again for Europe. By the time they got there, the Canadian seamen knew they would have to strike. Bud Doucette remembers every detail of this last trip.

"We got to London with a cargo that included grain. The following morning when the dockers came to discharge the ship to open up the hatches and remove the grain, we told them that a strike had begun worldwide. We asked them to leave our ship until we'd resolved this dispute with the shipowners. The ship was declared 'black.' In Britain that means a great deal. They won't work a 'black' ship.

"There was immediately a great to-do about that. Canadian Pacific doesn't take lightly any mutinous acts on the part of its employees. And we were very securely and safely berthed in the port of London. But the strike started out at a slow pace.

"It was a relatively unusual issue. There have been many battles on the London docks and the dockers there wage principled battles. They

Canadian Seamen's Union on strike, 1949. Photo: courtesy of Public Archives Canada 49-75-6

A Seafarers' International Union scab is hung in effigy, 1949. Photo: courtesy of Public Archives Canada 49-75-10

don't shy off a fight. But this was a little different. They were being fed two very different versions of the story. One was that the official union recognized by the shipowners, the Canadian government and by everyone but this little handful of seamen was the Seafarers' International Union led by Mr. Hal Banks. They were told that we were an outlawed group of subversives – communists – who were disrupting the shipping industry, slowing down the recovery of war-torn Europe and sabotaging the Marshall Plan. The other story, of course, was our own.

"We made contact with the Transport and General Workers' Union that looks after the dockers and also with the Lightermen and Bargemen's Union. We talked to militants down on the docks and explained our situation. I met with Willy Gallagher, the popular communist member of Parliament for West Fife, and with Phil Piratin, who was then an M.P. for Mile End. Gradually the support for us grew strong.

"We quickly discovered that three or four docks away there was another Canadian ship called the *Ivor Rita*. She wore a Canadian flag but there wasn't a Canadian in the crew. Some way or another they had conveniently switched crews and brought in East Indians to man the ship. We went over and declared her 'black' as well. And, of course, the grain handlers refused to discharge her.

"Within a few days another Canadian ship, the *Argomont*, arrived and berthed in the Surrey docks. Her crew immediately joined the strike. They joined with our ship's union committee to establish a Canadian Seamen's Union Central Strike Committee.

"Then we had another strike that had been in progress three or four days before we arrived in London. It was up in Avonmouth in the Bristol channel. A Canadian 10,000-ton ship. There was a great battle fought there. The port workers showed their loyalty to the old principles of trade unionism. It went on all summer until the men were evicted from the ship and the *Gulfside* got away. In Liverpool and Southampton there were west coast vessels and, of course, they struck, too.

"We had quite a number of ships in Europe and the natural place to send the crews who had refused to sail them was the U.K. All summer long we received the crews that had been taken off Canadian ships in

Norway, Belgium and France. From all over Europe they converged on London. The police would remove them and the government would then deport them to the mother country. At one stage we had about 350 seamen to house and feed and clothe. In some cases they were taken off the ships in the middle of the night and they came to London with just the clothes on their back.

"We rented a church hall and converted it into a sort of barracks. Then the British trade unionists, the salt of the earth characters, started to come down and announce: 'We have a spare room, a spare bed. We can take two, or four, or six.' And they meant not only taking them in but sharing with them their cigarettes and their meagre foodstuffs.

"The *Daily Worker* printed our story and an address, and every day we'd get mail from a union local or perhaps from the retired members of a local exhorting us to continue the battle. They'd express their support and enclose five or ten shillings toward the strike fund.

"The central strike committee had headquarters at the rear of a barbershop down in the port area of London. British barbershops aren't the sterile, sanitary places that Canadian barbershops have become. They swept the floor daily and swept the hair over into a corner. Then they'd do a sort of tidy-up job on Saturday evening. The strike committee slept on the floor to be near the telephone in case a call came in from one of the other ports. I must say that in the entire period of the strike we made no more than a half dozen calls to Canada. The telephone was still regarded as a very great extravagance.

"We had our own borrowed typewriter and wrote our leaflets and engineered our demonstrations from there. All with the help, of course, of an active and dedicated trade union movement from all over the island.

"The strike went on and we were charged. It was a peculiar charge under the British Shipping Act. We were charged with disobeying the lawful commands of the master, combining with others to disobey the lawful commands of the master, usurping the authority of the master, impeding the progress of the voyage, and so on.

"In all, 111 people were charged with combining with me. I was charged with inciting 111 others. The case went to court and the Canadian Pacific Steamship Company had its array of very learned legal people who were prepared to make quite a case of it and remove us from the ship.

"Halfway through the trial, which took place in West Ham courthouse, our little solicitor Jack Gaster, a brilliant man whose sympathies with labour were obvious, asked me: 'Do you think the captain has the certificate of registration?' I told him I not only thought he had the certificate of registration but also the first pound note he'd ever made!

"It seemed to me to be a shot in the dark. The captain had a great, bulging briefcase and all of these stern and learned men backing him. I was sure they had every document there they needed. Gaster asked the captain if he had the certificate of registration for the vessel. The captain told him that the certificate of registration for a merchant vessel is usually kept in the company's safe. 'Where is the head office of the company?' Gaster went on. 'In Montreal,' he was told. Then Jack Gaster said: 'It is my submission that that is where your case rests. In the safe in Montreal. Not here.'

"The captain hadn't been able to prove that the ship was a Canadian ship. We were all turned loose and left the courthouse in great glee. We had many celebrations about that. But it wasn't long after that proceedings were begun and we were removed from the ship.

"We had big meetings every working day at the docks to explain the latest developments. In England they have a shape-up system on the London docks. They call so many men for such and such a dock. If the men want to work a specific ship they go and throw in their cards. Show-up time in the morning is the time to hold a meeting.

"In the hour preceding the time jobs were called we'd arrange to address the dockers who were gathered in that area. And there were several areas where they gathered. You might meet with 1,300 dockers at one end at the Royal docks, or over at Millwall or Surrey you might meet with 2,000 who would stop to listen to the latest news. Two or three of their rank and file spokesmen would usually be on the platform with us. I say 'platform' but it might have been the roof of a car or the top of a fence.

"As the government and the shipowners combined to take countermeasures against us, then massive meetings were called in places like Victoria Park where 15,000 workers showed up. One of the days Harry Davis was in England we had the biggest meeting of all. Between 15,000 and 20,000 to listen to the president of the Canadian Seamen's Union explain what was happening at home and what we hoped to accomplish by the strikes in foreign ports.

"The May Day 1949 march in London was an experience I'll remember for a long time. The route was lined with police cars, paddy wagons, mounted police and so on. They were kept out of sight in the side streets. We got down to the Nelson memorial in Trafalgar Square and spoke at the foot of Nelson's column. The strike was the key issue at that moment. It was less than a month after it had begun. The workers came out to hear our interpretation of the problem: how we felt, what we intended to do and what we asked of them. It was a great inspiration for young fellas like us to see the size of the support that we had in England from people we'd never encountered in our lives.

"The British dockers were given an ultimatum by Lord Ammon, who was the head of the National Dock Labour Board at that time. They were told to either unload the Canadian ships in the port of London or they wouldn't be offered any other work.

"The next Monday morning they called only two ships – the *Beaverbrae* and the *Argomont.* No cards were thrown in so a lockout developed. Instead of having a couple of hundred men and three or four ships involved, it eventually grew to a point where thousands and thousands of dockers were forced out of work. Hundreds of ships were tied up. And this, of course, became part of a communist plot that they blamed on the CSU.

"The press had grave rumblings about the necessity to end this anarchy by bringing in the Emergency Powers Act. They said there were perishable cargoes involved and England needed to recover from her war wounds. The Emergency Powers Act was in fact declared by the Labour government. It outlawed gatherings of support for the seamen's union, outlawed meetings of any kind.

"Fourteen thousand troops were eventually put in the London docks to move cargo. I might say that 14,000 grade-school children would have moved more cargo because the troops didn't really have their heart in the matter either. And they didn't know anything about unloading cargo. But the point was made.

"The press went on a really delirious campaign of red-baiting. Members of Parliament began to investigate red plots in the docks. The British MI5 – Military Investigation of Fifth Column Activities – had all sorts of 'evidence' of a conspiracy led by me, Joe McNeill, Bill Arland, Nick Carter, Alan MacIsaac and so on – fellas who weren't too involved with plotting on the international level. We'd been at sea most of our adult lives.

"By this time the *Ivor Rita* had gone. It had slipped out, been towed out into the stream at night and discharged over in Germany. It was towed over there and then they put on a scab crew. We've never heard of the ship since. But the *Beaverbrae* stayed and the grain was beginning to sprout in the hatches.

"From April it had now come to the middle of July and the ship was still very tightly held. Bill Arland, another of the ship's crew, and I met with the representative of the Canadian High Commissioner. He phoned Canadian Pacific and one of the other companies involving another ship. He assured us after talking with the owner's agents that they would be glad to have a settlement of the issue.

"If we'd go back to the ships and take them back to the port of signing, we'd go at the same wages and conditions as we had come. On that basis we were willing to agree. It was apparent to us by then that the strike was lost."

While Bud Doucette and his shipmates were holding out in the European sphere, back home the tide had turned against the Canadian Seamen's Union. The shipping companies and a number of international unions were determined to put an end to the CSU. The armed violence, the intimidation, the red-baiting continued. A Canadian seaman was found dead in San Francisco harbour. A coroner's jury ruled death accidental, drowned while drunk. But CSU activists were dubious about the verdict particularly when one of their own officers was informed by a friendly policeman in Montreal that the word was out that he was to be dumped and thrown into the harbour. The coroner's report would rule his death accidental, too. Drowned while drunk.

The waterfront in Montreal became a jungle. Petty criminals were hired down on the Main and paid $15 and $20 a day to go out and harass CSU militants. The police often seemed to work in conjunction with the strikebreakers. Seamen had to develop their own protection. But lurid stories in the daily press painted them as thugs and lost them a great deal of public support.

As the year went on the CSU felt theirs was a lost cause but desperately they sought some way to salvage the organization and maintain the fleet and their jobs. Neither the Shipping Federation nor the government made any overture toward reopening negotiations. The most consistent criticism throughout the strike period had been of communist leadership in the union. Now the entire national executive offered to step down and allow a rank and file leadership to take over if the shipowners would sign the old contract again. That offer was never accepted.

Finally, unable to withstand the constant pressure from the international AF of L unions that threatened to withdraw en masse from the Trades and Labour Congress, Percy Bengough succumbed. He begged the CSU to resign so he would not have to expel them.

The seamen's national executive reluctantly agreed to do so on September 1, 1949. As much as they wanted to see a strong independent trade union movement in Canada they did not want to be responsible for the destruction of the country's central labour congress.

In England, Bud Doucette and the crew of the *Beaverbrae* prepared to sign on for the journey home.

"On the day set to re-sign for the return voyage it was announced that eight of the ship's crew would not be permitted back in the ship. I was one of the eight. We were told to appear in an office up in central London to discuss with the ship's officers and the company representatives the details of who would be going back in the ship and under what conditions. It was at that point we were informed there would be no Canadian Seamen's Union. The ship would go back without a union.

"Then two Criminal Investigation Department officers came out and arrested me as chairman of the European strike committee and Alan MacIsaac who was the picket captain. They also arrested Bill

McPhedren, Bob Easton, Vern Walker and Benny Fisher who were all members of the central strike committee. We were taken to Brixton Prison and charged with assaulting some scabs in a tavern a couple of nights before down in the London docks.

"The strike ended with emotions very high. We had been betrayed by some of our own Canadian shipmates. They sold out. I make no apologies for any rough treatment handed out to traitors under those very trying conditions. There's not much doubt that there had been quite a battle in the London docks over that weekend.

"Traditionally in England, at least up to that time, the British working class was relatively nonviolent in direct contrast to the tenor of the fight here in Canada. During the 1948 Great Lakes strike I remember that almost civil war conditions ensued up and down the inland waterways. There it was more peaceful, everything according to law. And when we decided in the heat of battle and perhaps in the passion of defeat to have a settling of issues with some of the scabs when the strike ended, I don't think it was a popular form of retaliation in England. But we weren't in a popularity contest at that time. We had lost our jobs. Our dreams of building a bigger and better union and of holding the industry were blown. I don't apologize for what we did. Today, I might have counselled differently. But it's easy to pick the winners of yesterday's horse race. It's more difficult to pick the winners for tomorrow.

"The *Beaverbrae* sailed a few days after we were arrested. We officially called the strike off. She discharged the cargo and went over to pick up refugees again in Germany. The crew would have kept that ship in Britain forever if it had been necessary. But the greatest fighters in the world couldn't reverse what was then apparent. The strike was lost. We had too many enemies. The tide had changed irreversibly and was running against us. Holding the ship for another three or four months wouldn't have changed the situation at all. As a matter of fact, it might have led to an even greater division.

"There was a split in the British unions between those who were prepared to go to the end of the road and those who had succumbed to the propaganda barrage from the right wing of the labour movement, from the sell-out artists, from the shipowners. We didn't want to take the responsibility for widening this rift.

"The ship got away about the first week in August. Back in Canada most of the crew were discharged and barred from sailing forevermore because they were members of the CSU.

"We were held without bail in Brixton Prison although bail was offered. Then we were tried in Old Bailey in October. After two and a half months it was decided that four of us were to be acquitted. MacIsaac and I were convicted. In a fair court at a different time, we'd have been acquitted too. We were sentenced to eighteen months.

"The picture that the press and the shipowners like to convey was that we were a drunken irresponsible lot who derived a great deal of satisfaction from creating havoc and disruption in the industry. The odd contradiction is that five or six years before we were very highly regarded as the heroes of the North Atlantic, the people who were sailing those ships under very uncomfortable conditions, often with very little escort and delivering cargoes to the various war ports. I think it was C.D. Howe who compared the ratio of losses in the merchant service with those of the armed forces. Our numbers were smaller but we lost many more men.

"We did our time in prisons all around the country. We started off in the old Wormwood Scrubbs but after a couple of months we were moved because we were creating too much attention. We were shackled together with another dozen people and sent way up to North Yorkshire to a place called Northallerton, way up in the Yorkshire moors. Coldest goddamn place I ever spent a winter. Our tactic was to start study sessions in the prison. Here again in short time we had tables and tables of prisoners listening to our proposals for social change. So one morning very unceremoniously and with no prior notice we were told to pack our bags and we were sent over to the other side of England, to Stafford in the pottery district.

"We finished our time in Stafford and came down to London in the late fall of '51. We worked for a while in the docks there and then we were given one chance to be repatriated home and we took it. Canadian Pacific was bound to repatriate us to the port of signing. They took us to Montreal but they were so afraid that I came back the only passenger in a twelve-passenger ship, and MacIsaac was sent back the same way in another ship. That was the extent to which the hysteria had gone by that time.

"It wasn't a happy scenario back home. The SIU and Hal Banks had got hold of the waterfront. We were blacklisted. There was an economic downturn in that period. Jobs were hard to get. The union hall was still open because we still had two or three contracts remaining with lakes carriers. The national office on St. Francis-Xavier Street was still open and Harry Davis, Conrad Saurus and a couple of the other officers were there to meet us when we returned. But the union had no funds. It no longer had any function. There was very little hope that we could make a comeback. We didn't want to accept it but that was the way the land lay."

The Canadian Seamen's Union held on as long as it could. Finally it went under, swamped by a shipping industry that found it more convenient to deal with a U.S.-dominated "business" union run by known racketeers.

In December 1950, the Canadian Labour Relations Board revoked the CSU certification on the grounds of communist domination. Seamen in Canada were to be represented in the Trades and Labour Congress by the SIU under Hal Banks.

Since that time the same violent raiding tactics employed to overthrow the CSU have been used again and again by the SIU against other unions in Canada. This has caused continual friction between the central labour bodies in Canada and the United States and more than once has sparked serious charges of interference in Canadian union affairs.

About 80 percent of the CSU membership were blacklisted and were never allowed to sail again. Like Harry Davis and Bud Doucette they took shore jobs where they were able and settled down finally to make a living as best they could.

It has been close to thirty years since most of them have sailed the ships but in their hearts they are seamen still. Any one of them will point out quickly how the government stood by while their fears about the future of the Canadian fleet became a tragic reality.

At the end of the Second World War, Canada had some two hundred vessels on the high seas. Today, this country no longer has an ocean-going fleet.

8

HOMER STEVENS

West Coast Fishermen from the Fifties On

As early as 1893 fishermen working off Canada's West Coast found that their only hope of getting a fair deal in a fickle and expanding industry was to band together. The fishing industry vigorously resisted their attempts to unionize. It sought to keep them divided and fanned petty ambitions by insisting fishermen were small businessmen, "co-adventurers," or at least sharesmen in a business enterprise.

Over the years the battle has continued to rage. Repeatedly, fishermen have fought to clarify their legal status as workers but neither government nor industry has been willing to concede this.

The first fishermen's associations were usually based on gear lines which meant there were unions for gill-netters, unions for those using seines, and other unions for trawlers. There was also a tendency for each ethnic group to form its own protective association. On the West Coast the Japanese guarded their interests with one organization, the native people had a separate group, Finns had their own co-op and so on.

Isolated attempts were made at unity but the competitive nature of the industry made this difficult. Fishing companies always tried to play them off one against the other. But in 1945 as the degree of monopoly control of the industry became more formidable, British Columbia fishermen, tendermen and shoreworkers joined together in a new industrial union to protect their interests.

The fishing companies were compelled to bargain with the United Fishermen and Allied Workers Union. It was the only way to solve disputes and ensure a bumper season. Fishermen for their part learned that their only weapon in the battle for a fair price for their fish was the strike. They would start off the season getting a certain price per fish and as soon as the run hit heavy the canning companies would turn around and slash prices. Since fishermen bargained on their collective strength, the important thing was to keep organizing and expanding the membership.

By the 1950s, the UFAWU was a formidable pressure group among fishermen and shoreworkers in the West Coast fishing industry. Their developing strength was a threat to the big industrial monopolies. But the first attack against the union did not come directly from the industry, but indirectly from the nervous, anticommunist elements within the labour movement itself.

Homer Stevens was secretary-treasurer of the UFAWU in this period. He had grown up a fisherman's son in Port Guichon, a part of Delta not far out of Vancouver on the south bank of the Fraser. Homer's early experience had taught him firsthand the cutthroat competitiveness of the fisherman's life. From this reality he emerged as a strength to fishermen and a nagging thorn in the side of the fishing industry in British Columbia.

I speak with Homer Stevens when the fishing fleet drops anchor in Port Alberni on Vancouver Island. As he tells me of the continued threats to the UFAWU I am conscious of his calculated calm. It is as if the man waits for history to absolve his union.

"Prior to 1953 there was a campaign going on to force every union inside the Trades and Labour Congress to conform to a dictum that was laid down in Washington. This said that no officers of any trade union, or executive committee members, or members of a negotiation team, or anybody else could be suspected of being either a communist or a fellow traveller. It was the McCarthy era. In Canada it meant the expulsion of a whole number of unions like the Mine, Mill and Smelter Workers, United Electrical Workers and so on. They got booted right out when the American counterparts of those unions were kicked out of the AF of L or the CIO.

"Our union took a consistent position that no one should be thrown out because of the politics, or the suspected politics, of its officers. It was the right of the membership to decide whom they wanted to elect.

That was democracy in action. When the Vancouver Civic Employees, the outside workers, were thrown out in '51, we stood up and protested. We protested again in the action against the Canadian Seamen's Union which was being thrown out. Then in 1953, several months after the convention of the Trades and Labour Congress of Canada we just suddenly got a notice.

"I was on the union boat heading around Cape Scott at the top end of Vancouver Island with the business agent when it came over the news. Somebody called us and we turned on the news broadcast and found we had been suspended. We were suspended unless and until our union cleaned house.

"There was a raid on us then by the Seafarers' International encouraged by the Congress. They came out to try to take over our membership. They were issuing press releases every day saying that our membership was all defecting and going over to the Seafarers. It was right in the middle of the season and everything was pretty uptight. They said they were running out of cards they were signing up our members so fast.

"The only thing was they made the mistake of letting it be known that some of these goons they had hired were carrying side arms. That did it. The membership drove them right out. They ended up with their tails between their legs. There was no violence, though there were threats of it. Most fishermen always carry guns on their boats for shooting seals and so on. They weren't going to be intimidated by some American gangsters with a little pistol.

"The next year we had a strike of tendermen during the peak of the salmon fishing. The fishermen decided they'd tie up their boats. They wouldn't produce any fish while the tendermen were on strike.

"We had some people out scabbing and the following year the fishermen took pretty strong action on the grounds. They refused to deliver their fish to the packers that were handling fish caught by the people who had scabbed the previous year. The result was that some of those who had scabbed were driven right out of the industry."

Though the fishermen did not suspect it at the time, all of these events were setting the scene for the drama that was to follow.

"Some time along in the spring of 1956 I was sitting in my office in

Vancouver when two people appeared. They asked to see me and introduced themselves as representatives of the Combines Branch of the Department of Justice. They said they wanted to look at some documents having to do with the organization of the union and the kind of contracts we'd signed. I referred them to a study that was made by a parliamentary committee in which they'd gone into the background of the union and published a report under the Department of Labour of Canada.

"They insisted they'd come to search my office. I said that right then I was a bit busy. I had a meeting coming up in an hour or so. I asked them if they could come back the next day when we could discuss it further and see what they really wanted.

" 'You misunderstand us,' they told me. 'What we're going to do is start searching your office. We must warn you that if in any way, shape or form you resist the search we have powers that lead to penalties under the act.'

"I was tempted to throw them bodily out of the office but I phoned the lawyer. He said: 'You're in for it. And not only you but the union you represent if you challenge them in any way. These people have pretty wide powers.'

"The upshot was they started in at my desk drawer which was a mess. I don't think they could find much there. Just scraps of paper and bits of junk decipherable to no one but myself. Their intent was to take all the documents they thought might be of interest back to Ottawa for photocopying. They were apparently going to transfer all that onto microfilm. They said they were going to keep the documents for up to six months.

"As they started to go through the office it was apparent they weren't just going to look here and there and pick the odd sample document. They were taking original files going back fifteen or twenty years and also a lot of up-to-date material. It meant we'd be virtually stripped of our correspondence files, agreement files and a whole number of documents that were vital to the continued functioning of the union.

"I was surprised at this attack. Everybody in the union was taken by surprise. We'd conceived of the Combines Investigation Act as legislation to curb monopolies, cartels, big business combines. We'd never heard of it being used against a union. With one exception. In the United States some ten years before there'd been an attack on a union that was then called the International Fishermen and Allied Workers of America. A local branch of that union down in California had been attacked under the Sherman Anti-Trust Act. We didn't expect the same type of legislation would be used up here."

The Combines Investigation Act was promulgated in Canada in 1910. It revealed Labour Minister Mackenzie King's ingenuity. He explained shrewdly at the time that it was not meant to curb the combines, mergers and trusts developed by free enterprise but simply, "the possible wrongful use or abuse of their power." It was exactly the same type of legislation that in 1834 had sent Britain's famous Tolpuddle Martyrs to a penal colony in Australia when they tried to organize a union of agricultural workers.

"The attitude of those two investigation officers was sharp and arrogant. As time wore on we applied to the courts for an injunction that forbade them from taking any documents out of our offices. They finally had to do all the photocopying in the building.

"We set up a watchdog committee that watched their every move, followed them from one part of the office to the other to see what documents they were taking, watched them while they did the photocopying and then while they put them back. They were more intimidated than they might have intimidated any of our people. We weren't threatening them bodily. It was simply moral pressure. Our people were pretty hostile at the very thought that anybody would come in and challenge our right to be a union.

"That procedure resulted in thousands of documents being photocopied. There must have been ten thousand pages of material that they copied. They took just about everything. Records of minutes of the general executive board, minutes of negotiating committees, minutes of strike committees. They took copies of contracts, of correspondence relating to the agreements and how they were being enforced.

"They also took other things that seemed unrelated totally. Materials having to do with the regulation of the fishing industry by law. Federal Department of Fisheries bulletins. Copies of injunctions that had been made against us in the past.

"Once they actually started we did link it up with the attack that had been levied in the United States. Following the anti-trust actions down there the courts upheld rulings against local union after local union, all up the coast from California through Oregon and Washington and into Alaska. The upshot was that they were stripped of their bargaining rights and the union was virtually smashed. We were well acquainted with that. We estimated we were going to follow the same route here.

"After they'd completed the photocopying there was a period of three years where the only thing that happened was a hearing. Their position was that they had the right to cross-examine us with counsel but with no other people in attendance.

"We didn't know just how far this thing had gone.We had no inkling where they'd gone for other information. Later we found out that they'd gone to just about every anti-union element they could find, starting with the Employers' Association, through to the Fishing Vessel Owners and a number of other splinter organizations that were still in existence. They'd brought them in one at a time, questioned them and got information that would lead in the direction of saying the union was doing everybody a hardship by occasionally tying up the industry.

"The labour movement gave us some legal assistance but there was a kind of hands-off policy. They were concerned but the TLC leadership wouldn't go any further than simply saying they'd have a lawyer stand watch and try to get in with a listening brief. We didn't want to go into this closed session but we ended up going in there and giving evidence.

"Everyone was sworn in like in a court. But it was more of an inquisition. You had no rights there at all. They had the hand stacked. They had all their documents plus newspaper reports and everything else.

"Their line of questioning was one that would incriminate you, if it were a court, every time you opened your mouth. It was almost like a memory test without your knowing where it was leading or what the charges were. I remember our lawyer getting frustrated. Time after time he tried to object to questions which under law couldn't have been asked in an ordinary courtroom. They just brushed him aside. The chairman would overrule any objection and you either had to answer or be subject to the penalties provided for failure to answer.

"It was a kind of charade. People who had done part of the investigating were sitting there handing forth documents to another person acting in the capacity of prosecutor. They were representing the investigation part of the committee. The chairman of the hearing was a man who represented the Restrictive Trade Practices Commission. He was supposed to be neutral. He made a pretence at the start that he was there to see there was fair play. But that was pretty much of a farce.

"After the hearing everything went quiet. There was nothing said. No one charged. Nothing. Then three years after the original investigations started, in the spring of '59, the director of the Combines Investigation Branch, T.B. MacDonald, brought out a signed report. This was presented along with the statement of evidence – two rather huge volumes of material where they'd stacked together copies of union contracts, some strike bulletins and parts of evidence they'd got either in the oral examination I was put through or from companies, and so forth.

"At the end of all this was a statement of allegations which listed the activities of the union in signing agreements for minimum prices on behalf of fishermen, and division-of-catch agreements dividing earnings between the owners of boats and the crew. They also went into a curtailment programme we'd adopted to slow down production of the halibut catch and spread it over four or five months instead of having it all caught in twenty or thirty days.

"All of these activities, particularly those having to do with strikes and picketing, were considered to be in restraint of trade and detrimental to the public interest and therefore illegal under the act. In other words they were wiping us off the board as a trade union.

"That statement of allegations was given to us sometime in late April or May of '59. At the same time it was provided to the Fisheries

Association of B.C., the Native Brotherhood and perhaps to other people as well. In itself it was a charge. It meant the next stage would be a hearing before the Restrictive Trade Practices Commission.

"The first people to react were the companies. They immediately served us notice that they were ceasing all negotiations having to do with fishermen. They intended simply to post the prices they were going to pay. We weren't surprised at this reaction. We were in the midst of two disputes over what the prices for herring and salmon would be for 1959. It was a subterfuge to get out of collective bargaining which they never wanted to enter in the first place. We decided that we would have to put the issue to the membership. That meant taking a strike vote.

"While the vote was being prepared, I was sent down to Ottawa to see the Combines people. I went in and talked to a fellow by the name of Quinlan in the Justice Department. I told him what we intended to do. He said: 'The penalties are strong enough. I could put you in jail for two years for what you've said, let alone for what you say you're going to do.' I told him that the way our membership felt he could put me in jail and throw the bloody keys away. It wouldn't make any difference. If they were going out to destroy us we'd go down with all guns firing.

"At almost the same time, the companies had got into the act. Jimmy Sinclair, who'd previously been minister of fisheries but who at that time had been defeated in the federal riding of Coast-Capilano, was given the post of president of the Fisheries Association of B.C. He requested a meeting with us. His questions were pretty much to the point.

"'What are you going to do about the Combines Branch?' he asked. We told him we were intending to go on strike. It wouldn't be long before he'd get the notice that we were going out. We intended tying the goddamn industry up as long as it was necessary to get our bargaining rights back.

"All he said in a very calm way was: 'Thank you very much. That's just what I wanted to hear.' He adjourned the meeting and took off. We didn't learn till later that he was headed for Ottawa.

"In the meantime, union officers and organizers went all over the coast taking a vote on one clear-cut issue: Are you prepared to strike in order to establish your bargaining rights? I went into Rivers Inlet and up into the Skeena area. It was one of the liveliest sets of meetings that I can remember. Everywhere I went there were tremendous turnouts at the meetings, tremendous debates. We brought out as sharply and clearly as we could that this was a question of the survival of the union. If the Combines Branch had its way with us there wouldn't be a union at all.

"We got an excellent vote – something like 85 percent in favour of strike action in the largest turnout we've ever had of the membership. A lot of people who'd hung back to that point even joined the union then because they were concerned.

"In Ottawa, Sinclair pulled every string he could on both sides of the House and persuaded the government that something had to be done. Within six days they adopted an amendment to the Combines Act which placed fishermen in virtually the same category as any other workmen. We always considered ourselves workmen but the legal beagles take the other position that fishermen are not necessarily workmen but possibly sharesmen, possibly co-adventurers or small businessmen.

"This amendment provided that all fishermen in the province of British Columbia would be exempt from the provisions of the Combines Act unless one of two things happened. Either the government should decide to alter that in future, or at the request of fifteen members of Parliament the matter might be opened up for further discussion.

"It was a yearly amendment, expiring approximately within twelve months of the date it was introduced. It had to be reintroduced each year until, three or four years later, it was finally made a permanent part of the Combines Act. The amendment was eventually broadened to refer not only to the fishermen of B.C. but to fishermen in other parts of Canada.

"This took the Combines Branch out of the scene though the Restrictive Trade Practices Commission did start a hearing on the evi-

An investigator from the Combines Branch sorts through documents at UFAWU headquarters, 1956. Photo: courtesy of The Fisherman

UFAWU patrol boats on the Fraser River in the 1959 strike. Photo: courtesy of The Fisherman

Strike relief sales—UFAWU fishermen sell directly to the public. Photo: courtesy of The Fisherman

Homer Stevens (bearded) enters police wagon after his conviction for contempt of court, June 1967. Photo: courtesy of The Fisherman

dence. They were claiming that there'd been some price fixing on the part of the companies. But the companies went into court and got a ruling stopping the further hearings.

"They said that information in the transcript of evidence given already had been made public by the union to their detriment. They claimed that if they were compelled to go further in a hearing it could happen that they'd be forced to disclose the names of confidential sources of information inside the union.

"There were other allegations, too. The Combines Branch eventually dropped the case. They never did try to appeal that injunction brought by the companies or proceed with any action against them for the price fixing they'd indulged in, even though the act is specifically designed to deal with that.

"We came out of it a lot stronger as a union. Our membership was elated that they'd done it themselves. The solidarity they'd shown in their decision to tie up the industry for an extensive period of time had sent the companies running to Ottawa to get that amendment.

"We were sure it was the companies who were behind the Combines Branch's attack. It interconnected with other things that went on. For instance, later on a statement by the Fisheries Council of Canada, to which the Fisheries Association of B.C. belonged, said they had made a terrible error not to oppose the amendments to the Unemployment Insurance Act which brought fishermen under that act in 1956.

"At that time, Jimmy Sinclair was minister of fisheries. He was a politician looking for votes. He could see the writing on the wall. So, he supported our union against the Combines attack and he backed us also in our right to be covered under unemployment insurance. He was the one who pressured the companies to go along with it.

"In their bulletin they said they could have kicked themselves in the rear all down the street for ever having agreed to it. That amendment made possible amendments to the Labour Code which would grant fishermen the right to bargain and to be certified. It would make us eligible eventually for such things as vacations with pay, workers compensation, statutory holiday pay and all the rest of it.

"Once the amendments were passed we stepped up pressure on the government for amendments to the labour legislation which would enable us to become certified. We knew we had to do something about the Labour Code. The one gap in the whole thing was that nowhere in Canada was there any legislation which definitely said that fishermen had the right to organize, the right to bargain, the right to strike. We weren't accepted under the Labour Codes of any province or of the federal government.

"The only thing that existed that gave us any leverage in law was Section 25 of the Fisheries Act of the province of B.C. That act was to regulate the operation of fish canneries and fish production plants – business operations on shore. It really wasn't designed to deal so much with fishing. All it said was if in any year the fishermen hadn't yet agreed on the price to be set for pilchards or herring or salmon, there could be arbitration established. It was an unused section. We attempted to make use of it once in a dispute in the fall of 1952. We tried to use it again in the winter of '52–'53 but the government wouldn't actually invoke the use of the act. We were without legislation.

"We started two campaigns – one in Ottawa and the other in Victoria – to try to get changes in the codes that were then existing. We got the same old shunting from pillar to post, from Ottawa to Victoria. Passing the buck. Ottawa saying it was provincial jurisdiction, Victoria saying it was federal. Neither government being prepared to take action.

"In 1965, we made presentations to a federal-provincial fisheries conference where all the governments were represented, proposing that both the federal and provincial laws should be changed so that the basic right to be certified would be written into law on behalf of working fishermen. Then it would be up to fishermen and the government to decide which fishermen came under provincial jurisdiction and which under federal.

"We could envisage a combination. For instance, if fishermen fishing in a lake or in river systems or anywhere that the province claimed a certain amount of jurisdiction were to apply for certification, it would obviously be under provincial authority. But where fishermen crossed provincial or even international borders to do their fishing, then it very likely would be federal. We proposed this and didn't get anywhere."

Fishermen were unable to force any clarification of their legal status. The following year the same question of certification and bargaining rights came up again, though indirectly. The UFAWU were going after their first contract in the trawl section of the industry. Twice before, in 1947 and in 1952, they had been on strike trying to get a contract and each time they had lost out. But by 1966 it was obvious that with no written contract the old oral agreements were being violated again and again. Fishermen were being fired indiscriminately or they were getting less and less for their share of work on the boat.

"The strike started in March. Five boats stayed on the grounds in defiance. They were all fishing for the Prince Rupert Fishermen's Co-op. One way or another the skippers either tricked or cajoled or even forced the fishermen to stay out. They came back with their loads of fish.

"Then an injunction was issued ordering the union to order somebody to order somebody else to tell the workers to go back to work. It was a very complex sort of order. We called a meeting of our executive and decided that if the order was to the union, then the union would have to vote on it. Later on the courts moved with a contempt action saying that the union had no right to vote. The order to the union was an order to the executive – the president, secretary and business agent. The union was sentenced to pay a $25,000 fine and each of the officers to spend twelve months in jail.

"In the appeal, the business agent was let off on the basis that he wasn't present at that meeting and therefore couldn't be held responsible. The president, Steve Stavenes, was also shown not to have been present. He was up on the coast on a boat at the time travelling back toward Vancouver. However, the court ruled that even though he wasn't there he should have done something about it. So he also spent the year that I did in prison.

"I was jailed in Oakalla. We were there from the beginning of November to sometime in mid-December, just before Christmas. Then they shipped us out to a camp, part of the Oakalla system. We spent the rest of the time there. There were fifty in each camp, and there were four camps. Two hundred people in the valley working on forestry projects.

"Conditions at the camp were better than inside Oakalla. But jail is jail. You don't get out and you don't see anybody except to visit once a month. The petty officialdom in there is stupid.

"'We've got to know what your national origin is?' they told me when I first went in. I said I was a Canadian, born in Canada, my parents born in Canada. That didn't satisfy them. They kept talking until finally the guy told me he wanted to go off duty and get to bed but first I'd have to tell them what my parentage was. I said again that my parents were Canadian, but it went on and on. Finally, I said that I had one living grandparent, my father's mother, who is an Indian. So they put me down as an Indian.

"I was housed with the Indians. The Indians knew I was raised in a white man's society but the fact that I respected them meant something. They were in one cabin, the French Canadians in another, and so on. The guards play on that and, if they can, work them one against the other."

All his life Homer Stevens had been fighting bureaucracy and injustice. He saw no reason to stop just because he was in prison. He tried to speak to the guards, to the warden, and even wrote letters to the director of corrections about the treatment handed out to younger prisoners and the lack of rehabilitation programmes.

"The director of corrections came out and told me in a very strong English accent: 'Don't think you're here to represent these prisoners.'

"The Indians in the valley had meetings and we used to consider our conditions in the jail. We were able to meet without the guards present. Other groups usually had a guard sitting in but the Indians had a better system. When there was a guard present nobody spoke. They just sat there and didn't say a word. It drove the guards crazy. They just couldn't take it. So after a while they left us alone.

"We got paid 10 cents a day at the start, 50 cents later on, and then we got 80 cents a day. But if some little thing happened they'd cut you back down to 30 cents a day. You get remission of sentence, too, for your work. I lost some of mine.

"For having a watch I lost three days. You're not allowed to have a watch in prison. I lost another nine days for refusing to work when they tried to send us up to Campbell River. Both Steve and I refused to go. It was going to cost our wives $40 or $50 every monthly visit just to come up and see us. There were camps in the Fraser Valley so why force our families to go all the way up to Vancouver Island just to see us? We sensed they were just throwing the knife into us. We said we wouldn't work. They put us in the hole for twenty-four hours but we managed to get the lawyer to see us and there was a public outcry. They had to back off."

Homer Stevens and Steve Stavenes were re-elected as secretary-treasurer and president of the United Fishermen and Allied Workers Union while they were in jail. That same year, 1970, the UFAWU was at the centre of a long drawn-out controversy at the other end of the country.

It was the same old fight. Fishermen in the Canso Strait area of Nova Scotia were struggling to break free of the "co-adventurer" label that branded them as partners of the fishing companies rather than employees entitled to a trade union and an hourly wage. On March 30, they tied up their boats and began to man picket lines.

The UFAWU had started organizing in the East three years earlier when the fishing companies started telling the West Coast fishermen that they could get cod and other fish processed in the Maritimes for less than a third of the wages they paid in British Columbia. The union knew then they had to organize their East Coast brothers. There had been no fishermen's union in Nova Scotia for over twenty years since the Canadian Fishermen's Union was smashed in 1947.

During the three years of organization hundreds of fishermen from all over the province signed UFAWU cards, eager to win the advantages unionized West Coast fishermen had managed to achieve. When they went on strike in the area of Canso, Mulgrave and Petit de Grat of the Canso Strait they were out for seven months. Striking fishermen were jailed and served with court injunctions. An intense campaign was mounted to pressure them to join the Canadian Food and Allied Workers Union, the Canadian branch of the U.S.-based Amalgamated Meatcutters and Butcher Workers Union of North America (AFL-CIO). When he was released from jail, Homer Stevens went east to lend moral support.

"It still hadn't been decided by federal or provincial governments where jurisdiction for fishermen lay. When the employers – Acadia and Booth fisheries – after using every trick in the book failed to break the strike they went to the government to see if they might be able to bring about some kind of settlement. The federal and provincial governments came together and made certain recommendations. One of them was to set up a one-man enquiry commission which would be responsible to both governments at the same time.

"A fellow by the name of Green took on the job, a judge in the lower courts in Nova Scotia. He failed miserably. He called me into his office. We had a lawyer at that time by the name of Green, too. All the two Greens wanted us to do was to go back fishing while they investigated. I tried to explain that there was no way fishermen were going to go back fishing until they had some of the basic grievances settled and a contract they could work under. Once that was done they'd be quite willing to go back fishing and deal with the other issues that would take more time for negotiation.

"Judge Green thought I was exaggerating. So he went down into the Straits area and held three hearings. He started in Canso, then went to Mulgrave, and ended up in Petit de Grat. At times it was uproariously funny because the people spoke in four-letter words and the judge wasn't used to hearing them. But the fishermen were deadly serious about the deaths that had occurred at sea, injuries that had happened, and the fact that they were getting paid nothing on trips and were coming back owing the company money. All the age-old grievances. They told him clearly he should bloody well realize they weren't going back fishing until some of these things were straightened out. When he tried to give them his assurance he would do something, their response was: 'Who the hell are you?'

"The political atmosphere was such that there was a great wave of support for the idea that fishermen really did have the right to bargain. There were any number of public spokesmen, including this Judge Green who was appointed, who said it might have been all right at one time to label the fishermen as entrepreneurs or businessmen but the whole structure of the industry had changed. With the greater centralization, greater ownership and control by a handful of large fishing companies the time had come when some kind of legislation needed to be adopted.

"We had sent representation of a dozen fishermen who accompanied me down to Ottawa to meet with Bryce Mackasey, the then minister of labour. He had in fact agreed that something had to be done but he wasn't prepared to put it before Parliament at that time. The provincial government was on the spot. They were going into an election campaign. There wasn't any legislation introduced.

"The strike went on but in the course of it the Liberal government came into power. Gerald Regan who had done some work for trade unions as a lawyer became premier. He'd made the promise that if he were elected, the fishermen would get bargaining rights. The following year, 1971, Nova Scotia adopted amendments to the Trade Union Act of the province making it possible for fishermen to certify.

"Newfoundland did the same thing. They, too, could see the handwriting on the wall and there was some concern to what extent our union might sweep the Maritimes. They adopted the legislation in a hell of a hurry and another union was in there before we were able to do anything about it."

The United Fishermen and Allied Workers Union continued its battles on the West Coast. Whatever the issue, the crux of the matter was always the same – there were no legal bargaining rights for fishermen. The court injunctions served on striking fishermen could not have been issued to a trade union certified under either provincial or federal law. A fisherman could stop work but he did not have the right to persuade anyone else to stop.

The constant refusal to clarify their legal status made it doubly difficult for fishermen to win the benefits that most workers in other industries now took for granted.

"We had quite a battle over workmen's compensation. We had no coverage under the provincial Compensation Act, though some fishermen were covered from the time the act was written in about 1916. If you fished on a company-owned boat, or a boat you rented from the company, then you were covered. If you didn't, there was no compensation. We started a public campaign in '52 – massed fleets into Victoria and that sort of thing. Step by step, we finally won it though it wasn't until around '75 that we got universal coverage.

"We had all kinds of cases, prior to that, of widows and orphans being left with no compensation as a result of industrial accidents –

people drowning or getting killed or dying by fire. Fishermen get injured. On the seine boats there are strong tides and heavy boats towing under. People get crippled up that way. There are always boats going down. We lost a lot of men here three years ago on herring. Fourteen men were lost in one series of storms.

"We're workers and we work hard for our living. But when we got to the end of the season or we were laid off, we weren't allowed to draw unemployment insurance. Nobody. It didn't matter whether you were working on your own boat or anything else. We were at that for at least fifteen years, battling with the government until 1956 when we managed to get a breakthrough.

"Many fishermen have to supplement their earnings. Those that can get into the herring fishery, and it's a limited fishery, can probably survive without doing any other kind of work. Also those fishermen that have extremely good seasons. But the average fisherman and those on the lower end of the bracket either have to find some other job in the wintertime or go under economically.

"Canada's economy is such that there are a lot of other seasonal industries and not many fishermen can find other employment. Some have regular jobs ashore and that's become another kind of problem. Those of us who figure fishing as our number one occupation feel that something should be done to eliminate those who have shore jobs and who fish at the same time. They work their regular shifts and then when they know there'll be a fishery on Monday and Tuesday they arrange to get those two days off. Then there are the other people – doctors and lawyers. My own local doctor had a boat out commercially fishing."

These part-time fishermen moonlighting at sea do little to help the cause of the fisherman who must make his living through his catches. The professional fisherman has nothing to rely on but his own hard work and the experience that tells him where and when the fish are running. The tools of his trade are his boats and equipment.

"Whether or not you own your own boat or work a company vessel you're never truly independent. The Davis Plan came in a few years ago. They started making fishermen what they said was going to be an elite group. They'd all own their own boats. They licensed the boats and added a cost for tonnage. It got to the point where people can't afford it and where fishermen only own about 55 percent or less of the fleet. In other words, the company owns not the 12 percent they used to but about 45 percent of the fleet, or better.

"It's the company that controls everything. Not only the price of fish but also where you're going to deliver your fish, how you're going to operate. They have massive controls. If you come into Port Alberni, for instance, the only place you can get ice is through Westons.

"McCallum Sales deals at the head of the dock and B.C. Packers have a plant across the way. McCallum Sales is a direct subsidiary of B.C. Packers which is owned by Westons. If they want to turn on the screws they can say you won't get any ice. Or they'll put you in the position where you'll get ice but you'll wait till all the others get their ice first. There are international connections, too. We don't know yet how deep the links go between Westons here and Maribeni in Japan or Mitsubishi or any of the other big companies."

More than ever the fishermen who must confront these big international monopolies are convinced a strong union is their only chance of protecting their livelihood. But still the attacks on the fishermen's union continue.

In November 1975, Homer Stevens was stepping off a plane in Toronto en route to Ottawa. He was handed a message asking him to call the union office. When he spoke to Vancouver he learned that the Combines investigators were back there again searching through files.

"We went through almost the same procedures though we didn't have to go to court on whether or not they'd take the documents away. Once they got it all photostated they wanted to proceed to a hearing. One of these closed-door hearings. We decided we were not gonna take that lying down.

"We organized a demonstration in front of the building and went into the rooms where the hearing was to take place – the Immigration courtroom in Vancouver. We went in and wanted to know what was going on and why we couldn't be seated there.

"After three days they adjourned the hearings then laid charges of obstruction against us for impeding the enquiry. We've had two members found guilty and fined $350 which we're appealing. And the Crown is appealing the dismissal of the cases against the other five including myself.

"The act is worded in such a way that they can hold all kinds of secret hearings, have secret allegations and not let anybody know what's going on. It's set up to deal with a system of private corporations that get together. But they're not doing that. They haven't broken up a single cartel. They haven't smashed a single monopoly. They haven't changed anything as far as price fixing goes. But they have the power to do it.

"They've got this power of life and death. Fines that range in thousands of dollars per day. Two years of prison for refusing to answer a question, for refusing to go into a secret hearing. They need that to deal with corporate structure. But for a union they don't need anything of the kind. Almost everything we do is like an open book. They can go read it in the union bulletins. We put out a newspaper. In order to deal with anything effectively we have to have mass meetings. We don't do anything in secret.

"Their intention seems to be to force us into those closed-door hearings. They're bound and determined to get convictions and penalties, no matter what.

"There has been more direct support from the labour movement this time. We're now members of the Canadian Labour Congress and the trade unions have set up a defence committee. They've paid a good part of the legal expenses we've incurred.

"What the companies have done parallel to this attack is go out and try to weld together all the anti-union elements helping to create associations of fishermen and split them off from the union. They're saying there's no place for a trade union in the fishing industry."

Whatever the ultimate outcome of this latest Combines investigation, Homer Stevens is a fisherman with a living to make. After thirty-one years working for the union he went back fishing when he stepped down as UFAWU president in 1977.

"There's more hectic competition now than once there was. Though it's still the same basic project of going out there and pulling fish, mending nets and working in all kinds of weather in order to catch any fish and pay off the mortgage and the debts you've incurred. You can't employ other people to do it for you. We're just workers like any others."

9

GRACE HARTMAN

Organizing Public Service Workers in the Sixties

In recent years, many working people in Canada have come to see trade unions in a new light. The old fears that once separated workers are breaking down. Now, men and women in offices and colleges, the so-called "white-collar" workers, are taking up the struggles that their brothers and sisters in "blue-collar" jobs have carried on alone for over a century.

A dramatic example of this change in the dynamics of the labour movement is the public servant. The very idea of a public servant as a trade unionist was almost heresy until the early Sixties. But in September 1963, when 77,000 public employees across Canada, from garbage collectors to office secretaries, swallowed their differences and formed CUPE – the Canadian Union of Public Employees – trade unionism in Canada was jolted into some fresh thinking.

The new union was a merger of two small national unions – the National Union of Public Employees and the National Union of Public Service Employees. CUPE was given immediate recognition and a charter by the Canadian Labour Congress but its first few years were awkward and uncomfortable.

Governments at all levels were all too ready to move in when their public employees tried to bargain collectively the way other workers do. And the community was usually content to sit back while court injunctions and no-strike legislation ensured as little disruption as possible in its daily routine. In addition, CUPE had to struggle through bitter internal strife to overcome the natural allegiance of its members to each of the two original unions.

For ten difficult years CUPE endeavoured to find its place as a real trade union among Canadian workers. This was more than a historic battle for union recognition or first collective agreements. It was a fight to change the face of Canadian labour. Once the professional and clerical staff of public institutions realized that they were every bit as subject to the whims of an employer as the workers sweating it out in garbage-disposal dumps and hospital kitchens, a new day had dawned in Canadian trade unionism.

Among those who have worked to pull these diverse elements together is CUPE president Grace Hartman. Both Hartman and the union she leads have had to break a lot of new ground and for that they have needed to be strong. This strength sometimes has made her an unsettling adversary in a world where, until recently, women seldom reached the top. I am aware of both the strength and a disarming directness as I sit in the living room of the Hartman's bungalow in a Toronto suburb while Grace tells me about the fight to make CUPE an effective trade union.

"In 1954 we had just bought this house in Willowdale. Joe, my husband, was a construction worker and sometimes would spend as many as five or six months unemployed. Our two boys were in school and in order to carry the house payments and meet all the other expenses I went to work full time again. I started to work in the Township of North York as a typist.

"I discovered very early in the game that there was a union in North York. It had a very young, energetic president. I think he was about eighteen. And I had some background. I hadn't been active in a union before but I had married into a union family. I suppose the greatest influence at that time was my mother-in-law who was a longtime fighter. All her family were members of unions. My husband had been born in a small Scottish mining town where everybody belonged to a union. I certainly didn't come from that kind of family. I came from a southern Ontario, Orange Tory family. My first brush with a strike was when my father broke one as a boss.

"It seemed to me a lot of things could be done in this union in North York that weren't being done. And I always felt that if I was going to belong to something I participated in it. When the first elections rolled along after I started there I hadn't quite completed a year, and they had to ask for a waiver of the constitution so that I could run for office. I started work there in '54 and was a member of the union executive in '55. In May that same year the National Union of Public Employees was officially formed and we were a part of that union, Local 373.

"Three years earlier the National Union of Public Service Employees had been formed. We were part of the Trades and Labour Congress and NUPSE was part of the Canadian Congress of Labour. In '57 when the two congresses merged there was an apparent overlapping of jurisdictions.

"NUPSE was more in the utilities, Hydro Ontario and areas like that. NUPE was more in the municipal field and school boards and hospitals. Unions within the public service were new. We had very little strength, very little recognition. And for a long time it seemed to be a ridiculous way to operate. The staff representatives from the two unions were like ships passing in the night. One would be going into Hamilton to look after a civic group there and the other might be coming away from Hamilton after meeting with a hospital. We began to feel it was nonsense to have that happening. It was expensive too and neither union was really able to provide properly for the membership.

"We began to feel it would be better if we merged and formed a stronger union. But within these two national unions you had a lot of local unions that were years and years old. Some of them had been independent unions or had belonged separately to the congresses at an earlier time. There was a very strong feeling of local autonomy and of little empires that had been built. It took several years of meetings with breakdowns in discussions before there was a strong enough feeling amongst the leadership that they could now start laying the basis for a new union.

"Through the local unions and our district councils we began talking about the merger and its benefits. More and more active in my own local union, I became a delegate to the NUPE District Council. I was the first woman delegate to that council.

"The first night that I attended as a delegate one of the fellas said:

'Oh God, we won't be able to adjourn to the pub tonight to finish our meeting.' As a woman I was very unusual in those days in union gatherings.

"About 70 percent of my own local union were women though usually they were not activists. We had to be very careful about union meetings because we all recognized that women had those extra responsibilities at home. We used to meet at seven thirty and we tried to be finished by nine. If there was some very important issue like negotiations and we knew the meeting was going to be longer, we would appeal to the people to stay and they would decide whether or not we'd go on.

"I became president of the local union. We had interesting turnouts at union meetings. I remember in the early Sixties there was a group, all male, in the engineering department who felt they'd had enough of female leadership. They couldn't complain about their contracts, we had good contracts. They couldn't complain about what the union was doing for them. But somehow they got it in their heads that they should run someone against me.

"I was oblivious to this, it must have been a busy day, and some of the women came to me about four o'clock in the afternoon and said: 'There's going to be opposition tonight but don't worry, we've taken care of it.'

"When I got to the union meeting, and I was always there early, the place was packed. One of the men came in and said: 'My God, this looks like a women's auxiliary.' He was promptly told there was nothing auxiliary about this group. I think the other candidate hardly got the votes of his nominator and seconder. I was president of that local for eight years.

"At that time I was secretary of the Ontario Division of NUPE and in 1963 was elected president. It was the same year the merger took place. I remember how I felt my responsibilities were very heavy because in the Toronto area in particular we had a lot of old local unions that had strong feelings about whether we should merge or not.

"In discussions over the past little while we had seen the merger getting closer but there were still those people who didn't like the idea of a constitution being drafted by the merger committee and simply imposed. I had some fear about it too but I couldn't see any other way for the first convention.

"The merger convention was set for September in Winnipeg. Each provincial division caucused prior to the convention to decide who its candidates would be for the national executive board. In the Ontario region eight of us ran and I was the only female. I topped the poll. Two of us were elected from that caucus and we became the regional vice-presidents representing Ontario at the merger convention.

"The merger committees pre-decided the new president and secretary-treasurer. One from each union. The president, Stanley Little, was from NUPSE and the secretary-treasurer, Robert Rintoul, from NUPE. They were four-year terms for the first term, then those positions became open to anyone.

"The convention was very well attended. Even small locals sent delegates. My own local at that time in North York would have been about 275 members and we sent a delegate. It was very costly for us but we felt the importance of what was happening to us.

"Each union had their own convention for one day and then we came together after that as a merged union. There was no great harmony in that last NUPE convention. The decision to merge had to go to a roll-call vote, which was most unusual. But there was no question about the final decision.

"Still there were a lot of hard feelings. The large clerical group in Vancouver would not stay within the organization. They withdrew and are still independent. And there was one other local in Vancouver and the outside workers in Toronto who withdrew but who eventually did come back.

"There was a fear of merger, a fear of losing their identity. If you believe in a union you develop certain feelings for it. We had those strong feelings for the two older unions. And there was some feeling in my own union, which was the larger one, about the new president coming from the smaller union. But after we all sat down and looked at it seriously we felt it was the right thing to do.

"It was the art of compromise. Everybody had to go into that convention prepared to compromise in the interest of a stronger union for our membership. If it meant that the president had to come from

NUPSE, then that was part of the compromise. The president of NUPE, I should say, was not a full-time position.

"Public employee unions were not really of great news interest at that time. Our new union caused little reaction in the labour movement because I don't think the industrial unions took us too seriously at that time. And they were busy, involved in struggles of their own. The public employee was not an important person in the scheme of union affairs. I think there may have been more concern on the part of employers who now saw the two unions they might have been able to pit against each other merging to strengthen and grow.

"Once we were able to put together our service departments, research, education and so forth, we were in a better position to provide real service to the membership. But the biggest problems we had were the political problems within the organization. You just can't put two organizations together without having to cope with different methods of operation, different people, all the petty jealousies about who had certain jobs. And that had an effect on the organization in the very early years.

"There were all the misgivings that everybody had about whether or not this person or that was politically acceptable. We had just come through the McCarthy era and people questioned if some of the activists were left-wingers, or were they right-wingers.

"There were observers of the scene who said NUPE was a more left-wing organization. I don't know if that was true because in a public employee union at that time outside politics played a very, very small role. People weren't interested. They didn't think they should become involved in any way. They considered the elected people, the councillors, as their employers and they didn't feel they should do anything to oppose them.

"Special legislation was in effect for public employees at that time in Ontario and still, I think, in New Brunswick. A municipal council could pass a motion-in-council, opt out of the Labour Relations Act and take away our right to have a union.

"In some places we had to fight it. And in some cases we had to strike to have it done. Our very first strike in CUPE came when the municipal workers in Perth, Ontario, organized and wanted to form a union. The Town of Perth used Section 89 of the Labour Act which took away their right to have a union. And the workers went on strike.

"Perth, you must remember, is not a particularly strong union town. It's where International Silver went from Niagara Falls at one time when their employees had organized and they wanted to avoid a union. So we were facing pretty tough odds there when the municipal workers struck for union recognition. The Perth workers lost the strike but they are now members of CUPE. It took changes in legislation and some changes in thinking but they eventually gained recognition and we got rid of Section 89.

"People always said: 'Public employees don't need unions. They're there because of who they know. It's all political patronage.' And in some areas it was. But that disappeared when the unions became a little stronger. The aim at the end of that first merger convention was to restructure the new organization to better fit the needs of public employees, to start helping eliminate this legislation that was preventing us from having the right to form unions if a municipal council felt they didn't want us to.

"We didn't have the right to run for political office. We didn't have decent pension plans. Many of the sick-leave plans weren't too good either. We didn't have much in our contracts at that time. We were just beginning to develop them. We had to strengthen our union locals and convince people they should be members. We were looking at dues checkoff too. In the majority of our locals it didn't exist.

"We were building a brand new union even though there was a lot of experience. Some of the union locals had voluntary recognition from the employer and in a lot of cases we went back and got certification at that time. We then had to apply to all of the labour boards across the country to recognize CUPE as the new employee organization. There were many technical things that had to be done to establish that union. But the main thing was to fight that feeling that existed in both the old unions of: 'We did things right in our union. Why do you have to change it?'

"The two original unions had a lot of blue-collar workers in them. And then we began to see that the area that was requesting organization was the white-collar sector. Where we had the maintenance and caretaking staff in school boards organized we didn't have the clerical workers and they were beginning to see they were slipping behind in wages and fringe benefits. More important, they were beginning to see that there was some job protection under a union agreement.

"You have to constantly point out to these people that whether they like to accept the fact or not, they too are workers. That was a little difficult to get across to some of the white-collar groups. Maybe not so much the clerical workers in the municipalities who knew the fellas outside. They weren't somebody separate and apart. But when we'd get into other areas, say a university library or a municipal library, then we began to get into a whole different kind of person. And they didn't always fit too easily with the municipal groups. Once we began to move into universities you found a new type of discussion taking place on a convention floor.

"Many of these people were more concerned about the atmosphere of the workplace and their involvement in the operation of the library or the office or whatever it was. Our people in municipalities and school boards and hospitals and Hydro hadn't thought too much about that before.

"One of our first university library groups, in Queen's University in Kingston, in its very early stages developed some interesting clauses in their collective agreement. They fought for the right to take education courses in the university on company time and also the right to sit down with a new member, a new employee, and talk to them for a couple of hours about the union and about their involvement in it. All this on company time! They were important changes that we started to look at."

As the union grew and began to find its way, Grace Hartman was becoming known as a union leader. At CUPE's 1965 convention she was elected a general vice-president.

"It took a lot of time and energy and a lot of cooperation from my family. However, Joe always said to the two boys that there was no such thing as women's jobs and men's jobs. And that helped.

"At the same time that I was developing more within the union I had gone from a clerk-typist in North York to a top-grade secretary. I was secretary to the chief planner and the subdivision engineer in the planning department. North York was mushrooming as a municipality and I really loved the work I was doing. But there were great pressures because my department head wasn't too anxious to have me running around fighting governments and so forth when certain work within the department passed through my hands.

"The union was beginning to shake down a little bit. Still, there were great differences between the president and the secretary-treasurer and that was no secret. There seemed to be a constant struggle going on and some of us couldn't help but be caught up in it because we were officers. There were policy differences and there was still that mistrust. Each one wanted things done their way and each one thought they were right. You still had the two unions there trying to live together under the same roof.

"We were coming up to the '67 convention. The secretary-treasurer hadn't been well and he decided to resign. His resignation caused a lot of internal strife. It was obvious there was going to be some kind of power struggle for that position. One of the vice-presidents indicated he was going to run against the incumbent president. The two old sides were competing for all the new members who had never been in either of the former unions.

"In the meantime I'd been chosen from among the five elected general vice-presidents to replace the secretary-treasurer until the convention. It was a highly explosive period. I had from May to November to decide whether I would run for the job in the election. After discussions with my husband and sons we decided it was a challenge that I should take up.

"It was a very political convention. And very exciting. We had over 600 delegates there. They were fantastic, though we probably didn't have more than 20,000 members then. I remember that Hydro Quebec had become members just at the time.

"I had no opposition but the presidential position was highly contested. I supported Bill Black of Vancouver who was running against the incumbent president Stan Little. There was a feeling that we needed some changes. It ended up with only 10 votes difference be-

Grace Hartman presents Bill of Wrongs to the Ontario provincial government, February 1969. Photo: courtesy of the Toronto Star

CUPE hospital workers demonstrate in Edmonton, Alberta, 1969. Photo: courtesy of Grace Hartman

CUPE president, Stan Little, in the front lines of garbage workers strike in Ottawa, 1971. Photo: Murray Mosher

tween the two but I think now in retrospect it was the best thing that happened to the organization that Stan Little was re-elected at that point.

"However, the day after the election there was a story in the *Globe and Mail* where a reporter asked the re-elected president if he was going to do anything about the staff who were involved in the elections. He answered that heads might roll.

"The staff had taken sides, no question about it. It had been a bitter battle. I remember saying to someone at the time: 'If only he'd remembered the story of the English king on coming to the throne. When he was handed the list of the barons who had worked against him, he threw it into the fire.'

"That convention was like a bloodletting and it was from that point on that we really began to settle as a union. There hadn't ever been a woman as one of the two top officers before and the men were unsure of it. There are always those people that feel threatened by that sort of thing. And because of that I had to work much, much harder to prove I could do the job.

"There were many groups sitting very uneasily in CUPE at that time. But I had a clear mandate. I'd had no opposition. I felt I was in a strong position to go to the membership and try to heal whatever rifts there were. I set myself that as a personal goal. But it wasn't easy. We didn't smooth that out in a short time. However, at the next convention held in Toronto you could feel a settling down of the organization. There was opposition to both Stan Little and myself but both of us won our positions handily.

"Our real concern by '69 was to provide increased services for the membership. We launched a programme of increasing our per capita tax so that we could add field staff and strengthen the research department. Employers' organizations were beginning to form and those that already existed were getting stronger. We found they were hiring so-called public or labour relations people and lawyers to negotiate. There was a real need for better backup service and research was a key.

"There was also a decision made to start driving ahead on the organization of hospital workers and improve their working conditions.

We had a fair number of hospital workers already in the union. So the membership gave us more money and we were able to add staff.

"The international unions had very little use for us. We weren't really considered a very important part of the labour movement. Our position within the Congress didn't really start coming to the fore until the early Seventies when we were a little more sure of ourselves and of the problems we were facing.

"There were differences with the Congress regarding our jurisdiction. According to what they laid down for us when we were formed in 1963, provincial government employees could organize in CUPE. But in the early Seventies a lot of these provincial employees said they didn't want to come into our union. They were used to their associations and had very close links with the provincial government.

"By that time we were emerging as a militant union in their eyes and they didn't want to join an organization like that. The Congress certainly wasn't on our side. They argued that we didn't have the jurisdiction though it's very clear in the printed jurisdiction they established for us. They wanted the provincial associations to come in as separate groups.

"We resisted their direct affiliation to the Congress. We said it was going to create a jungle of unions in the same area and we didn't feel unorganized workers needed the added hassle of having two unions pulling them one way or the other.

"Federal public employees had been granted bargaining rights in '67 by the Pearson government. They had formed the Public Service Alliance of Canada. And they sat in with us on the many meetings we had with the provincial associations trying to find a way out of the problem. I remember there was a point when our membership were so up in arms about the question that they were ready to pull out of the CLC. We did withhold our per capita tax for a while. Finally the suggestion came forward that they form a national union of the provincial government employees which would give us three large unions within the public sector who could eventually form a council within the Congress.

"There was no question about it. As public employees we have a lot in common. The negotiations, the dealing with your employer in the public sector, is quite different from the private. When you negotiate with an employer in the private sector you're negotiating with him for your share of the profits. If you have to take strike action, you're eating into his profits.

"When you sit down with a municipal employer it's a whole different kind of bargaining. It's not his money and if there's a strike in the municipality he saves money. He's not paying wages and he's not giving you a tax rebate.

"The fact that a public employee is also part of the general public and has to pay taxes doesn't seem to make much impression on the media and the people they influence. They say our nursing-home workers, our policemen, are essential servants. But when you come to the bargaining table and you want wages and working conditions for those people, there's no such thing as essential wages.

"Nursing-home people, I have always found, are something else. They go on strike, in most cases, because their employer is a private enterpriser who makes a profit out of the sickness of old people and who is not prepared to pay decent wages to his employees. And yet when you walk the picket lines of these people they don't talk about their problems. And they have problems. Lots of them are single parents struggling on really low wages. But they are wondering if some of their old patients are receiving their medication or if they're getting out for a walk.

"You have to understand the trauma they're going through in having to withdraw their services and then for them to pick up newspapers and listen to the radio and hear themselves condemned all over the place. That's very difficult.

"I've walked in a picket line with women in a nursing home that struck for three years before they obtained a contract. And they only obtained a contract because the NDP was elected in B.C. and they took over the nursing home!

"I firmly believe that every worker should have the right to strike, to withdraw his services. It's the only weapon he has. Yet in 1966, the government of Ontario took away the right to strike from hospital workers and workers in homes for the aged. Those workers know now that the employer doesn't really have to bargain with them because he can ultimately go to compulsory arbitration.

"In any case, for a public employee what is the right to strike? The Hydro workers in Ontario struck and the government called a special session and by an order-in-council put them back to work. But despite all these difficulties we always were conscious of the great need to organize and there were still a lot of people unorganized.

"There was that period in the late Sixties and the early Seventies when the women's movement was really developing. I'd been involved and while I couldn't make that my main focus, I felt I had to speak up. But generally there was no understanding of the women's issues that I was trying to raise.

"The number of women in the membership was increasing. We began to see more and more participating in struggles, in conventions, on the picket line. Sometimes they'd say to me: 'I wish I could speak like you can.' And I'd tell them that it wasn't really long since I stood up at my first national convention with my knees knocking, making my first contribution and asking my first question.

"I was on the original committee that pressed for the establishment of the Royal Commission on the Status of Women and after the commission report came out we took a number of its recommendations that could deal specifically with our membership and developed a policy paper called 'The Status of Women in CUPE.' That was presented to the 1971 convention in Edmonton. It dealt with equality in pension plans, health and welfare plans and job opportunities.

"We started a campaign for equal pay in the hospitals between certified nursing assistants and orderlies. I suppose ever since those positions were created, orderlies were male and nursing assistants were female. And because the orderly was male he received more money always even though the woman had to have a certificate and he was more or less trained on the job.

"Even our own CUPE pension plan discriminated against women. We quickly eliminated that. And further down the road we took the plan and eliminated all the 'he's' and 'she's' within the text despite the fact the actuaries said they didn't think it could be done.

"Consciousness was beginning to develop. Maybe it developed in the staff and some of the elected people first. Then as more women were coming into the organization, younger women, women in the universities, women in the libraries – that was a whole new breed. They were more aware of their rights and were prepared to fight for them."

In its first ten years, CUPE signed more than 3,500 collective agreements. Only about 100 of them, less than 3 percent, took public employees out on strike before the agreement was signed. But those strikes were given a great deal of publicity. Some of them were far from the run-of-the-mill union conflicts.

"The employees of the Don Jail in Toronto became members of NUPE before the merger. They were mainly matrons and jail guards. Then following the formation of Metropolitan Toronto there were a lot of changes being made in jurisdictions and the jail guards were considered provincial government employees. As such they were not supposed to be represented by us.

"We raised the issue many times because their pay cheques were coming from Metropolitan Toronto. But we didn't receive any satisfaction. Then there was an incident in the jail. One of the guards whose hair had gone white and who was only thirty-three decided to dye his hair because he felt he'd then look more his age. One of the other guards helped him with this process through a friend who was a hairdresser. When the guard got back to work he was fired for having dyed his hair. The chap who helped him was also fired.

"They were under some constraints about going to the press so, as I was then the president of the Metro Toronto Council of CUPE, I took up the issue on their behalf. We knew that we had to determine if they were indeed provincial government employees or were they municipal employees. The CUPE Council wrote a brief and presented it to the chairman of Metropolitan Toronto who was then Fred Gardiner. It was the first brief I had ever presented of that size. It was a pretty important day for me and we won that situation. They were declared municipal employees and those people were reinstated.

"There were many changes being made at that time by the provincial government. They were talking of taking over certain municipal services and they decided that the Don Jail would be one of them and our members would definitely become provincial employees. Our members in there were really upset about this. We tried to fight the legislation through the usual channels but come December no decision had been made. This changeover was to take place on January 1. So the guards at the jail went on strike in December. It was a very cold December that year and they walked the picket line daily.

"We were getting close to Christmas and I found out that the people who did the cooking for Christmas dinner in the jail were prisoners. Most of them spent more time in the Don Jail than they did outside. They were usually picked up as vagrants and drunks. We thought it would be interesting to see what would happen if we got them out on bail.

"It was going to cost us twenty-five dollars to get each one of them out and there were two or three of them, key people, we wanted out. I went down to the strike headquarters to try to raise enough money to bail out these prisoner-cooks. It must have been Christmas Day or close to it because I remember I was having my family for dinner. I was expecting thirty people at home and I spent most of my day at strike headquarters!

"We managed to get enough money to bail them out. The administration within the jail soon were wise to what we were doing but there wasn't anything they could do about it. It was very disruptive for them. They had no one to cook the big Christmas dinner!

"We kept up the struggle till the end of the year but they eventually had to go over to the provincial government. We retained the right to represent them until the end of the agreement then they became provincial government employees."

The City of Ottawa was another employer that came under CUPE fire. Since 1963 they had been contracting out their garbage pick-up to a private contractor. With each contract renewal there would be a different contractor and CUPE would have to start afresh, organizing the workers and bargaining a new agreement. There was strike after strike, until finally in 1971 a particularly vicious clash took place as CUPE workers fought to retain pension and sick-leave rights as well as a decent weekly wage.

"There were a lot of incidents on that picket line – people hit by cars, scabs coming in, strikers turning over a car. But we managed to keep the garbage trucks in. The construction workers in Ottawa had agreed to support us and they were on the picket line every morning. It just happened that my husband was working for a Toronto construction firm in Ottawa at that time. He'd been sent there by his company. My son was also a construction worker, so the three of us were on the picket line every morning.

"Then the City of Ottawa decided they were going to take a chance and put the garbage trucks out on the street. They went around to all of the dives in Ottawa and Hull and picked up whoever they could find there to drive the trucks. And they got the trucks to roll.

"That only created more and more problems and one day we arrived on the picket line to be faced with about twenty-five members of the Ottawa police riot squad in full battledress. They didn't intimidate the workers. What they did do was strengthen the resolve of other workers, the construction workers in particular. They felt, it's you today, and us tomorrow. The next day there were about fifty of the riot squad there. This contractor's building was in a little back street so that most people didn't realize what was going on there.

"We won that strike but have had difficulties every time the contract is renewed. They renew the contract with the contractor who will do it for the least money. And the only way private enterprise does that cheaper than the City of Ottawa is by paying lower wages, if they can get away with it.

"I've often felt that the invention of the green garbage bag has helped employers hold out on garbage strikes. In 1972 when the City of Toronto manual workers went on strike, Toronto allowed the people to dump their garbage in city parks. I remember driving by Allan Gardens and feeling disgust at seeing garbage piled around the statue of Robert Burns. He didn't deserve that and neither did that park or any of the others.

"People feel public employees shouldn't have the right to strike. But if the general public and the taxpayer are not prepared to give us the same things they have then a strike is the price they have to pay.

"As early as 1966 we could see in CUPE that we were going to be facing more strikes. We didn't have a defence fund yet which meant that we had to send out appeals to our own union locals and then to other unions. We decided we had to establish our own defence fund. We started off with an assessment of a dollar per member. That was the seed money – then ten cents per member per month went into it.

"But in 1969 we had to put a moratorium on the defence fund because we had strikes in Vancouver, Toronto, Hamilton and Montreal. There was no money left. We had to let it build up again. Since that time the membership has realized the importance of the fund. We now will be putting eighty cents per member per month into it.

"Some people ask why pay into a defence fund when we have workers who don't have the right to strike? We've talked a lot about this and we believe that all workers receive the benefit when some are forced out on strike. From the fund we also pay legal fees of locals that get into difficulty with serious and important arbitration cases. Sometimes we've used it to enlighten the public when we're having difficulty negotiating in a town or city. And we've used it for public relations money to try and prevent a strike."

CUPE found out quickly that politics was an integral part of any bargaining procedure for workers in the public sector. In 1969 the union marched on Queen's Park to present the Ontario government with a Bill of Wrongs listing ten pieces of legislation discriminatory to public employees. The next year CUPE challenged the Saskatchewan government.

"During the Thatcher regime in Saskatchewan there was a Bill 2 which was called the Essential Services Act. All they had to do was declare hospital workers or school board workers, whatever, essential services, then they didn't have the right to strike. Our members suffered through this. Their inability to make any gains made their frustration build up. They went on a catch-up campaign and part of that campaign was not only to catch up on what they had lost over a period of time, it was to get rid of Bill 2 and the Thatcher government.

"That was one of the important times when CUPE membership took real political action. They went out to defeat the Thatcher government and elected the NDP government. I don't think there is anyone in Saskatchewan who won't admit we were the greatest influence.

The Thatcher government was defeated and Allan Blakeney became the premier. In the first session of that government they rescinded Bill 2 and gave us back our bargaining rights.

"Our local unions have complete autonomy and sometimes it almost stands in their way of progress. We developed regional and provincial bargaining which was new for us. But in order to bargain on a regional or provincial basis you have to give up a little bit of that autonomy and work as a team. In our hospitals now we bargain provincially in pretty well every province and it makes a difference. You have a more solid base because this is the way the employer operates."

CUPE kept expanding its horizons. As the union grew it had to learn how to deal with the exigencies of life as a Hydro linesman, a CBC announcer, a set designer, a hospital orderly, a professor, a policeman, a typist, a municipal worker. Long before most other unions in Canada were ready to deal with the question of Quebec's identity, CUPE formally recognized the two-nation concept of Canada. In 1965, the union acknowledged the two official languages of the country and from then on all CUPE material appeared in both languages. In 1971, a formal resolution recognized the right of self-determination for the workers of Quebec. This was a touchy issue within the labour movement and CUPE's forthright position did not sit too well with many of the other unions in the CLC.

By 1973, ten years after it was first formed, the union had 175,000 members. The convention that year was a milestone.

"What a satisfaction it was. There were people in '63 who didn't think we'd last ten months let alone ten years. But here we were bigger and stronger than ever. We'd come through our first decade and that has to be the toughest period of any organization. And we came out of it united. Now at last we were truly CUPE. No one talked any more of the two old unions. A third of the delegates on the convention floor hadn't ever been in either of them.

"Discussion was interesting because we had such a wide group to draw from. On one microphone we'd have someone whose job was picking up garbage, on another there'd be someone from the CBC or a professional librarian or a hospital worker. It gave us a real cross-section and we got to see things from everybody's point of view.

"There wasn't any longer the feeling we used to encounter when we'd talk to a group of white-collar workers about joining the union and someone would ask: 'Why do we have to belong to the garbageman's union?' Now people were burying their differences. They didn't seem to care that they were a social worker and the member sitting at the next table cleaned out ditches.

"Now we were realizing that we were all workers, public-sector workers, and we were all under fire. We'd been under fire as public employees ever since our union came into existence. And we didn't see that letting up. We saw it intensifying. What's more, our members were beginning to realize what the struggles of the other workers were and how important it was to support them at a time of crisis."

In 1975, CUPE elected Grace Hartman as national president. It was the only Canadian union to have chosen a woman as its top officer. That same year, CUPE topped the United Steelworkers of America in membership. The fledgling Canadian Union of Public Employees had become the country's largest labour body.

10

YVON CHARBONNEAU

The Quebec Common Front 1972

In the spring of 1972, less than two years after the wave of hysteria that took away their civil liberties and put the armed forces to patrol their streets, workers in Quebec shrugged off their fears and together took a giant step forward. The Common Front was organized by the three central labour bodies – the Confederation of National Trade Unions (CNTU), the Quebec Federation of Labour (QFL) and the Quebec Teachers Corporation (CEQ). It demanded the right to negotiate for the very real needs of some 210,000 public and para-public employees.

Such massive solidarity across conventional trade union lines was new and disturbing to an uncertain, recently elected Robert Bourassa. A head-on political confrontation quickly became inevitable.

The Confederation of National Trade Unions was a development of the old Confederation of Catholic Workers of Canada and had nine union affiliates. The Quebec Federation of Labour was the provincial federation of unions affiliated with the Canadian Labour Congress. Each of these two central bodies represented unions of public employees who collectively made up a little more than half of the Common Front workers. The rest were members of the Quebec Teachers Corporation – a federation of French-speaking teachers whose dynamic young president found himself in a situation with no precedents to guide him.

Yvon Charbonneau had barely two months experience as president of the CEQ when he was thrust into the Common Front arena. It was a rare chance to put his ideals to the test. Just a few months prior to his election Charbonneau had chaired a special committee on the future orientation of his union. The report that he presented to a special convention in June 1970 proposed among other things that teachers must become more involved in Quebec politics. The report provoked intense discussion and when in August that same year Yvon Charbonneau ran for the presidency of the CEQ he was elected by a slim 16-vote majority.

Charbonneau headed the CEQ for eight years and in that period they made labour history. Social and political events hurtled them forward, forcing them to find new ways to protect their mandate. And the teachers rose to the challenge. The year 1970 was the starting point and Yvon Charbonneau remembers still the excitement of Quebec at that time.

"Teachers were making the necessary connections between their actual struggles and the proposals we'd put forward for a new organization. We determined to do away with the old corporation status of the CEQ and to reorganize ourselves on a real trade union basis. Some of the older teachers were fearful of this but we gave ourselves a time period of four years to do it in. However, the main problem was not one of structure but rather of the kind of presence we, as teachers, were going to have on the Quebec scene and among the working class in general.

"Quebec teachers had had to face the fact that there was no specific attitude to education. The government had its own way of looking at everything. And behind the government, of course, lay the state apparatus.

"In the previous three or four years, moves had been made to standardize the wages of each group of workers in the public sector. At the end of 1966, the new Quebec Department of Education, established only two years before, tried to impose provincial ceilings over education expenditures. And the main expenditures in education are teachers' wages. Up to then all negotiations took place at a local level.

"If you heard of a clause that was in some other local agreement and it was better than your own you tried to get it in your agreement, too. From one place to another demands gradually mounted. It was advantageous to a certain point for the strongest unions, but big gaps were being created between those unions and some of the smaller regions.

"From the government's point of view it was an intolerable situation. They were paying 80 percent of the bill without being present at the bargaining table. So they came out with their ceilings. This led to a lot of strikes right across the province. One third of all teachers were on strike, though at different periods of time.

"Then in February 1967, the government adopted a historic piece of legislation. It was referred to as Bill 25 and it had two main effects: it imposed a uniform grid of salaries across the province for women and men, for the primary and secondary level according to two main criteria – the number of years experience and the division of teachers into nine categories according to the number of years of schooling.

"On the question of salary, the teachers were sharply divided – those who had more and those who wanted more. Negotiations were now going to be centralized across the province. No more local bargaining. It was a moment of truth for teachers. For twenty-eight months we negotiated and tried to amalgamate four hundred previous local agreements.

"In May '69, while negotiations were completely deadlocked, we organized a massive demonstration before the Parliament buildings. It was the culmination of a week of marches all converging on Quebec City – 22,000 people walking silently behind a coffin with flags held downwards. We were going to bury the Reform of Education.

"Later that year in November, in a climate of disillusion, Raymond Laliberté, the president of the CEQ, signed the first collective agreement. But nobody was really happy.

"This was the background to my being elected. When I became

president only half the officers were elected with me. So the change was not radical. I had to consider the points of view of the former officials who were still there. I also had to consider the union staff – at least half of them were former teachers who didn't hesitate to give advice. I needed time to become acquainted with the domestic functioning of the office and of the organization. But almost immediately after my election we lived through the October Crisis in Quebec.

"There was no time to read any handbook about controlling a crisis. I had to take a firm stand. Our membership was divided. They were afraid, shocked by the imposition of the War Measures Act and the patrolling of the army and the police everywhere. Even though in June they had voted for the involvement of the union in politics, in October most of our members seemed astonished that we would have a union point of view in the crisis.

"The evolution of an organization is determined by discussion among the most interested of its members, those who are more open-minded, more involved. So we felt a gap between the official position and the grass-roots resistance and reluctance. For me, personally, it was like a bath in cold water.

"I had to take the initiative so that the CEQ might join the movement of resistance to the War Measures Act. We tried not only to regroup with the other unions but we had meetings with people like Lévesque, Parizeau, Morin, Burns – the people who are now the important figures in the present Parti Québécois government. At that time they had just been through their first election and had only seven people elected. Even Claude Ryan was a member of that ad hoc Common Front and the leaders of the Société St. Jean-Baptiste – the national movement of Quebeckers.

"It took all my energy to try to develop a position. As a trade union we were very new and I was a young leader neither known by those I had to deal with nor by my own members. I succeeded in getting approval from our general council for a statement requesting the withdrawal of the War Measures Act only by a 1-vote majority – my own vote. The vote was something like 47 to 47 and I had to put the flag on the right side.

"I got a pile of protest letters after that but in all it was a positive move. I had no problem after that and we received a congratulatory motion at the following convention for the position we had taken. After that the chair was firm.

"Many of our members, however, were still not convinced that their professional corporation should be involved in such a delicate affair opposing the government. After all, Laporte was dead. But that period was an important one for the union. Immediately after, in December, the provincial government set up a special commission of enquiry concerning the involvement of teachers in the October Crisis. It was presided over by Gérard Dion, a university professor.

"The minister of education, M. St. Pierre, said he'd received hundreds of complaints concerning teachers. The press at that time certainly carried many letters from parents saying that such and such a teacher had discussed the October Crisis and the meaning of the FLQ Manifesto with students. It was the most normal thing in the world. There were many young intellectuals involved in left-wing groups in the society and, naturally, there were teachers among them.

"But teachers were shocked that they had been singled out by the government. They began to see that they were perhaps more important in the government's eyes than in their own. Politically, it was an opening and the beginning of a better understanding of their importance in society."

After October 1970 many Quebeckers felt nothing would ever be the same again but as the drama wound down the society found itself confronting the same old problems. Teachers still had to find a way to deal with Bill 25 and the new centralized process it imposed.

"The classification issue, according to the number of years of schooling, became a real problem especially in the Montreal area where many teachers found that they were now getting less money. Years of schooling that had been recognized before were now not considered valid.

"There were strikes in Montreal in early February and March '71. Illegal strikes, but strikes anyway, and we had to confront the minister of education and a parliamentary commission to open special rounds of talks.

"It was a tough period because the movement on the classification issue started from Montreal. I had to explain the Montreal problems across the province and try to mobilize other groups. It wasn't easy. In Montreal, if 5 percent of the staff is hit by an issue like this it could mean 100 or 150 people. In Rivière-du-Loup, 5 percent might only be 2 or 3 people. So it becomes difficult to mobilize. But the principle was important. Still, it was a tough experience to face that diversity.

"While we were facing these problems in education, hospital workers and civil servants had similar problems to contend with. So when in 1971 the government told us that it was going to extend this standardization and set up a common framework in its wage policy for all employees in the public sector, we knew we had to work in a solid front with the other unions of workers. The organization of the salary scale, the social security clauses, pension funds – they were all going to be planned according to a general principle for all types of workers in the public sector.

"When we made the decision in CEQ to become a genuine trade union, rather than just a sham of a professional corporation, we started to recruit new categories of members. So now we had teachers in our union, professional nonteaching staff, and we had maintenance staff, too. Some of the teachers were a bit hesitant at first to be in a union where they had to discuss issues with maintenance people.

"Up to this time, a blue-collar worker in a hospital and a blue-collar worker in a college had had no formal contact. They thought they were in separate worlds. Now they were forced to join their negotiating committees. We all had to organize in a different way. Teachers had to start discussions with nurses, with professional nonteaching staff, with blue-collar workers.

"The very early promoters of the Common Front were the CNTU. After all, they knew what it meant. They had a lot of different categories of workers within their own body. In a way they had to operate a type of complicated internal common front with their own members. We were immediately convinced that the idea was sound and must be given very careful consideration.

"Even before I was elected there had been some talks held between the three union centrals. Laliberté, the former CEQ president, held preliminary talks with the other two labour bodies in May and June and during the summer of 1970. They were talks only in general terms because everybody knew there was going to be a change in the leadership of the CEQ. These talks continued after my election.

"As president of the CEQ I was dealing with the presidents of the other centrals – Louis Laberge of the QFL and Marcel Pepin of the CNTU. We tried to build a wage policy for all categories of workers, blue-collar and professional, including teachers who are not easily comparable to other categories in the public sector.

"We ended up adopting some priorities common to all categories. First, a minimum weekly wage of $100 for everybody in the Common Front. This was very important because many workers at that time were earning only $65 or $70 a week. We also had specific demands concerning social security, pension funds and the security of employment. But the most important demand was that the government set up a central table for negotiations. Sectorial negotiations would still take place where each category of worker would bargain on specific issues. But the central negotiating table – *la table centrale* – was our first demand.

"The government was very reluctant to do this. For almost a year they refused this one point. A government always has advantages in keeping workers isolated.

"In my own union as we were preparing the Common Front we put out a special document concerning the political commitment of teachers. We stressed that teachers had to consider themselves as salaried workers. We presented this to our 1971 convention where it was accepted though there was a lot of resistance. Perhaps we were at fault. We were imprudent enough to use the term 'political cell' and that was a period when there were 'cells' all over. So that wasn't a good thing. But it was indicative of deeper resistance from some of the older, more conservative teachers. Still, the idea attracted many of the young teachers who had begun teaching with the education reforms that were introduced in the mid-Sixties and who now had five or six years experience.

"The other trade unions looked at us as newcomers on the scene, apprentices in genuine unionism. Laberge and Pepin had more experience and union background than I. They were more classic unionists. I was only thirty. They'd been in the union movement for twenty-five years and more. But they made a real effort to understand our problems and we became better at explaining ourselves.

"I had to become familiar with a more complicated approach than I was used to when I was president of a local union. But with the help of my colleagues we were able to play a role as one big third part of the Common Front. After all, our members represented 45 percent of the 210,000 Common Front workers. The CNTU with Pepin was the most important central in the social sector – hospitals, etc. The QFL had no more than 15,000 public-sector workers. So I was in a good position to intervene. At the same time they knew, with their experience, that I was in a very delicate position. This kind of militant approach was very new for a group such as teachers with a tradition of remaining separate.

"In February, we held huge meetings all over the province in fifty different locations ending with an enormous rally in the Montreal Forum with 15,000 people. It gave us an opportunity we'd never had before to reach directly out to other workers and to hear firsthand of their problems too. Those meetings made a deep impression on me. We chartered a plane and about nine or ten of us travelled about. There was a kind of instant communication. Usually Pepin opened the meeting, I spoke second and Laberge concluded. One of us would explain the state of negotiations, another would remind the members of our main demands and the third would give some perspective, some indication of the strategy to follow. There were local speakers, too, to add to the fire. This was the euphoric period of the Common Front.

"Finally on March 9, 1972, we took our first important joint step. We had a general vote for a mandate to organize together and even to strike in order to force the government to discuss with us at the Common Front level.

"The vote was taken in every workplace – schools, hospitals, offices – on the same day. Workers all over the province had the feeling they were communicating. A new network of human relations was set up. The vote took place during the day and the results were tabulated at night. We'd prepared a centralized system of collecting the data in Montreal at the CNTU offices and also in Quebec City with a special hookup for our union. It seemed like the opening of a new era, a new way of doing things here in Quebec.

"The atmosphere of that vote was like the end of an important electoral campaign where everybody comes together. We knew we'd achieved something unusual, something symbolic. The government was very nervous. What's more it was a new government. It had no more experience than we did. It had only been elected in April 1970.

"The teachers were very supportive of the Common Front and of the idea of going on strike if necessary. The big Montreal local didn't take part in the action. They'd already spent a lot of energy and money the year before in the big battle over reclassification. Their attitude now was: The province didn't help us much last year so now we're exhausted and can do nothing else.

"Their nonparticipation meant a great deal to the struggle but it was a situation that we overcame. Teachers here always used to say that without Montreal nothing could be done. We began to say that if everybody else did something it would still be possible. And we proved that to be true. Even without the big Montreal local that didn't take part in the Common Front – and it had close to ten thousand members at that time – we did it.

"For us the vote was an unexpected success. Just three months before there wasn't one line of agreement between the unions, yet we'd not only succeeded in getting a good vote but the pressure from the membership was so strong that we felt they were ready to go out on a general strike.

"One of my biggest concerns was to build the Common Front in each region. I knew that at the top level it would look strong for a while but it could be dismantled very easily. In fifteen or twenty different regions we set up very well structured committees. The Common Front was a reality, not just a media phenomenon.

"About ten days after our vote the government agreed to meet with us. But the offers they made concerning salaries were unacceptable. We made a report to our members and called for a one-day strike around March 24. There was a severe snowstorm that day so we postponed the strike until four days later.

"There's a regulation in Quebec making it obligatory to send a

Yvon Charbonneau is interviewed on his release from Orsainville prison.
Photo: courtesy of Yvon Charbonneau

The Common Front resurfaces in 1975 to demonstrate against wage controls imposed by federal and provincial governments. In the front row, left to right: P. Lemaire (CEQ), M. Pepin (CNTU), L. Laberge (FTQ), Y. Charbonneau (CEQ), P. Laroche (students' union) and C. Charron (Parti Québécois). Photo: courtesy of Yvon Charbonneau

From left to right: Jean-Guy Morin, secretary, CNTU; Norbert Rodrique, president, CNTU; Yvon Charbonneau, president, CEQ; André Lavallée, secretary, CEQ. April 1978. Photo: Guy Turcot

notice eight days before going on strike in the public sector. We hadn't waited the eight days so technically the strike was illegal. But we were very sure of our support by that time and that didn't make us nervous. At this stage the government and employers started requesting injunctions against us.

"Of course, a one-day strike has no real effect in itself. It's symbolic. But that strike in March shocked Quebec. It was an expression of an important new strength on the Quebec scene. It was also the first opportunity our members had to express their resentment toward the government offers. After the one-day strike the government made some minor amendments to their proposals concerning salaries. They took a few cents from one place and put them in another. They were trying to widen the gaps between different classes of workers, to broaden the range of the salaries paid.

"When we saw it was useless to keep bargaining like this we did a second tour of Quebec. There were more big meetings. We told our members that there was nothing more to be done. We didn't need to get a new mandate. The mandate had been very definite. And it was as strong from the teachers as from other workers. They had voted 70 percent overall but in some regions it ran to higher than 90 percent.

"We were all in unknown territory. We knew that after a certain time the government would intervene. That was certain. But we had to go out. Laberge, Pepin and myself were being carried by the movement we had initiated. We became good friends. Both of them are very strong personalities. Very sincere.

"I especially became very close to Marcel Pepin. He has a quick, sharp mind and was a very powerful leader for us. He was the main spokesman for the Front. Laberge and I were on either side of him but Pepin was the central figure. He was very conscious of the social aspects of any issue. Sometimes I think it's easy for a union to negotiate forgetting the very real problems of the worker, but Pepin was constantly sensitive to the situation of the poorest, the most neglected categories of workers. The strategy was always oriented toward them.

"Finally it was decided. On April 9 we went out on a general strike in the public sector. It had a devastating effect. The first week everybody was expecting it to collapse but when, getting into the second week, they saw it was serious, then the press started its barrage. They began quoting examples of the lack of health services. More than five hundred hospitals, clinics and psychiatric jails were involved and, though in principle workers are obliged to give minimum services during a strike, we had problems convincing some of the workers they should do this. It was all front-page news and meat for the editorials, too.

"We set up picket lines. They were more necessary in other sectors than they were in education. When a school is closed, it's closed. There's a symbolic picket line in the morning for one or two hours. But it was different for hospitals and other places. There were some bad incidents when people tried to go through the picket lines at hospitals. I remember in Sept Îles that a car driven by an administrator of a hospital tried to go through the lines. A lot of people were hurt.

"At the end of the second week we had serious problems. The premier had come out very harshly against us and the Liberal party itself had organized special squadrons everywhere in the province to force the picket lines and try to dismantle local organization. The Liberal party became very aggressive during the strike. They tried to form a counter-organization to the Common Front. But they didn't seem to understand that a common front has no power from the top, it draws its power from the grass-roots structure.

"Some of our own members tried to block the highways for a couple of hours. Workers occupied radio and TV stations. They did that in Sept Îles, in Thetford Mines and in Victoriaville. In some cases they were expelled by the police force after a few hours but in other places they kept control for two or three days. They took time to explain their problems to the population and would receive the public's comments over the phone. It was a mini-social revolution.

"That social dimension of the Common Front was very important. People had to organize themselves in long meetings at night and then go and do things they'd never done before. They had to openly confront not only their employers but the forces of law and order. Dozens of militants were taken before the courts.

"Every night the union officers would have long meetings too. We'd have to interrupt them to record a special broadcast that was presented nightly at eleven o'clock. The three presidents would deliver a message to our members and to the listening public as well. There was a tremendous audience for those broadcasts. Everyone was interested in knowing what orientation we would propose to our members. At the same time we were censored. When you buy air time the law provides that the station is responsible for the content of the broadcast as well as the person presenting it. The company's lawyers were always there and they obliged us to record in advance. Twice they insisted we rearrange our speeches because they felt there were some legal implications. We had to accept their conditions otherwise no message would have been possible at all. We could have held press conferences but then we would have been subject to misinterpretation.

"Everyone was aware of the Common Front. To certain segments of the population it was a kind of monster. But it meant something to the workers. For more than a year we'd been saying teachers had to consider themselves as other salaried workers. Now it was no longer a theoretical idea. It was a reality.

"By the second week of the strike the premier was threatening us with special back-to-work legislation with heavy fines and other penalties. At the same time he was inviting us to negotiate. But the negotiations were never serious on their part. It was just a matter of taking some money here and putting the same money somewhere else. It was obvious that Bourassa's strategy was to break the Common Front and not give it any importance at all.

"The negotiating meetings were always held at the same place – the Holiday Inn at Ste. Foy. But after we'd been on strike ten days we had a special meeting at the Château Frontenac. It started at eleven at night and went on till three in the morning. It was on the eve of the special legislation.

"This was, as we say in French, *la nuit des grands couteaux*. All the big knives were there. Everybody was trying to sharpen their arguments. Garneau, the finance minister; Castonguay from Health; Cloutier, the education minister; L'Allier of the Public Service; and Cournoyer, the labour minister. They were all there. They were very hard with us. Distant. They had their information from the two main networks they had in hand – the school board administrators and the hospital administrators. They knew we were at the limit of our resources.

"They legislated us back to work and we were caught in a very difficult position. Would we recommend to our members to go back or were we going to defy? To defy the legislation needed a lot of organization and politicization. The strikers were angry at the government but after ten days the government propaganda was beginning to have some effect. We decided to hold another ballot. We held it the next day.

"With hindsight I would say it was a mistake to hold the ballot so quickly after the legislation. We should have waited two or three days so that the fever would have cooled down. We should have organized another tour of Quebec as we'd done twice before. But we were in too big a hurry. We were nervous and exhausted at the same time. The vote was held in general meetings. There was no time to organize a vote in the workplace as we'd done before. As far as the CEQ was concerned, most of our unions had time to consult their general assemblies. In other sectors they consulted only with councils of delegates. The joint committee recommended to go on but without the necessary explanations.

"The result of that consultation wasn't positive enough to give us a clear mandate to go on with the strike. Fifty-five percent of the teachers voted in favour. But only half the members voted. In the hospital sector only 35 percent took part in the vote but with a majority of 65 percent or 70 percent in favour. But 70 percent out of 35 percent.... In the QFL participation was very low. When you consult just the officers you have a good majority but it doesn't mean much.

"We had to announce to our people that the struggle was finished. They had to turn the page. It was one of the most emotional moments of my life. It was a dismantling of all we'd been building. All the hopes, the objectives, all the personal involvement we'd had in this thing was coming to an end. It was like a dream that was coming apart. I wasn't even certain I was making the right decision.

"When I look back now I realize that we weren't organized to go on further at that time. We recommended going on but if you consider that it meant going against legislation, against the government, against popular opinion – that was really something. Obviously we didn't have a sufficiently sophisticated strategy to take on all those opponents at the same time.

"In certain sectors we were criticized a lot and called traitors. But in other areas people refused to go on. The movement couldn't be considered massive any more, it had holes all over the place. Even with some fervent militants on our side we had to face a brutal reality.

"From this point on, April 21, 1972, the story becomes a legal one. Laberge, Pepin and I were obliged to go to court. Notices were served on us at the Holiday Inn. We weren't surprised. We'd been expecting it. The government representatives disappeared at this time. For a month we had no contact with them. We weren't much interested either. We had no more mandate.

"We were charged with having recommended to our members to openly defy a court injunction concerning the one-day strike at the end of March. But the three presidents were not the only ones before the court. Fifty workers who had also been charged in connection with the strike were there, too. They were all responsible for having organized the defiance of the injunction in the hospital sector.

"Superior Court Judge Georges Pelletier was very arrogant and scornful. Pepin was called into the box as a witness for the other workers but Pelletier refused to deal with our case. His wife was not well and he said he could not be objective.

"Several days later our case was to be ruled on by Judge Pierre Côté. But we never saw him. The courtroom was very crowded. The atmosphere was charged. But the judge was more than forty minutes late. When we saw he was not there on time we took the opportunity to leave. It was a way of getting more publicity for our cause.

"I'm sure the fact that we left didn't help us but we left anyway. When the judge finally came in he condemned us to one year in prison. And we weren't even there!

"On the ninth of May we went to jail at Orsainville. The other fifty militants were jailed with us. They were given sentences of one month or two weeks or five days, with very heavy fines.

"If I try now to tell you how I felt I would have to say I felt proud. On the day we went to jail there was a massive demonstration in the streets of Quebec City. The feeling among the workers was that something unacceptable was taking place. Although officially the strike had been called off, workers were walking out in our support. And the strike movement was spreading. Miners, port workers, construction workers – they were all going out. Even if they weren't involved in the negotiations themselves, they saw their confederation being attacked politically."

From the time the three labour leaders turned themselves in at the courthouse in Quebec City, workers right across the province rose up in a solid wave of solidarity. Longshoremen in Montreal, Quebec City and Trois-Rivières, teachers in the Gaspé, Sorel, Joliette and Mont-Laurier staged walkouts along with nurses and hospital workers, bus drivers and steelworkers. In St. Jérôme north of Montreal several hundred employees of Regent Knitting Mills walked off the job. In Thetford Mines, Black Lake and Asbestos, miners joined in the protest as did thousands of construction workers at the big Manicouagan No. 3 dam.

It was evident that a new militancy was afoot among workers in Quebec. From one end of the province to the other, by the hundreds of thousands, they defied court injunctions and contract agreements proving beyond doubt that the Common Front was alive and well and had the support of a sturdy rank and file base.

This growing strike movement in the private sector was heartening to the jailed labour leaders but Yvon Charbonneau remembers the concern they all felt about dissension within the CNTU.

"The CNTU public-sector workers were very militant as were the two executive committee officers, Pepin and Parent, who'd been involved in the negotiations on their behalf. But the other three executive officers were much more conservative. Dalpé, Dion and Daigle – the three D's they were called. *Les Trois D.*

"For a long time they'd felt that a union shouldn't be so involved in confronting the government. Now with Pepin caught in jail, they managed to call the decision-making bodies together and at the end of

May, they organized their own union central. They formed their own confederation called *La Centrale des syndicats democratiques* – the Central of Democratic Trade Unions. It was a breakaway within the CNTU.

"They took with them at least thirty thousand workers from the most conservative elements of the private sector. It was very serious. Pepin was not only shocked, he was also in a situation where he had to get out to look after his confederation.

"Up to that time we had decided not to appeal our sentences. We were going to serve the time and try to use that as a means of broadening the base of the movement. But with this new kind of division within our own ranks we changed our minds. Around May 19 we announced we were ready to go to the Appeal Court. With that, the government decided to release us. We'd been in only about two weeks. The premier himself had appeared on a special television broadcast appealing to us to agree to resume negotiations. We were in jail and he was telling us that our place was at the bargaining table!

"When we got out of jail the only thing to do was to go back to negotiate. Pepin was certainly obliged to go back. We resumed talks about the beginning of June. The government had a new set of negotiators. They had changed the ministers and their spokesmen. Cournoyer now took L'Allier's place as minister of the public service. But there were no new compromises from them.

"We spent all the summer negotiating, but when you're in a situation at a bargaining table without any possibility of building pressure, negotiating becomes a series of superficial exchanges. No one among us had any preparation for all this, not even if he had more experience than I did. Nobody had an exact scenario of what might happen in mind. There was a great deal of improvisation.

"By this time most of the population was expecting a stand from the government. The most militant, the most politically conscious were supporting us but not in any active way. It was over. Now our only mandate was to save what we could.

"The CEQ held its convention in Ste. Adèle in June. There were more than six hundred delegates and the feeling among them was very militant. It was here that we adopted our famous manifesto: Our

Schools Serve the Ruling Classes – a charge against the system in general.

"Essentially, we envisaged our work through an educational process. We would set up a network of political action committees to create a bridge between the school and society and an understanding of the links between the political role of the state and the function of education. We wanted to explore the forces at play behind governmental policies and the connection between politics and multinational economics.

"We were anxious to have local studies done about two categories of students in particular – so-called retarded children and those students streamed into vocational training. Our delegates were ready to take the most progressive steps.

"There was very intense support for me personally from the people who were there and they were even ready to consider the possibility of refusing to sign an unacceptable agreement. But the special legislation adopted in April included stipulations that after so many months if no agreement were signed there'd be a decree to determine the working conditions.

"In the opinion of the CNTU and the QFL we had to try to settle something even if it meant making important compromises. In their concept of trade unionism, a good union always terminates its work by signing something. In our opinion it was rather different.

"By August the two other organizations were pressuring us to come to a settlement. But as far as the CEQ was concerned there were not only problems at the central table but our sectorial negotiations were also completely blocked. That wasn't the case with the other groups of workers. At least at their sectorial tables they were able to come to agreements.

"So we came to a kind of mutual decision that they'd sign what was acceptable to them and we'd refuse to sign. It was the fifteenth of September – the deadline set down in the special legislation by which we had to reach an agreement.

"The government agreed to give the CEQ a thirty-day supplementary period so we kept negotiating. But in the middle of October they adopted a first decree covering our salary scales and then in December, after setting up a special board to hear the parties involved, they adopted a second decree for all aspects of the collective agreement.

"The form was different but as far as the content was concerned we had the same result in the decree as the other centrals had been able to achieve. It was full of holes. Concerning the salaries, our demand for a minimum of $100 was accepted but for the fourth year of the agreement, not for the first year. The teachers had an increase in their work load, an increase in the pupil-teacher ratio, a deterioration of their working conditions. But in other aspects like the social security and insurance systems there were some gains made. There were some advances, too, concerning the security of employment. It was a mixture but the main impression was that it was not a good contract. But we did not accept it. It was imposed by decree.

"Politically, we felt we had the whole power of the state against us. Not only the government but all the apparatus of the state including the media. Only by emphasizing the political aspects of our struggle could we hope for a better deal in the future. We knew we had to intensify the work of our political action committees within the union to further analyze the situation in terms of class relationships and the real nature and role of the state.

"The Supreme Court refused our appeal. On the second of February we went back to jail in Orsainville. This time it was winter from all points of view. There was no more visible support. There was a solidarity meeting the evening before we went in but otherwise it was quiet. I think the average union member was trying to forget the whole episode as quickly as possible. There was even a feeling among some workers that we'd serve the sentence on their behalf. We were paid for. It's not something I like to recall. We were alone to pay the bill after the fiesta."

It looked as if labour in Quebec had retreated but it was only catching its breath. Sporadic support for the three jailed leaders was mounted here and there during that winter. Then, on the first of May, Quebec workers got their second wind.

Although labour's May Day celebration is not a long-established tradition in Quebec, that year there were big demonstrations outside the jail at Orsainville, in Quebec City, in Montreal and in some fifty other centres across the province. The consensus seemed to be that workers had to regroup their forces and start to fight again.

And they did. Despite intense rivalry and continual friction between the QFL and the CNTU in their bid to represent Quebec's construction workers, the Common Front surfaced again in 1975 when the public sector renegotiated their contracts. The Quebec government had set wage controls for the province but by bargaining together the three labour centrals managed to win a 6-percent increase above the set guidelines. Again, in the 1979 contract talks, it is *la table centrale* negotiating for the province's public-sector unions.

In political terms, *Le Front commun* is not quite the force it was in 1972 but its point has been made. Workers in Quebec showed they were prepared to take on more than a fight for better wages. They know now they must battle on the political front for social justice, as well.

As Yvon Charbonneau explains it to me across a dinner table in Quebec City: "We tore down the wall between unionism and the political scene. In my own union those who were still wondering if there was any need to politicize our members in order to achieve our mandate were in the minority from then on. Teachers stand now with other workers in Quebec. That's the most important thing I was able to be part of during my years as president of the CEQ."

In September 1979, Yvon Charbonneau takes up a new post as special adviser to the leadership of the Quebec Teachers Corporation. It is one more indication that the fight in Quebec is still far from over.

11

MARTIN SAUNDERS, GERRY DWYER AND JANE MERCER

Asbestos Miners at Baie Verte 1978

Today, workers who have established their right to bargain collectively and negotiate their terms of employment are looking critically at other aspects of their working lives. Health and safety has become a prime issue in contract agreements. More and more, trade unions now question an employer's integrity and focus on the responsibility of private enterprise to the whole community.

In November 1978, American asbestos companies and their Canadian subsidiaries were accused of having withheld from their workers the knowledge of the potentially deadly effects of asbestos exposure. The accusations were made in a series of lawsuits brought against asbestos companies by families of disabled workers. Documents brought in as evidence showed that Johns-Manville Canada Incorporated maintained a company policy of not informing workers they were suffering from asbestos-related diseases until they became physically disabled.

This was chilling news to the miners of Local 7713, United Steelworkers of America, in Baie Verte, Newfoundland. Just a few weeks before, one of their members had died in the Baie Verte Peninsula

Health Centre. They believe asbestos killed him.

Gus Lewis was fifty-eight years of age. His family was told he had cancer of the spleen, the liver and the bowel, and that he was suffering from bronchitis and pneumonia. The cause of death was cited as heart failure.

Gus lived with his wife and five young children in the coastal village of Fleur de Lys on the northern edge of the Baie Verte peninsula. To get there from the Trans-Canada Highway you travel sixty-eight kilometres on a paved road which runs through Baie Verte, up over the hill and out past the Advocate Asbestos Mine on the edge of town. After the mine turnoff, Highway 410 turns into a dusty, gravel road.

This was the road Gus Lewis took to work every day of the thirteen years he worked at the Advocate Mine. The last twenty-eight kilometres leading to Fleur de Lys wind past the tailings from the mine. This waste pile is a little higher now than most of the hills around it. And it grows still, despite the wind that keeps blowing the fine grey dust and scattering it over the whole countryside. A recent environmental count on the Fleur de Lys road showed a frightening concentration of asbestos – 1,400 times the levels now being found in North American cities.

Asbestos is a killer. Many people in the Baie Verte area fear for their lives. Safety is the number one priority for the union at the Advocate Mine and the miners resort to increasingly militant tactics in their attempts to force the Johns-Manville Corporation to admit the health hazards and take precautionary measures against them.

In 1958 when Johns-Manville came in to test-drill and run the chrysotile samples through a pilot plant, Baie Verte was a sleepy logging town of about six hundred people. It was a Bowaters town. They cut the wood here and exported it overseas. But when the Canadian branch of Johns-Manville Corporation were satisfied that an asbestos mine-mill in Baie Verte was a worthwhile investment, Bowaters moved out.

Construction crews were brought into Baie Verte. A permanent mill was built. Roads, sewers and sidewalks were blasted through the solid cliff rock. The company built apartments for its employees and management set up comfortable homes in the area known as Barn Hills. Schools and churches were established, businesses moved in to service the booming economy. Within five years the town's population had grown to three thousand.

The $1.50 starting rate for labour that the company was offering was a lot better than the $1.00 or $1.20 an hour most places on the island paid their workers. Rumour had it the company wanted to go even higher but the government was anxious not to upset the economy of the area. Still it was good steady money to Newfoundlanders who had been trying to subsist on a dying fishing industry and odd jobs in logging and construction. Even more important, there was ore there for a good forty or fifty years.

Johns-Manville took their pick of Newfoundland labour. They recruited on radio, television and newspapers all over the island. Psychologists with building blocks and Rorschach tests were sent around to interview prospective miners who passed the rigorous medical. Baie Verte, Newfoundland, had hit the big time.

Martin Saunders was an orderly in a TB sanatorium in Corner Brook when Johns-Manville were looking for workers for their new operation.

"I'd never worked in a mine and I didn't really understand what it was all about. But I was willing to take a chance on anything. I had a wife and three kids and needed the money. I got hired as a senior tester in quality control because I had Grade 11.

"The first morning I was taken in on the job, 'twas muck up to your eyes. We needed to almost tie rubbers on to get around. I went in with shoes on and a pair of dress pants. I soon realized I had to change my attire real fast.

"It was exciting for a while. In 1964 the union was organized and I was elected secretary-treasurer. In 1966 I became president. It was after that I first remember reading an article in some kind of male magazine about the effects of asbestos and how bad it was on the people workin' into it."

Gerry Dwyer who worked with Martin in quality control remembers this article very well. "It was in *Stag* magazine that used to have those girlie pictures in it. There was one of those in the lab with an article about asbestos. Somebody had done a study down in the States and found out that asbestos was harmful.

"Now when we started the mine first it was all mainland people came in and did the supervising. We were the Indians. We were the blacks. Only we were white. They came in and they thought they could give you a little bit of this and butter you up. Our supervisor was from the mainland and this magazine was there and Martin showed it to him. 'Jeez,' he said, 'don't be showin' that around. The next thing you know the place will be closed down.'

"So that's all we thought of it. We didn't know nothin' about mining. Martin come from a hospital, I come from a railway – just got out of school. The rest were fishermen and none of them had any experience in this kind of thing.

"The next time we heard about it was in '68. An editorial in the *Western Star* said about asbestos bein' a health hazard. So we brought it to the company in negotiations. Stupid-like, we figured this was worth more money to us. We weren't sayin': Clean up the health hazard. We didn't know. None of us was in a union before.

"I can remember Sampson from the company saying" 'You don't need to worry about that. They're not talking about mining. They're talkin' about manufacturing. Insulation workers.' We sort of believed him. Maybe because we wanted to believe it.

"They said we were never exposed to the levels of dust that asbestos workers were in the Forties. But I remember takin' samples in Advocate Mines in 1963, '64 and '65. We stopped takin' 'em. Not because the dust was hard to breathe. We didn't know anythin' about the dust then. It didn't come to us our lungs was bein' affected at all. We refused to take those samples because the dust was so strong and thick we couldn't see through it. And it was burnin' our eyes.

"Some of us were afraid we were goin' to be fired over that. Then they used to tell us the white asbestos we got in Canada is not hazardous. It's the blue asbestos comes from Africa that's the killer, they'd say."

But Martin Saunders found it hard to put the danger out of his mind completely. "I was sort of leery of it myself because I'd been a

TB patient before I worked in the sanatorium. The doctors had advised me they weren't too fussy about me goin' to work in the mine. But they realized that I did have a financial problem and they didn't really try to talk me out of it. But when I came to work here and seen how the dust was goin' around I wore a dust mask if I could get one. Some of the guys used to laugh at me because I used the mask more often than the rest of 'em.

"While I worked in quality control we were usin' jute bags. What they call the bren bag. Then every once in a while we would get a special order to have the fibre put into paper bags or plastic bags. A hundred ton or a thousand ton of it. After a while we saw them not only puttin' 'em into plastic bags and paper bags but also puttin' little tags onto 'em sayin': Caution. This material could be harmful.

"When we questioned the company about that we were told: 'That's just certain customers. They won't buy it unless it has that type of package.' When we questioned them about the tags they told us that some of the stevedores refused to handle it unless this was on the bag.

"At that point we started diggin' into it more. I did a lot of travelling. The union sent me away on conventions. While I'd be there somebody would ask me where I worked. I'd tell 'em and they'd say: 'Oh, you're workin' with all that dangerous stuff.'

"Under provincial law we had to have an annual miner's medical in order to work. We were never told that anything had ever shown up. We questioned that. We complained we weren't gettin' satisfaction. We made recommendations and all kinds of suggestions as to what we wanted done. But it wasn't until 1974 after we had made numerous presentations to them that the government met with us and started talkin' to us about the problem. We found then that half of the X-rays that had been taken here were never read. There was too many. The person that was readin' the X-rays in St. John's just couldn't keep up with 'em.

"About this time Gus Lewis had problems with breathing. He went to a doctor who mentioned the fact to him that he had lung problems and he might have to be moved from the dust area. But somewhere along the line the doctor wrote a letter to the company's public relations officer and advised him that Lewis' lungs were progressively gettin' worse.

"Gus never knew that the doctor had written the letter to the company but a photostated copy of it got into his hands. Whether somebody in the main office was a friend of Gus' and passed it on to him I don't know. But the word got about that somebody had picked up the letter on the garbage dump."

January 15, 1974

Mr. Ron Goodman
Advocate Mines
Baie Verte, Nfld.

RE: Mr. Augustus Lewis
Baie Verte, Nfld.

Dear Mr. Goodman:

I am writing you to advise you of the medical condition of the above employee of yours. He has been seen here several times this fall and was last seen on January 14, 1974. Subjectively, this man is quite healthy and indeed on physical examination, he is certainly capable of performing his duties on the "tailings" at the mine. However, three successive X-rays have shown increasing thickening and markings in the lungs, which are suggestive of a developing fibrosis. His pulmonary function tests on the machine here are compatible with X-ray findings, in that they are just slightly decreased.

Generally speaking, the indications are of potential or incipient pulmonary disease. He is certainly capable of continuing heavy work and is in no way distressed. However, I feel that he should not be working in the area with a high density of dust or fibre. With your current precautions, he may well be able to continue in his present location; however, I would appreciate it from a medical standby point of view if you would have his immediate environment checked for these qualities. It may be that an area of minimal dust and fibre content is advisable for this man.

If you have any further questions or would like to discuss his condition with himself or myself do not hesitate to contact me.

Yours sincerely
(signed) R.J. Riddle, M.D.

Gus Lewis was moved from the tailings area down into the mill, a site where the dust count is also very high. He worked there for a year until he became too ill to go on. But he was never able to claim compensation. No one could ever prove that his condition was related to his work. Gus had to support his family on a $425 Canada Pension he got as a veteran of the Second World War. Then, less than five years after Dr. Riddle wrote that letter to Advocate Mines, Gus Lewis was dead.

Martin Saunders began to realize how many men had died in Baie Verte since he had been there – all of them from cancer, heart disease or respiratory problems.

"The first one was Kenny Shea, an oldish man about fifty-five. Ken worked in the pilot plant and then stayed after the mine started up. In '69 he died from lung cancer. He had cancer all through his body. Bill Doyle who worked in the pilot plant as well was sick when I came here. He died soon after from cancer of the throat. Andy Bryant from Coachman's Cove, he worked on tailings and he died from cancer. Garret Jones, a shovel operator. He was only in his twenties. A strong, healthy man. He got sick and within six months he was dead from cancer. There was also Ches Filtree. Ches worked in the crushings. There was always an awful lot of dust. He had respiratory problems and was off sick for over a year. One day all of a sudden he died. They said it was a heart condition. But he was off not because of his heart but because of the respiratory problems.

"Mike Gould certainly had breathin' problems. He died supposedly from a heart attack but according to his wife and people who were there, he choked to death. Then Raymond Hoven. Ray died from cancer. It went all through his body. He was a man in his early fifties. And Eric Jones. He worked at the pit in the pilot plant and he certainly worked there afterwards as a millwright. He left Advocate Mines and he died up in Montreal from cancer. He was only a young man, probably in his late thirties.

"When I questioned Dr. Black, our resident health officer, about this he was unaware so many people had died in that short period of fifteen years. None of these people had autopsies done on 'em. I think Garret Jones may have. His wife was sent some kind of letter and they'd known he'd worked with asbestos. Other than that there seemed to be nobody concerned. It was just a matter of he was dead and they buried him. They did an autopsy on Mike Gould. I tried to get a report of that but I couldn't.

"Even when they do autopsies, they're not lookin' for the fact he died from asbestos. They're lookin' for the fact he died from heart trouble. They don't check into his lungs to see how much asbestos damage is there. Medical people should be able to keep records but records haven't been kept. Right now the only compensation allowed is for asbestosis. The only way to prove asbestosis is through a biopsy. To my knowledge, no biopsies have been done on anyone in Baie Verte.

"I started thinkin' about all this and gettin' more information. The final blow came when I went to a United Steelworkers Policy Conference in Toronto in 1974. The theme was: Stop the Slaughter in Industry. They had invited Dr. Selikoff as a guest speaker. He's known all over the world for his studies on asbestos.

"He suggested if I was concerned I should ask for a study to be done. So when I came back home I got to the membership and asked them to send in letters to their M.P.'s. We wired messages to the provincial government, to the minister of labour, the minister of mines, the opposition as well. Finally, the company and the government agreed on bringing in Dr. Selikoff."

Irving J. Selikoff, M.D., of the Environmental Sciences Laboratory, Mount Sinai School of Medicine of the City University of New York, went to Baie Verte in June 1976. In the long, flat, brown Baie Verte

Peninsula Health Centre he and his staff did a wide range of clinical tests on 485 employees of Advocate Mines.

They didn't expect to find much evidence of abnormalities in the Baie Verte workers. The mine had been operating too short a time. Experience had shown that the disease does not normally manifest itself for fifteen, twenty-five, or even thirty-five years. But even with a limited fourteen-year exposure, 10 percent of the workers studied had one or more radiographic abnormalities commonly associated with asbestos. As Selikoff had proved before, the prevalence of abnormalities increased with the duration of employment.

Selikoff suggested that dust emissions be monitored and controlled, the roads paved with asphalt to cover asbestos-content crushed rock, a car wash provided to prevent workers' cars from spreading caked mine dust or mud, and clothes-changing and shower facilities installed so that the men would no longer bring the deadly stuff home to their families.

Once the report was made public the local evidence began to pile up. Incidents that had seemed merely bizarre now were given more importance: the fish, filled with asbestos fibres, caught in the open pond at the mine where the men get their drinking water; the potatoes grown locally with the sparkly stuff clinging to their skins; the burning eyes and throats and the shortness of breath that were a common complaint in the area. Maybe there was something to it after all.

"No one had really thought before that children and other people in the town were bein' affected. People began to be concerned about their families. Before that they didn't know the difference. They'd come home and haul off their clothes and spread 'em all around and the kids would climb all over 'em. People started to be more careful.

"We had the water tested and found we have a very high count of asbestos in the town water. We've got no filtration system on it. The public health people who came in here told us we were tryin' to create panic. They said there was no proof there was any danger in drinking water with asbestos in it. But they wouldn't tell us there was proof it wasn't harmful!

"We were in negotiations at that particular time and had already

Martin Saunders, president of Local 7713, United Steelworkers of America. Photo: courtesy of Martin Saunders

Strikers of Advocate Mines, spring 1978. Photo: courtesy of Martin Saunders

Picket signs on the road to Advocate Mines. Photo: courtesy of Martin Saunders

Women Behind the Miners prepare for a bake sale in support of the striking miners. Photo: courtesy of Martin Saunders

Women Behind the Miners present their donation to the strike fund of Local 7713. Photo: courtesy of Martin Saunders

written into our proposals that we wanted to discuss the recommendations of Dr. Selikoff once the report came out. We asked for a main dry or change-house. We asked for that even before Selikoff's report came out. We'd asked for a car wash the last time we had negotiations. A lot of people laughed at us, negotiating for a car wash. But we wasn't lookin' for one of those elaborate city-type car washes. We wanted something that would take the dust off the cars so we wouldn't be bringin' it all home.

"In the pit our lunchroom was pathetic. It wasn't fit for animals. You'd be sittin' there eatin' your lunch and there'd be ten or a dozen rats in the corner. The building was fallin' down with leaks into it and everything else. So we asked for proper lunchroom facilities with wash-up. And a proper locker room."

The company agreed in principle to most of the union's demands. However, they would not be tied down to any time schedule for the construction of the car wash and the main dry. But the workers felt they could not afford to waste more precious time. After all, Selikoff had made it quite clear that the dust inhaled in six, twelve or twenty-four months would remain in the lungs leaving the lung tissue vulnerable to continuing damage, even without further exposure.

Talks broke down at the end of January and on the third of February, 88 percent of the workers voted in favour of a strike.

"We set the strike deadline for February 13. That was ten days. We figured that would give the company plenty of time to call us in and sit down with us and get down to this business of bargaining. They'd already told us they were goin' to do these things. It was just a matter of getting some dates. But when the ten days was up we found that we had to go and set our picket line up.

"The Steelworkers' strike fund is set up on the basis of twenty dollars per member. When we got our first cheque, we started figurin' it out. We felt we weren't goin' to be able to keep our members out on strike on that amount of money. The fact was we couldn't get none of our members to work. A few managed to get jobs. They started cuttin' wood for small contractors. But a lot of them didn't get paid. So we still had to meet their expenses even if they were workin'.

"We had a certain amount of money in our own local fund. So we decided we were goin' to subsidize our strike fund to the tune of $2,000 a week. After the strike dragged on we found we had to put out a public appeal for funds. We got a lot of support so we came through pretty good. Myself, I had seven children. My wife, myself and seven children. Before the strike my grocery bill ran anywhere from $120 to $135 a week. Now we had to manage on $53.

"The town split. Some of the business people didn't want to offend the union but at the same time they wanted to help the company. We sent letters to the town council askin' for them to make a bylaw sayin' that no company vehicle would leave the company property without being washed off. What was happenin' was that the company staff was goin' in using their own vehicles in around the mine and they were bringin' out all kinds of asbestos mud around town. The council took the position they wanted to sit on the fence. They didn't want to get involved.

"The council was not elected. They went in by acclamation because they couldn't get enough to have an election. Most of 'em were business people. They were afraid their business might be affected if they took sides.

"I don't think I had many friends in the community outside the workers at that time. There was some people around town that were not workin' with the company that would give me a pretty hard time. I had some of my own union members phone me and call me pretty hard names. There were some that were opposed to the strike.

"Some of the older Newfoundlanders, they'd worked in the lumber mills and they'd worked under pretty strenuous conditions. Newfoundland has a tradition of people that thought they always had to be beholden to the employer. For instance, before the mine started up here if you wanted a job in the lumber mill you had to shop at the company store. The guy that had the contract also had the store. If you didn't buy your groceries in his store, you didn't work in his camp.

"One guy during negotiations came to me and said he had rumours about how bad the company was doin' financially. He said he was willing to take $1.50 an hour cut in pay to help the company! People with that kind of attitude never want to go out on strike against management.

"Right from the start the RCMP was involved. They phoned us and said they were goin' to be checkin' the picket lines. They wanted to keep tabs on what was goin' on. They wasn't goin' to interfere or anything like that. Just friendly visits to the picket lines.

"One evening the Mounties phoned me and said the boys had this truck held up. What happened was this dump truck was comin' out around one thirty in the afternoon. She was all full of asbestos dust. The boys figured they weren't goin' to let 'er out till she got washed off. So the guy went back to wash it off. But apparently he was sent back out again and she still wasn't washed off. The boys said: 'You're not goin' out.'

"When the four o'clock shift was comin' off, the pit superintendent, the head leader comin' out, stopped by the truck although it wasn't in his way. It was towards the side. He wouldn't move. He held up all the staff. When I went in there at four o'clock the staff was held up. I went down to 'im and told 'im he could go. He wasn't bein' held up. The boys just wanted the truck washed off. He told me: 'I'm not prepared to negotiate here on the picket line.'

"Anyway he never moved. I went behind him then and I talked to some of the other people. I got wavers to wave them out but they wouldn't move. So I left then. I went up and told the Mounties the guys were not holdin' up the staff. It was the guy there at the head who wouldn't move. The Mounties said there was nothin' they could do.

"At six o'clock the staff were still sittin' there. The company was passin' out emergency lunches then to the people that were held up. From six to six thirty I waved 'em out three times. All the picketers were standin' back except a couple were standin' in front of the truck.

"At six thirty the Mounties came in and said they had word from the company that they were goin' to press charges. They were goin' to write out a notice to appear in court in the morning if we didn't let 'em go. I talked to the boys and we decided better than gettin' arrested we'd let the truck go through.

"When the truck started to go through, the pit superintendent that was sittin' there all this time holdin' up the staff, he started a big laugh. He and the other guy that was in the truck they were havin' a big laugh. It got my goat. For two and a half hours they'd had the staff held up there and there was the Mounties comin' in and doin' their dirty work for 'em. So I picked up a picket sign then and I started walkin' back and forth in front of 'em.

"I said to the Mounties: 'He's not goin'. He's stayin' for another two and a half hours before he gets out of here.' The Mounties said: 'Back away, or we're goin' to have to arrest you.' I told the boys to stand back and I kept walkin' back and forth in front of the truck. I felt sorry for the sergeant because I put him in a very awkward position. He didn't want to do it but the pit superintendent started up the jeep and as I jumped in front of 'im the Mounties clapped me on the shoulder and told me: 'You're under arrest.'

"I didn't resist. They took me out and put me in jail. The sergeant came in a few minutes later. He had a form and he told me: 'I'm not goin' to keep you locked up. This is a release form that you can sign yourself out on bail.' So I signed myself out.

"When I got arrested three other guys on the picket line jumped out in front. They didn't arrest them but they charged 'em. We were charged with interfering with private property, wilful mischief, somethin' like that.

"The next morning there was about three hundred showed up on the picket line. They were ready to start a riot. But I said no. That wasn't goin' to help. As I see it when you're in that type of situation you're no longer fightin' the company, you're fightin' the law. If you take on the company and the law at the same time, you're battin' zero. But they had a bit of fun in there on the picket line that morning.

"I had to appear in court at ten thirty. So they all left the picket line and followed me out to the courthouse. The magistrate was a bit shook up. It was the biggest crowd he'd ever seen in the courthouse. There's only a small courthouse here in the basement of a church, so there wasn't that many could get in. But I guarantee they had quite a crowd. They were all lined up outside. I was remanded. They never did convict me. They put me on probation with two years good behaviour.

"We got a court injunction after that. They made us reduce our pickets and move them outside the company property. So the whole thing changed."

It was a grim, discouraging battle. The company was not negotiating at all. As the cold weeks started to slip by with no money coming in nor any end to the strike in sight, the men started to lose heart.

Gerry Dwyer's wife Maureen had gone to school with Brian Peckford, Newfoundland's minister of mines and energy. She wrote asking him to intervene to help the striking miners in their fight to gain adequate safety precautions. Peckford's answer was tentative. Maureen Dwyer refused to let it go at that. She wrote again and again until finally the minister of mines wrote her crossly to say that he had been elected by the loggers and not by the miners.

The miners' wives began to realize that the men were becoming discouraged. They decided to do something about it. The women knew that the oil truck kept going up to the mine and filling up there. So they arranged for a small group to go down and picket the Golden Eagle gas station.

Jane Mercer, a young mother of two and wife of one of the striking miners, tells how they prevented the oil truck from going out: "There was a police sergeant in there told us we couldn't stop the truck but we could stand in front of him. As long as we didn't make him stop we could make him go as slow as we liked. One lady, Louise Tulk, she got in front of the truck and she'd make out she had to pull her stockings up or she had to haul up her pants. I never laughed so much in all my life.

"The young fella in the oil truck he wanted to get out so bad. And it was icy, really icy. So he come out from the gate. He speeds his tires and hits the fence. Was he mad. He'd get so far and rev up the engine then we'd start walkin' back and forth. We just let him inch up, inch by inch. He got through but it was about an hour later.

"This was just a spur of the moment thing. Nobody knew what else to do because we weren't organized. I went to Martin Saunders and asked him what he would think if the women had a meeting and had someone from the union come and explain what we were allowed to do and what we weren't. He said it was a good idea.

"That Thursday night he had a film about Harlan County. It was about coal miners who suffered from black lung disease and went on strike when the company wouldn't sign a contract. I was really mad after seein' how the men in the movie were. And the asbestos was just as bad.

"I got up and told the people there that this thing didn't just concern the miners. It concerned everyone in the town. Even the foremen. It was their families we were tryin' to protect too. It was a matter of everyone's life and the men needed all the support they could get.

"At our first meeting we had something like twenty-two women. At our second meeting there were fifty or sixty. Women Behind the Miners – that's what we called ourselves. We decided to have a big demonstration April 29.

"We sent a letter around publicizing how the asbestos was hurtin' everybody. We told people there was no such thing as neutral ground. You had to be either for life or against it. We got almost every business store to close down for two hours during the demonstration.

"The Saturday come and it was rainin', hailin' and snowin'. But when the demonstration got underway we had almost fifteen hundred people there. As we went along more people joined in. And what wouldn't walk, came in a car.

"One of the women, her husband's an electrician. He made up a coffin with white panel board. We figured there was no better way than a coffin of symbolizing that we were tryin' to save lives. It's asbestos that's the killer.

"I was so proud. I'd never done nothing like this in my life before. After that we had bake sales, tickets on a variety box, a bingo and a rummage sale. In less than a month we raised between $1,800 and $1,900.

"My husband was surprised. For a while there the men were figurin' the women weren't goin' to do anything. What could the women do? they thought. We showed them we're not puny, little things to sit home all day long. Where the men haven't got the guts to get out and really fight, we have.

"We went out to the mine and joined the picket line. We weren't allowed to go in with the men. The union said they could get in trouble for it. So we stayed so many feet away and stopped the foremen when they came out. We talked to them and told them how we felt. We told the radio how we felt, and the TV.

"The strike was too quiet. The men were up here twenty-four hours a day picketing but there was nothing on the news. Once we got goin', it was in the news continuously. That brought the men's morale back up. They got encouraged again. And it made the government really sit down and take notice."

Martin Saunders agrees that the Women Behind the Miners was a big factor in ending the strike. "The other thing was the fact the spring of the year was comin' on and the strike was after draggin' on longer than most folks realized, especially the company. The minister of labour appointed a mediator, a lawyer in Corner Brook, Gordon Easton. We went out to Gander for a week.

"There was a complete news blackout on proceedings in Gander. It was a very tense situation. Even up to the last minute. Even when we felt we'd got almost to the point of agreement there was one moment where we broke off the talks. But it wasn't on conditions of occupational health. It was some contract wranglings. So we reconsidered and we settled.

"We wanted the right to pull people out of high dust-count areas until the dust count was lowered. That was one item we never got. But we did settle for the fact the company offered a utility crew that would be concerned only with environmental matters. Five days a week, any place there's any serious problem they'll go in and clear it up. What's more, we'll have our own union guy spend eight hours a month monitoring levels over and above what the company does. They finally agreed to that.

"Every once in a while Johns-Manville sends in people that do a whole count of the area but the actual counts are not made public. What they come out with is the average and the government is inclined to go along with this averaging bit. The minister of mines during the strike made a statement to the effect that the average dust count in Advocate Mines was only two fibres per cubic centimetre. That may be true but we know for a fact that we got people workin' down there in areas that are nineteen, twenty, twenty-three fibres per cubic centimetre.

"The Newfoundland government has never had a regulation saying what the standard of fibre count was supposed to be. In Ontario the regulation now is for two fibres. In Quebec, I think it's five. It used to be twelve."

The strike had lasted fifteen weeks but the union had won almost everything they had wanted. The company agreed to put in a main dry worth $1.7 million. This would give the men the change rooms, showers and two-locker system they need to cut down on the amount of asbestos dust they carry home to their families. The car wash went ahead and the company put in a filtration system which is supposed to eliminate the dust coming from the stacks.

Despite these successes, the battle lines have been drawn now in Baie Verte. Most of the miners are painfully aware of the experience just a couple of hundred miles away on Newfoundland's south coast in the village of St. Lawrence. The fluorspar miners there were told that their dust was harmless, too. It was only when the graveyard grew almost as big as the town itself and nearly every family had lost at least one member that words like "silicosis" and "cancer" were taken seriously. But the damage had already been done.

Baie Verte still has a chance but people in the town know they will have to remain vigilant. They have learned that you cannot rely even on government health standards. An emission count of two fibres per cubic centimetre of air has been set in Canada as a safe measurement in asbestos control. But according to tests done by the Air Pollution Directorate in Ottawa, this figure is simply what the existing filtration equipment can handle. In the United States where 1978 statistics show that 17 percent of cancer deaths are caused by asbestos, federal health agencies want to bring the allowable level down to .1 fibres per cubic centimetre.

There are still days in Baie Verte when the dust is so thick you have to scrape it off your windshield before you can drive your car. Gerry Dwyer says the local people deal with this reality as best they can.

"There's some days down at the mine when the sun is really shinin' bright as can be. It shines right through the window down there. Well, there's some guys duck under the rays that shine through, or hold their breath till they be right past where they can see the dust in the sunlight. I've almost done it myself. You can't help it. You just feel you're somehow savin' yourself a bit."

AFTERWORD

Looking back through the stories of these labour militants, I find it amazing how much of Canada's last sixty years is represented by their experiences. Each of them has in some way helped shape the country as it, in turn, has played a part in the unfolding of their lives.

This was made dramatically clear to me when I met Bill Pritchard. I spent several days talking to him in his Los Angeles home, piecing together fragments of a very long history. We traced the early days of the Socialist Party of Canada, the enthusiasm for the idea of the One Big Union among industrial workers, the extraordinary solidarity of the Winnipeg General Strike, and the ruthless forces that finally broke it.

Despite his ninety years and the fact that he confessed it was "a bit of a strain to bring it all back again," Bill Pritchard relived it all for me. He even quoted verbatim part of his own passionate defence of labour's rights in the speech he gave in the state trials which followed the strike. But still I was reluctant to leave him on the last afternoon. The story was somehow not quite complete.

In 1938, Bill Pritchard was only fifty years old. Canada had been the stage of all his battles – the labour wranglings, the political contests, the jail terms, the public debates. Yet he left Canada and has spent the last forty years in relative obscurity in Los Angeles. What could have happened to disillusion this tough-minded idealist?

I had heard rumours of personal tragedy and wondered how I might insist now that he talk about this when he was weary with all the talking we had already done. But as if he knew the long story was incomplete without these painful details, he began to tell me all about it.

He pointed out photographs on a small table. "See that boy up there. And that one. Well, in between there was a girl. She was just a baby at the time of the strike. I remember when I came home off the train she ran up to me crying, 'Daddy, Daddy.' That was Mildred.

"In 1928, I'd been out of jail about seven years and I'd just been elected that year to the Burnaby Council. I'd known for years that the wife was becoming unstable mentally. Finally, I went to a doctor. After examining her he brought in an expert and they had a long session. That very day they decided she couldn't go home. I had to take the papers down to the police station. She died in hospital some eight or nine years ago.

"Mildred, she got through high school and she did a little work for me when I was on the paper. This was a kind of supporting paper for the CCF. You see, the Socialist party was left without enough support to keep a paper going and finally dissolved in about 1927. That's why I turned my attention to the CCF. I knew a lot of them. I disagreed with a lot of them politically. I don't oppose reforms but I don't advocate them. But that was their ideology – reform. A step at a time would bring us closer than the stern revolutionary position, they said. But I wanted to tell you about Mildred. . . .

"She turned twenty-one. She was very introspective and sometimes I thought I saw elements indicative of her mother. Times for me were tough then. About a week after her birthday I was going out to where I was working. I said to her: 'We'll get through this somehow.' I might have made a mistake in saying that. I don't know.

"I came home late that night. It was a wicked night. Raining. We lived on the bottom of this slope. It was nine o'clock when I got home. We had a little dog. The kids adored the dog. Now, when a car would stop and there's some of us not home that dog would be down at the bottom of the street to meet every car. But he wasn't there that night. I trudged up the hill and the house is all lit up. The door was open and it was cold. I looked around and got whatever there was to make a fire and I put on the kettle. I wondered where Mildred was and thought perhaps she was down with her friend. The kettle was boiling so I thought I'd get down and light the furnace. I had installed the furnace only the year before. I opened the basement door. That was it. The dog was at her feet. That's where the dog was. Whimpering. And she was hanging from a beam. That is why I'm in California." He says these last words very deliberately and pauses for a long time.

Bill Pritchard had been only fifty but he says sadly: "It was no age to come to another country." He worked when he could doing this or that, as a Fuller Brush salesman, in the kitchen at Ptomaine Tommy's.

His voice is firm again now. "But it's good that I came down here. The boys had been in every relief camp in the country. What was there for them in Canada? They both followed me down here and both fell on their feet. It is better that I came.

"I have no regrets. Not for myself. It doesn't matter to me that maybe I sacrificed myself. But sometimes I worry that maybe I sacrificed my family."

Bill Pritchard's anguished questioning today underlines his extraordinary contribution to our history. It is an example of the kind of personal commitment it has taken to build a labour movement in Canada. We still have a long way to go but thanks to Bill Pritchard and the millions of working men and women who have struggled before us, the road has at least been mapped out.

INDEX

FURTHER READING

Abella, Irving, ed. *On Strike: Six Key Labour Struggles in Canada 1919-1949.* Toronto: James Lorimer & Company, 1974.

Abella, Irving, and Millar, David, eds. *The Canadian Worker in the Twentieth Century.* Toronto: Oxford University Press, 1978.

Bercuson, David J. *Fools and Wise Men: The Rise and Fall of the One Big Union.* Toronto: McGraw-Hill Ryerson Ltd., 1978.

Dumas, Evelyn. *The Bitter Thirties in Québec.* Montreal: Black Rose Books Ltd., 1975.

Hann, Russell G.; Kealey, Gregory S.; Kealey, Linda; and Warrian, Peter. *Primary Sources in Canadian Working Class History 1860-1930.* Kitchener: Dumont Press, 1973.

Laxer, Robert M. *Canada's Unions.* Toronto: James Lorimer & Company, 1976.

Lipton, Charles. *The Trade Union Movement of Canada 1827-1959.* Toronto: NC Press Ltd., 1973.

Liversedge, Ronald. *Recollections of the On To Ottawa Trek.* Edited by Victor Hoar. Toronto: McClelland and Stewart Ltd., 1973.

MacEwen, Paul. *Miners and Steelworkers: Labour Unions in Cape Breton.* Toronto: Samuel-Stevens Publishers Ltd., 1976.

McCormack, Andrew Ross. *Reformers, Rebels, and Revolutionaries: The Western Canadian Radical Movement 1899-1919.* Toronto: University of Toronto Press, 1977.

North, George Alexander. *A Ripple, A Wave.* Edited by Harold Griffin. Vancouver: Fisherman Publishing Society, 1974. The story of union organization in the B.C. fishing industry.

Penner, Norman, ed. *Winnipeg 1919: The Strikers' Own History of the Winnipeg General Strike.* Toronto: James Lorimer & Company, 1975.

Stanton John. *Life and Death of a Union: The History of the Canadian Seamen's Union 1936-1949.* Toronto: Steel Rail Educational Publishing, 1978.

Sheils, Jean Evans, and Swankey, Ben. *Work and Wages*! Vancouver: Trade Union Research Bureau, 1977. A semi-documentary account of the life and times of Arthur H. (Slim) Evans.